Through Narcissus' Glass Darkly

Through Narcissus' Glass Darkly

The Modern Religion of Conscience

David S. Pacini

FORDHAM UNIVERSITY PRESS

NEW YORK 2008

"Tear It Down," "Exceeding," "Going There," from *The Great Fires: Poems 1982–1992* by Jack Gilbert, copyright © 1994 by Jack Gilbert. Used by permission of Alfred A. Knopf, a division of Random House, Inc.

"A Walk Blossoming," "Horses at Midnight without a Moon," from *Refusing Heaven: Poems* by Jack Gilbert, copyright © 2005 by Jack Gilbert. Used by permission of Alfred A. Knopf, a division of Random House, Inc.

"Self-portrait in a Convex Mirror," copyright © 1974 by John Ashbery, from *Self-portrait in a Convex Mirror* by John Ashbery. Used by permission of Viking Penguin, a division of Penguin Group (USA) Inc.

Library of Congress Cataloging-in-Publication Data

Pacini, David S.
  Through Narcissus' glass darkly : the modern religion of conscience / David S. Pacini.—1st ed.
    p. cm.
  Includes bibliographical references and index.
  ISBN 978-0-8232-2964-2 (cloth : alk. paper)
    1. Conscience—Religious aspects—Christianity—History.
2. Philosophical theology—History. 3. Hobbes, Thomas,
1588–1679. 4. Rousseau, Jean-Jacques, 1712–1778. 5. Kant,
Immanuel, 1724–1804. I. Title.
BJ1278.C66P33 2008
171'.6—dc22

                                                      2008043309

Printed in the United States of America
First paperback printing 2012

In Memoriam
Pierce Louis Pacini

CONTENTS

FIGURES

ACKNOWLEDGMENTS

"Friends," wrote the poet Stéphane Mallarmé, "mysterious finger shown, appeared, chasing away the false." I have been graced by many such friends in the course of writing this book. Thomas Altizer, Karl Ameriks, Jon Gunneman, Dieter Henrich, Brooks Holifield, William Mallard, Rudolph Makkreel, Richard Velkley: each read portions of this manuscript and offered invaluable suggestions for revisions along the way. Mark C. Taylor and James Wetzel championed the book, offering decisive encouragements when I was beset with discouragement. Russell Richey, former dean of the Candler School of Theology, made funds available for my archival research.

Among my students, Trish Anderson, Elizabeth Corrie, Michael DeJonge, and Adam Ployd not only diligently pressed me for clarification, but also offered willing hands in various aspects of the technical preparation. Two of them lent keen editorial eyes: Sarah Alexander and Stacia Brown discern what for many of us goes unnoticed. They saved me from much infelicity of style, many errors of fact and reference, and logical incongruities. Their generosities of spirit—and Sarah's Promethean efforts—have helped make it possible to bring this book to fruition.

Helen Tartar and the good people of Fordham University Press have accorded me a welcome reception to their list of authors, and have extended to me every help imaginable along the road to publication. John Ashbery and Jack Gilbert graciously granted me permission to incorporate extensive portions of their creative work, for which I am honored.

My family retained a remarkably good sense of humor during the long hours that I secreted myself away in the study, never failing to remind me that the world consists of more than Kant, Wittgenstein, and Freud, and that life often instructs in more telling ways than books.

The first contours of this book emerged in a 1992 series of lectures that I shared with congregants at St. Luke's Episcopal Church in Atlanta. Our son, Pierce Louis, was born during the course of this series, and accompanied me, in infant transport, to a number of them. Death struck down this small creature, whose gaze is not among the dead, but always in us. Again, the words of the knowing poet: "A dead being lives in us, our thought—what is best in him happens through the love and care we take of his being in our thought—in this there is a magnificent beyond." As long as these words go on living, he lives with all of us: they are a memorial to him.

NOTES AND ABBREVIATIONS

For ease of reference, I provide the reader with citations to standard editions of English, French, and German works (noted below), although my own translations occasionally diverge from those in the English editions cited.

Karl Barth (1886–1968)

R   *The Epistle to the Romans*. Translated from the sixth edition of Edwyn C. Hoskins. London: Oxford University Press, 1953.
Röm   *Der Römerbrief*. Reprinted from the new edition of 1922. Zürich: Theologischer Verlag Zürich, 1984.

Sigmund Freud (1856–1939)

GP   "Group Psychology and the Analysis of the Ego." In *SE*, 18:65–143.
GW   *Sigmund Freud Gesammelte Werke: Chronologisch Geordnet*. Frankfurt am Main: S. Fischer Verlag, 1966.
LN   "The Libido Theory and Narcissism." In *SE*, 16:412–30.
M   "Mourning and Melancholia." In *SE*, 14:243–58.
N   "On Narcissism: An Introduction." In *SE*, 14:73–102.
O   "Types of Onset of Neurosis." In *SE*, 12:231–38.
SE   *The Standard Edition of the Complete Psychological Works of Sigmund Freud*. Translated and edited by James Strachey. London: Hogarth, 1981.
U   "Assessment of the Unconscious." In *SE*, 14:196–204.

Thomas Hobbes (1588–1679)

Lev   *Leviathan.* Edited by Richard Tuck. Cambridge Texts in the History of Political Thought. Revised student edition. Cambridge: Cambridge University Press, 2000.

Immanuel Kant (1724–1804)

A   *Anthropology from a Pragmatic Point of View.* Edited by Robert B. Louden. Cambridge Texts in the History of Philosophy. New York: Cambridge University Press, 2006.

AA   *Kant's gesammelte Schriften.* Edited by Königlich Preussische Akademie. 29 volumes. Berlin: Georg Reimer Verlag, 1910–. (Volumes IX, XIIIff have imprint: Berlin: Walter de Gruyter)

CJ   *Critique of the Power of Judgment.* Edited and translated by Paul Guyer and Eric Matthews. Cambridge: Cambridge University Press, 2000.

Cor   *Correspondence.* Translated and edited by Arnulf Zweig. Cambridge: Cambridge University Press, 1999.

CPR   *Critique of Pure Reason.* Translated and edited by Paul Guyer and Allen Wood. Cambridge: Cambridge University Press, 1998.

CPrR   *Critique of Practical Reason.* In *PrP*, 133–271.

G   *Groundwork of the Metaphysics of Morals.* In *PrP*, 43–108.

LM   *Lectures on Metaphysics.* Translated and edited by Karl Ameriks and Steve Naragon. Cambridge: Cambridge University Press, 1997.

O   "What Does It Mean to Orient Oneself in Thinking?" In *RRT*, 7–18.

OP   *Opus Postumum.* Edited by Eckart Förster. Translated by Eckart Förster and Michael Rosen, Cambridge: Cambridge University Press, 1997.

PrP   *Practical Philosophy.* Translated and edited by Mary J. Gregor. Cambridge: Cambridge University Press, 1996.

QeE   "An Answer to the Question: What Is Enlightenment?" In *PrP*, 17–22.

Rel   *Religion Within the Boundaries of Mere Reason.* In *RRT*, 57–215.

RRT   *Religion and Rational Theology*. Translated and edited by Allen W. Wood and George di Giovanni. Cambridge: Cambridge University Press, 1996.

Jean-Jacques Rousseau (1712–1778)

CSV   "The Creed of the Savoyard Vicar." In *E*, 228–58.
E   *Emile or On Education*. Translated by Barbara Foxley. Everyman's Library. London: J. M. Dent and Sons, 1972.
Ém   *Émile, ou de l'education*. 4 volumes. Francfort [i.e., London]: Strahan, 1762.

Max Weber (1864–1920)

Sci   "Science as a Vocation." In *From Max Weber: Essays in Sociology*. Translated and edited by H. H. Gerth and C. Wright Mills. New York: Oxford University Press, 1958, 129–56.
WB   "Wissenschaft als Beruf." In *Gesammelte Aufsätze zur Wissenschaftslehre*. Edited by Johannes Winckelmann. Tübingen: J. C. B. Mohr, 1951.

Ludwig Wittgenstein (1889–1951)

NB   *Notebooks, 1914–1916*. Second edition. Edited by G. H. von Wright and G. E. M. Anscombe. [German/English edition; English translations by G. E. M. Anscombe.] Chicago: University of Chicago Press, 1979.
TLP   *Tractatus Logico-Philosophicus*. [German/English edition; English translations by C. K. Ogden.] London: Routledge, 1990.

A Walk Blossoming

The spirit opens as life closes down.
Tries to frame the size of whatever God is.
Finds that dying makes us visible.
Realizes we must get to the loin of that
before time is over. The part of which
we are the wall around. Not the good or evil,
neither death nor afterlife but the importance
of what we contain meanwhile. (He walks along
remembering, biting into beauty,
the heart eating into the naked spirit.)
The body is a major nation, the mind is a gift.
Together they define substantiality.
The spirit can know the Lord as a flavor
rather than power. The soul is ambitious
for what is invisible. Hungers for a sacrament
that is both spirit and flesh. And neither.

—JACK GILBERT

Prologue: The Looking Glass Religion

Of course it was a disaster.
That unbearable, dearest secret
has always been a disaster.
The danger when we try to leave.
Going over and over afterward
what we should have done
instead of what we did.
But for those short times
we seemed to be alive.

—JACK GILBERT

Opposing the encroachments of others on individual liberties is a recurring theme in Western intellectual thought. More often than not, it has meant opposing various forms of political and/or religious zealotry and fanaticism while at the same time advancing the thesis that liberty is the equivalent of noninterference. Deriving from the teachings of Greek philosophy, the basic idea underlying this thesis is that individuals possess desires and inclinations to pursue life in a particular fashion and may seek after such pursuits so long as they align with what is best for the community. What counts as best for the community thus becomes authoritative for the individual's right direction of its inclinations and desires. At various points throughout the history of Western Christian thought, this contrast between desire and authority has been cast in theological terms as a tension or opposition between sin and God-given reason; or, again, between sin and what sacred text, religion, or God has ordained. Given the depravity of human desire, this argument suggested, the balances of liberty and human life in community could be achieved and maintained only through the pursuit of, and congruence with, the divinely ordained ordering of life. In more recent, less obviously religious times, the contrast has been struck in more psychological terms as a tension between freedom and coercion. Given that all individuals wish to be free and do not want to be coerced into doing something to which they do not subscribe, humans establish certain social arrangements and institutions to safeguard the majority from the unruly caprice of the minority. This way of framing the matter has tended to depict the task of protecting liberties as a struggle between 'inside' forces of desire and inclination and the 'outside' forces of communal authority.

There is another way to construe the issue. It maintains that safeguarding human liberty from encroachments is, instead, a wholly *internal* matter, a conflict between competing aspects of a divided subjectivity. This argument, deriving from classical Stoicism and its transmission through the Pauline theological tradition—including Clement of Alexandria and Augustine of Hippo, Bonaventura and Nicholas of Cusa, Martin Luther and John Calvin—emphasizes the tension *within* the subject between the remnant of the original divine ordering and the sense of alienation from that order. Classical theology portrayed this inner conflict in conjunction with the familiar and externalized distinction between the "City of God" and the "City of Man." On this view, the Christian experienced resolution of the inward conflict between desire and coercion by virtue of the awakening and promptings of 'conscience,' which, these thinkers suggested, imposes injunctions to right conduct on the individual subject. Thereby, the classical formulation argued, the human subject could be enabled (by grace) to conform to the form of the divine implanted within—often the light of Christ, portrayed by a candle reflected in a mirror, as in de la Tour's seventeenth-century masterpiece *The Penitent Magdalene* (Figure 1). So conformed, the human subject, like the penitent Magdalene, could forswear sinfulness and proceed to his or her appointed end.

Although they differed over the details of how this formula unfolded, the authors standing in this tradition remained united in the view that there is a link between the human and the divine orders of being. However hidden, this link was said to make possible the conformation (transformation) of the subject to the internal divine, and the movement of the subject toward a divinely foreordained end. Even Luther's paradoxical construal of the formula in which the subject remains divided (simultaneously justified and sinner) did not depart from this basic ontological commitment.

Figure 1: De la Tour, *The Penitent Magdalene* (1638–43). (Image copyright © The Metropolitan Museum of Art / Art Resource, NY.)

The modern variant of this approach to safeguarding liberty from the encroachments of others is what I will call the 'modern religion of conscience.' It rests on the claim that God 'speaks' to us through the directives of a self-governing conscience that guide moral conduct. What distinguishes the modern religion of conscience from its classical forbears is the severing of the ontological link between the divine and human orders of being—and the corresponding elimination of the assumption that the end toward which a subject moves is divinely preestablished. Instead, it proceeds from the conviction that there is a basic, albeit complex, unity inherent in the individual, in terms of which the conflict between desire and authority may be self-regulated through self-legislation of the ends toward which individuals are to move.

In this book, I aim to outline the contours of the modern religion of conscience as articulated in early modern and modern Western philosophy, and to delineate its gradual collapse under the delusion—as in Ovid's telling of Narcissus—that the commitments of self-reflection are transparent. I want to show that its attempt to construe the protection of liberties from the encroachments of religious zealotry and fanaticism in terms of the inner tensions of a basic self-reflective unity of consciousness, independent of the orderings of heaven or earth, was both brilliant and flawed. Brilliant, because it altered the nature of the question that had been asked before, showing the situation of the individual in a new light; flawed, because it confounded individual good with the just society.

In the nineteenth century, Renaissance historian Jacob Burckhardt and French historian Julius Michelet both noted that the modern sense of what it is to impose shape or identity on ourselves differs significantly from the classical senses. Once seen as conformity to a revealed divine order of being, in the seventeenth century 'religion' began to metamorphose into conformity to the coherence of thought—or into a particular way of associating ideas often organized around the activity of self-reflection. No longer revealing an 'inner light,' as in de la Tour's portrayal of the penitent Magdalene, reflection now 'shows' merely the appearance of ourselves. This shift is evident in the eighteenth-century portrait by Vigée-Le Brun of her daughter, *Julie Le Brun with Mirror* (Figure 2). Not all early moderns participated in this metamorphosis at the time, of course; my focus remains a select group of thinkers whose philosophical programs became highly influential for later outlooks, and which continue to permeate ours today. These thinkers were not alone in their turn to a religion of

Figure 2: Vigée-Le Brun, *Julie Le Brun with Mirror* (1786). (Private Collection, New York. Image © The Metropolitan Museum of Art.)

conscience; other sources included German Lutherans and German and English self-defense theorists. But they did stand among its most formidable and influential articulators: the views of Thomas Hobbes, Jean-Jacques Rousseau, and Immanuel Kant constitute the focus of much of what I attempt to say here. In the present study, I ask how and why their writings reflect shifting conceptions of religion, and I explore the significance of this metamorphosis for understanding the modern religion of conscience within early-twentieth-century philosophical and psychoanalytic thought.

The Structure of This Study

I want to offer a word of introduction about those portions of Hobbes', Rousseau's, and Kant's intellectual projects that constitute the centerpiece of the present study. Philosophical and political interpretations of these thinkers are prolific and wide-ranging; my focus remains the narrower purview of their theological articulations and the problems that emerged within them. I argue that Kant made explicit a sensibility or religious outlook that remained implicit in both Hobbes and Rousseau: he suggested that humans are neither suspended from heaven nor anchored on earth, but must have the courage to live 'in between.' All three thinkers shared a view that the natural drives of humans (e.g., self-preservation) work at cross-purposes with human fulfillment; and accordingly, all three assumed that humans yearn to modify certain aspects of their natural constitution in order to achieve higher aims or ends. At the same time, Hobbes, Rousseau, and Kant also circumscribed what humans could mean by 'higher ends,' suggesting that humans no longer could strive for transcendence of their earthly, temporal selves to achieve divine belonging in the same way that they once assumed. Human striving instead appeared to them to be situated 'in between.' Hobbes interpreted this 'in between' to mean between anarchy and order, between a state of war and the Leviathan, between self-destruction and self-preservation. Rousseau portrayed the 'in between' as a state of caughtness between selfish love and appropriate love, between culture and the state of nature. And Kant cast the 'in between' in terms of the subject's suspension between the sensible domain and the intelligible domain, between the Realm of Nature and the Realm of Ideas.

Theirs were less statements about dualism (or about the precise content of the poles between which humans were suspended) than evocations and articulations of what these thinkers all perceived as the 'homelessness' of the human subject. In the shift from a conception of religion as conformity to the divine order of being to a conception of religion as conformity to the

human ordering of ideas, which in turn serve the interests of self-interpretation, these thinkers saw the loss of mooring for the modern subject. To such
a homeless subject, the idea of a divine order of being appears illusory;
and in its absence, a human ordering of ideas that answers the longing for
orientation in uncharted territory becomes all-important. And given the
imperative to shape its own dwelling place, the homeless subject naturally
would seek an ordering of ideas that supported an equitable and just society
around it. Thus I suggest that Hobbes' Leviathan, Rousseau's social contract, and Kant's ethical commonwealth functioned not only as blueprints
for what they took to be a viable civil society but also as the penumbral basis
for a 'new' or modern theological outlook: the religion of conscience.

Understanding the inner workings of this new theological outlook—as
well as its gradual unraveling over time—remains a difficult task, in part
because we are so shaped by the thought traditions of Kantianism—and by
negative reactions *against* those same traditions—that our reading already
bears the marks of Kant's biases and the biases of Kant's principal critics.
Contemporary students of philosophy and theology do not so much read
Kant as they read through the eyes of these more recent spokespersons;
indeed, our view is so saturated by traditions of interpretation that we often
read him with what Gadamer called 'pre-understanding.'[1] Thus we blanch
at the metaphysical prospect of the Realm of Nature and the Realm of Ideas,
preferring to adopt the more palatable notion of 'differing perspectives,'
and we similarly cringe before the idea that self-legislated moral law could
be anything other than the valorizing of self-interest. Simply put, the ways
in which we read Kant—and, to a certain extent, Hobbes and Rousseau—
are already overdetermined by the discourses that we are proposing to examine and criticize. Thus the contemporary reader might neglect to note,
first, that however things might appear to us today, at the time of its first
articulations the Hobbesian-Rousseauian-Kantian religion of conscience
was intellectually emancipatory.[2] It sought to liberate religion from the preserve of revealed theology and the dominance of the confessional church.
The contemporary reader might also overlook, second, the expansive legacy
that the religion of conscience came to enjoy: the idea that religion is a kind
of moral ordering lent novel interpretations to human religious practices
across a wide range of nineteenth- and early-twentieth-century philosophical and theological thought, on the Continent as well as in North America.
Finally, just as we might fail to note the extent to which this way of thinking,

its terminology, and its derivatives once served a liberatory role, so also might we neglect to note the precise nature of the problems that the modern religion of conscience posed for its followers.

The essays in this book strive to make explicit both the remarkable achievements represented by the modern religion of conscience and these problems that came to accompany and destabilize it. In the first essay, "Unscaffolding Religious 'Madness,'" I introduce Kant's theological program by situating it within his intellectual and political contexts. I show how Kant established some of the theoretical grounds for a modern religion of conscience by routing traditional religious positions among his contemporaries (including orthodoxy, "enthusiasm," and Pietism). Historical and philosophical in approach, this essay introduces readers to the broader milieu in which Kant worked. It also suggests that Kant departed from the certitude of his own formulation of moral law that his contemporaries celebrated when he began to press beyond this law to ask about the inscrutable ground of moral choice. In effect, this departure reopened the question of the authority of conscience and its relation to individual liberties.

In the second essay, "Disenchantment and the Religion of Conscience," I shift the analysis away from Kant's political and intellectual environs and toward a conceptual analysis of that 'inscrutable ground' with which Kant and others struggled. I argue that the modern religion of conscience effectively made the modern subject a hostage to its own ways of thinking: Hobbes, Rousseau, and Kant each saw this modern subject as both charged with the responsibility to assert itself against the world and steeped in such loss that it attempts to appropriate to its own rationality some of the role that 'spirit' once played. A conceptual analysis of the philosophical psychology of the era, particularly the destabilizing effects of the clash between the world of science and the world of Christianity, the essay points out the modern religion of conscience's forgetfulness of spirit as one of the consequences and manifestations of the Kantian 'in between.' I also suggest ways that this Kantian position created a disconnected agent: the particular kind of 'in between' that Kant crafted had the effect of de-divinizing both God *and* the modern subject, deepening the isolating effect of the 'caughtness' of the subject in the tension between the inscrutability of freedom and the authority of self-legislation.

The third essay, "Disfiguring the Soul," continues the claim that the modern subject became a hostage to itself within the philosophical programs of these thinkers but reappraises this 'caughtness' from a different vantage point: I look at the figures of speech operative in the modern religion of conscience. The essay traces the ways in which Hobbes, Rousseau, and Kant introduced new rules of 'figuration' as they tried to broker the terms of meaningful discourse, or what is much the same, as they distinguished between those configurations of words that would count and those that would not count in making sense of the world. Literary-critical in method, this essay argues that by amplifying or 'writing large' the role of conscience in their moral philosophies, Kant and others fostered an impoverished sense of the soul: the modern religion of conscience takes inherited figures of speech and both disfigures and repositions them.

The last essay, "Life Without Enigmatic Remainder," makes substantive as well as structural departures from the essays that precede it. I shift away from an analysis of the modern religion of conscience as Hobbes, Rousseau, and Kant depicted it and toward an exploration of how their theological programs contained the seeds of an unraveling: the modern religion of conscience could not sustain itself, because its inchoate incoherence eventually showed. Working across philosophical, psychoanalytic, and theological lines, this essay explores how Wittgenstein, Freud, and Barth criticized the modern religion of conscience. I attempt first to show that Kant's endeavor to conceptualize ethical conduct as issuing in harmonious repose implicated him in overstepping conceptual limits that he himself had proposed. Or, better, I pursue a line of argument, from the perspective of the young Wittgenstein, that Kant did not conceive of his own boundaries radically enough. Not only did he commit himself to saying what he could not, but in doing so he also advanced a fundamentally problematic conception of conscience. Freud, in turn, affords us a perspective from which to understand the problem from a new angle: Kant's is a 'diseased' conscience. Bound to an ideal of its own devising, the Kantian conscience, on Freud's telling, veers toward a destructive form of narcissism. Unable to acknowledge the transitory nature of ideals, the Kantian conscience cannibalizes itself rather than mourning the loss of old ideals and creating new ones. Finally, I attempt to retrieve and to recast what remains of enduring value in those earlier articulations. Despite the problems that accrued to them, these thinkers did say, and say boldly, that conscience announces and advocates a just ordering of human life. To this end, I explore the young Karl Barth's insights into the features of "Otherness" that narcissistic self-reflection omits—but tacitly presupposes—that make transformation of its vision possible.

Each of these four essays stands by itself. Together, however, they form a structure that tries to remain faithful to my larger analysis. After creating the necessary scaffolding about the advent of the modern religion of conscience by which Kant sought to dismantle religious madness, I observe Kant's own adage: "then the scaffolding must be taken down."[3] The fourth essay 'takes down' what the first three essays build up in different ways; or better, it emphasizes the ways in which the fault line of freedom's inscrutability began to open up, progressively shattering the 'looking glass religion' from the homelessness of the mind to disenchantment and disfiguration. So the fourth essay turns Kantian criticism against Kant himself, showing both what must be dismantled and what remains left to call out to us. I argue that Kant's formulation of the conviction that conscience directs us to an unknown order of just and harmonious repose is incoherent; the 'truth' of this conviction rightly appears only in the moment in which the 'known' and 'unknown' intersect in relationship. For only in this moment is our angle of vision transformed from one within which the question of liberty and authority had been understood *as* a question to one within which we, now seeing in a new light, recognize its *dissolution*.

Ways of Reading

Earlier I noted that the attempt to read Kant fairly is troubled by the Kantian lenses that we bring to our reading. In one sense, the essays in this volume constitute an attempt to address some of the problems that this overfamiliarity with Kant poses. Cutting across the essays in this volume is thus a methodological question that I want to identify from the outset: how do such problems of reading emerge? To begin with, Kantianism depends on a negative movement of reading, a 'blotting out' of one entity or idea in order to permit something else to come into view: to replace the idea that the world constitutes me with the idea that I constitute the world is what it means to adopt the Kantian 'critical standpoint.' Now to annihilate certain premises in order to arrive at a particular conclusion might be called simple misreading. But it can also be described, following Paul de Man, as a subtle kind of 'blindness.'[4] Here I do not mean simply the inability to see. I mean, as well, that not being able to see is itself a kind of seeing: de Man's 'blindness' is a kind of 'not-seeing' that brings insight. De Man remains convinced that such sightlessness ought not to be corrected, because it is constitutive of insight. Put another way, interpretative reading is able to inch toward insight only as long as it is in the grip of a peculiar (and self-aware) sightlessness. We may adapt de Man's thesis for our own methodological concerns by recasting it: what makes reading Hobbes, Rousseau, and Kant difficult is partly our inability to see the way in which our own commitments are anchored in, and proceed from, the blindness and insights of the discourses that we are reading.

Formulating the problem of reading Hobbes, Rousseau, and Kant in this way cuts against the grain of some cherished intellectual assumptions. For one, we tend to assume—even when we proclaim to the contrary—that we can set aside our own biases when looking at different conceptual schemes. We also sometimes think that after learning a particular discipline or discourse, and becoming proficient in it, we can imaginatively adopt the perspective of different voices within that discourse entirely independent of our own pre-understandings. To grant these assumptions, even partially, is to subscribe tacitly to the view that there is some neutral standpoint to which we can retreat from our own perspective. It is to assume that, in some way, thinking can be separated from language, or that 'thought' is a place of neutrality from which one ventures in the different and easily exchanged dresses of language.

On my reading, this kind of 'critical-neutral thinking' gets things the wrong way round. For where studies of Kant are concerned, this outlook becomes the weaving of a particular kind of rhetoric around the idiosyncratic practices of a Königsberg sage, which are taken to be the essence of what good thinking is universally, rather than a reading of a particular way of thinking. And in embracing the values of essential and universal 'good thinking,' promoters of this outlook delude themselves into thinking that together with Kant, they constitute a vantage point that is not subject to the vicissitudes of history and language. But there is no standpoint outside the historically conditioned and temporary vocabulary that all of us are bound to use.[5] The student of philosophy and theology must therefore make the choice to recognize, and be wary of, the shortsighted attitude that 'critical-neutral thinking' fosters.

Michel de Certeau affirms this point when he argues that the assumption of neutrality remains one of the historian's greatest stumbling blocks to productive and self-aware reading. While he recognizes that the assumption of our objectivity and neutrality is not inherently malicious, de Certeau persuasively suggests that given the right circumstances, most all of us will revert to the belief that we can attain enough objectivity to assess our subject matter from a detached and neutral vantage point. Thoughts of this order are not far from hand for those who prepare to engage in a reading of Hobbes, Rousseau, or Kant: one has to have a certain amount of optimism about one's chances in order even to begin the attempt. But when de Certeau argues that our arrangements of thought are essentially fictions, he is attempting to surface this residual sentiment, what I have been calling our philosophical sightlessness, in order to make explicit those commitments in the reader that otherwise remain unstated or suppressed. Simply put, de Certeau invites us to begin to address the problem of reading Kant by asking what kind of fiction or arrangement of thought we are encountering when we read him.[6]

In these essays I try to remain cognizant of the kinds of philosophical or theological fictions that are entailed in reading Hobbes, Rousseau, and Kant on the modern religion of conscience. Some of these fictions are idiosyncratic, unique to the individual interpreter. Others are held in common: to the extent that all of us are immersed at some level in a Kantian framework, we remain mired in particular ways of seeing and interpreting Kant's theology. Getting clear about what our Kantian lenses have disposed us to 'blot out' in order to 'see' requires attention to the particularities and contingencies of the specific arrangement of thought that we are following—in our readings as much as in Kant himself. These thought patterns begin to come into notice as we compare one arrangement of thought with another, contrast figures of speech in one moment of Kant with those in another passage or another thinker, and differentiate the backdrop of one with that in another—whether ourselves or someone else. By committing ourselves to the practice or discipline of these comparative exercises, we at least have a chance to see through Kant's tropes, thereby bringing back into view some of what has been withheld in Kant's project. Indeed, for us to see that these tropes help to mask or 'cover over' the incoherence of Kant's vision is to begin to recognize the extent to which our approach to the modern religion of conscience is invariably shaped by our status as inheritors of the tropes of this discourse. Acknowledging the readiness with which we become complicit in this 'covering over' can facilitate an ethic of appreciation for the value of identifying the seductions—and costs—of philosophical sightlessness.

On Narcissism: Preliminary Reflections

I want to end these prefatory remarks with a word on narcissism. The problem of narcissism—of the personal and social commitments that may become distorted in the course of the subject's attempts, guided by an inchoate belief in the transparency and eternal truth of self-love and self-reflection, to establish a harmonious balance between self and world—is a thread that runs through these essays. When I suggest that the linchpin of the modern religion of conscience entailed the subordination of everything to the figurative self-interpretation of conscience, it will become clear, I hope, that one consequence of this subordination for philosophical theology was the formation of what I call a 'looking glass' religion, a phantasmic religious orientation in which the modern subject sees itself and nothing more. For Hobbes, Rousseau, and Kant, the decision to privilege self-interpretation over everything else was thus a costly one. Its purchase price was the setting aside of traditional talk about the individual in relation to a community— and to God. As such, these three thinkers obliged themselves to promote and defend a view of the modern subject whose most enduring trait was its dissociation from the world around it, and what was more, its subsequent transformation of that world into an image of itself.

The narcissistic turn within the theologies of Hobbes, Rousseau, and Kant evolved over the course of a number of steps in their arguments. For now, I want to state simply that each of their intellectual projects had the effect of making the image of the self into an image of world. In their arguments the world functions as the self writ large, which means, of course, that for any given individual, the world naturally looks and functions 'like me.' This use of self-perception to determine world perception derived, in part, from the ways in which Hobbes, Rousseau, and especially Kant made use of the signifier 'I.' They deployed the 'I' not just as a referential category for a particular person, but also as a kind of glue that bonded ideas together: every concept or thought depended on the 'I' for its ordering, function, and meaning.

This way in which Hobbes, Rousseau, and Kant portrayed the subject as associating ideas turned on a deeper, implicit description that isolated a core component of the self by according primacy to individual modes of being over (and against) social modes of being-in-relation. The individual mode is the identity of the 'I' in relation to itself, or the sense of being that a subject has about itself apart from the world. The social mode has to do with the identity of the 'I' in relation to the world, the sense of being that a subject has about its relations (as person) to the whole of the world. Neither mode is reducible to the other, which generates a tension that many of us know firsthand as the ongoing conflict between private well-being and social requirements. But Hobbes, Rousseau, and Kant laid such emphasis and privilege on the self-referential moment in philosophical discourse—the 'I' in the individual sense—that they effectively upended the entire way of navigating such tensions between self and world, by turning the world into self writ large.

This upending was an invitation to a thoroughgoing narcissism that, I will argue, culminated in self-worship. It obscured the difference between the first person or individual 'I' and the third person or social 'I.' In doing so, it obscured the differences between the self and the world around it. Whatever gain may have accrued to the suppression of such differences, the loss may have been incalculable. Without such distinctions, it became impossible for Hobbes, Rousseau, and Kant to recognize fully the ramifications of the conflicts between anarchy and community, apparent self-interest and appropriate self-interest, fanaticism and moral insight. However much dissolving the tension between liberty and authority by conceiving of liberty as self-legislation became the hallmark of the modern religion of conscience, it tended to confound the concern for self-righteousness with the welfare and righteousness of all humans. In the absence of these distinctions, the real prospect of distinguishing between the sort of person one wants to be from the sort one does not want to be appeared to evanesce. Of course, Hobbes, Rousseau, and Kant attempted to sidestep such losses by noting that idiosyncrasies attach to all assertions of the 'I': all individuals possess peculiar convictions that are central to self-image and lend differentiation to that for which we imagine ourselves to be living and striving. But to admit that self-interpretations sometimes change is not the same as saying that the world challenges and alters self-interpretation: the world is still an image of the self if that self continues to see only *itself* changing in the mirror.

It is within these concerns that 'religion' becomes enmeshed in the narcissistic turn already underway in the Hobbesian-Rousseauian-Kantian outlooks. Far from being a specific set of ritual or liturgical practices, religion for them was a way of construing certain human experiences that advanced a particular ideal of the human being. It was an imaginative construct, not an ecclesial community; its purpose was to orient and to complete the requirement for a comprehensive self-description. In sum: they assumed that their religion provided a better looking glass. For them, religion claimed both to differentiate and to link the individual and social modes of being by legitimating—via conscience—individual self-interest and the requirements of living in community. In reality, however, the religion advocated by Hobbes, Rousseau, and Kant would prove less a harmonizing among individuals and more a harmonizing *within* the individual. It was the inevitable outcome of their declaring liberty to be concordant with authority. In their arguments, religion's primary task consisted in reflecting a view of the self back to the self, and in the process, extrapolating from that self onto the world around it.

This generalizing or extrapolating movement assumed, among other things, that given the right uses of reason and self-reflection, all people necessarily would describe moral duty and the human condition in the same way. Hobbes, Rousseau, and Kant did concede the realities of particularity in such descriptions: different people will describe matters differently when considering whether the actions they would like to pursue are consistent with the principles of morality. As such, they recognized the particularity and contingency, if not of the human condition or its overarching descriptions, then at least of individual descriptions of proposed moral actions. A great deal hung on their capacity to maintain this concession, for without it, the prospect of moral deliberation would be lost. But Hobbes, Rousseau, and Kant only gave this concession infrequent mention; they offered little explanation of how and when this distinction was to be struck. In consequence, their more frequent and forceful appeals to universality overshadowed the discussion. By so orienting the description, their readings tacitly defined difference—anything that operates outside the looking glass—as a distraction or mistake.

I hope this point about universality will help us see, in the essays that follow, how narcissism came to haunt the theological conceptions that Hobbes, Rousseau, and Kant put forward. For the idea that the description of the 'I' is in some sense universal stands as essential to Kant's ground-breaking claim that all ordinary consciousness depends on the same fundamental conditions. It is essential, as well, to the notion that all men and women are capable of discerning true morality. And it is even essential to the Kantian requirement that everyone be able to compare his proposals for action with moral principles. In short, a universal description commits us to the notion that all individuals, by virtue of something shared and essential, will of necessity agree with one reading of the situation, whatever that reading, and the variants it permits, might be. Thus the Hobbesian-Rousseauian-Kantian description obligates us to become blind or 'sightless' to the intrinsic difficulty that all of us have in speaking responsibly about universal descriptions. It forces us to blur the distinction between the particular and the universal in order to arrive at the insight that the particular awareness of righteousness within us implies our tie to a universal order of accord. Hobbes, Rousseau, and Kant even went so far as to introduce the concept of God to imbue those persistent moments of particularity with a figurative sense of universality.

Inasmuch as this figural ground (universal description) to which the modern religion of conscience appeals is derived from the literal (particular description), it therein commits us to a linguistic procedure known as 'catachresis'—the forcible importing of a term from one domain in which it has meaning to another in which it stands for that which has no proper name for itself. In other words, the force of the literal sense of a particular description informs the figurative sense of the universal description. But the modern religion of conscience goes one step further. It argues that the force of the figurative significance of the universal description has the effect of altering the literal significance of the particular description. This is why the 'king' is construed as the voice of the Leviathan for Hobbes, why the stricken 'Savoyard priest' is the visible expression of appropriate love for Rousseau, and why the 'public citizen' is viewed as if she were a moral agent, an end-in-herself, for Kant. This adoption of catachresis and its peculiar adaptation marks another step in the narcissistic turn of the modern religion of conscience. By affirming in others what one most clearly sees in one's own moral, figural imaginations, the individual subtly engages in a tactic of depreciation of their otherness, reconstituting their literalness from his or her own imaginative strivings. The linchpin of the modern religion of conscience is thus the subordination of everything to the figurative self-interpretation of conscience: a religion that could not avoid the form of the looking glass.

This way of reading—or what is much the same, this decision to privilege self-interpretation over all else—became a catalyst for the unraveling of the modern religion of conscience in philosophical and theological thought. And as I suggest in different ways throughout the essays that follow, the cost of achieving a self-referential religion was dissociation. By casting adrift inherited discourses that treated the interiority and exteriority of the individual in terms of his or her relation to God and to world, Hobbes, Rousseau, and Kant would find themselves obliged to delineate some new ground for argumentation. Their choice was 'ordinary consciousness.' This move was altogether novel and bold. But it brought a host of philosophical riddles whose insolubility forced Hobbes, Rousseau, and Kant into strategies of linguistic catachresis as a way of developing—and saving—their arguments. Accordingly, 'religion' became fundamentally a declaration of anthropocentrism. Hobbes, Rousseau, and Kant each quoted from biblical literature and referred to 'religious' events in their writings. But their uses of Scripture, doctrine, and theology bore little relation to the theocentric traditions that preceded them. Rather, their descriptions served to recast Scripture, tradition, theology, and God himself into the parameters of the looking glass religion. So, too, the soul came to be recast, eventually as the tain or lusterless back of the looking glass. The presumptive binding ties between the individual and social orders of being, between the particular and the universal, and between the temporal and the eternal became an elaboration of the conditions that supported the interests of the subjectivity described and implied by the mirror: the emergence of the modern narcissist.

ONE

Unscaffolding Religious "Madness"

Flying up, crossing over, going forward.
Passing through, getting deep enough. Breaking
into, finding the way, living at the heart
and going beyond that. Finally realizing
that arriving is not the same as being resident.
That what we do is not what we are doing.

—JACK GILBERT

J. C. Lavater, the Swiss poet, mystic, and renowned physiognomist, wrote to Kant in 1775, seeking Kant's opinion of his book on faith and prayer, *Vermischte Schriften* (1774). An ardent admirer of Kant who often wrote encouraging him to bring his new work to publication, Lavater apparently anticipated a positive endorsement. To his dismay, Kant's 28 April 1775, reply was anything but favorable: "Do you realize whom you are asking? A man who believes that, in the final moment, only the purest candor concerning our most hidden inner convictions can stand the test and who, like Job, takes it to be sin to flatter God and make inner confessions, perhaps forced out by fear, that fail to agree with what we freely think."[1]

Kant then filled out his response, setting forth the principal lines of a perspective that would be published eighteen years later as *Religion Within the Boundaries of Mere Reason* (1793). "My presupposition," he wrote in a postscript to the letter, "is that no book, whatever its authority might be—yes, even one based on the authority of my own senses—can substitute for the religion of conscience."[2] Distinguishing between the teachings of Christ and the historical reports about those teachings, between moral teaching and dogma, Kant insisted that that the moral law alone tells us what we must do to be worthy of justification, whereas dogma merely reports what God has done to help us see our frailty in seeking justification. Hence as historical reports of what *God* does, neither dogma nor confessions of faith, neither appeals to holy names nor observance of religious ceremonies purported to be a condition of salvation, are of any avail in making *us* any more worthy of the good. Rather, despite the "insuperable evil of our hearts," nothing is needed for our "union with this divine force" beyond using our "natural God-given powers in such a way as not to be unworthy of His aid."[3] But we may only humbly rely on this "hidden supplement to our deficiencies" if we have done what is in our power "not to be unworthy of his Law."[4]

So confident was Kant in this view that he declared: "But once the doctrine of the purity of conscience in faith and of the good transformation of our lives has been sufficiently propagated as the only true religion for man's salvation (the faith that God, in a manner we need not at all understand, will provide what our frail natures lack, without seeking His aid by means of the so-called worship that religious fanaticism always demands)—when this true religious structure has been built up so that it can maintain itself in the world—then the scaffolding must be taken down."[5]

What is it about Kant's religion of conscience, the criticism it embodied, and its seemingly new sense of certitude that became a catalyst for radical change in the history of European high culture? The religion of conscience served simultaneously as an attack on both Enlightenment moral utopianism and historical religious dogmatism. Against those utopians who believed that after the abolition of religious and political institutions, the natural bonds of human solidarity would reemerge, or those who thought that human satisfaction could be achieved once 'Nature' was mastered through technological self-assertion, Kant showed that freedom inevitably entailed the possibility of evil. Against those religious dogmatists who taught that conformity of human conduct with the divine commands would lead to the establishment of the Kingdom of God on earth, Kant maintained that freedom implies the impossibility of eradicating evil. When, therefore, Kant called for the removal of "the scaffolding," he had more in mind than the practices of the Christian Church.

The subject of this essay is the broader reach of Kant's call for removing such a scaffolding. As will become evident, the reach included epistemological assumptions and their political ramifications that underlay not only Christian beliefs and practices, but also the Enlightenment thinking of the empiricists, the rationalists, the 'mystics,' and the 'common-sense' theorists. For Kant, in short, only the religion of conscience has the possibility of preserving free thought and free action, because it alone is grounded in self-giving law.

Four Preliminaries

Before proceeding to the body of this analysis, I want to dispose of several preliminary issues. To begin with, Kant's placement of the main point of enlightenment, of people's emergence from their "self-incurred minority," "chiefly in *matters of religion*" can be somewhat misleading.[6] After all, it was the religious and not the political domain in which Frederick the Great tolerated freedom of thought. Thus we might be tempted to assume that Kant's call for enlightenment remained circumscribed within the domain of traditional religious practices. But it is at least arguable that the way in which Kant speaks of religion permits him to use religious discourse as a foil for a broader range of concerns that included epistemological and political themes. Indeed, such themes, often having to do with the ways in which we are related to the 'heavens' and the 'earth,' were themselves the object of Kant's critical gaze throughout much of his life; their systematic reappraisal formed a basis of his own "Great Instauration," the critical philosophy. So understood, the religion of conscience examined in these pages provides a window into that *novum organum*—by which he sought to articulate the temper of his time—which Kant began to erect even while dismantling other philosophical positions. Kant's "Great Instauration" envisioned the proportions of human reasoning to conform to the conditions of self-aware-ness in much the same way as da Vinci had portrayed the workings of the human body as an analogue for the workings of the universe (*Vitruvian Man*, Figure 3).

A second preliminary concern emerges from the first. By linking Kant's religion of conscience with his *novum organum* and the so-called temper of his time, I am introducing overtones of that morass known as the modernity

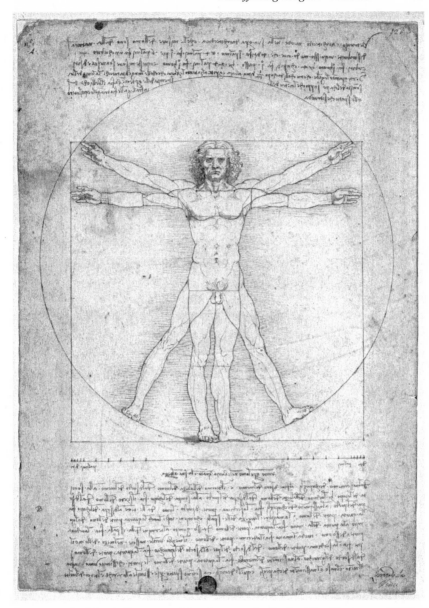

Figure 3: Da Vinci, *Vitruvian Man* (ca. 1492). (Scala / Art Resource, NY.)

question. To be sure, Kant is, in some sense, 'modern.' Thus it is tempting to posit an answer to the question of what modernity might be in order to determine more precisely what kind of radical change Kant's religion of conscience introduced. But important as the modernity question may be, it remains beset with seemingly insuperable difficulties that surface as soon as we begin to frame an 'answer.' For whether modernity is conceived of as a period of time or an ideology, as Western or global, as one or many, as self-extrication from naïveté or disenchantment, as the loss of the concept of a purposeful cosmos or secularization, as autonomy versus dependence, as the rationalization of economic behavior or the bureaucratization of social relationships, as the loss of the distinction between good and evil or the loss of taboos, as the power of domination or the power of self-preservation—to name just a few of the ways in which modernity has been cast—it is difficult to avoid falling into the traps of pragmatic antinomies that blur the very distinctions that we are attempting to strike. Given what Leszek Kolakowski has called "our incurable ignorance of our own spiritual foundation," we are hard-pressed to avoid the pragmatic practice of framing questions in a way that proves most useful to us, irrespective of their historical viability.[7]

We learn from these and other such difficulties, in part, that modernity's antinomic character is deeply unsettling, and, also in part, that we may be better served if we set aside the larger modernity question to focus on a more modest one. The question for us in this context would then become not so much "What is modernity?" as "What was Kant's particular philosophical perspective on the unsettling character of modernity?" On my reading, Kant perceives his age as characterized by the "ripened power of judgment," the "genuine age of criticism": not only are humans called upon to come of age and to think for themselves—thereby recognizing that enlightenment is a sacred right that has always been true—but they are also called to exercise their innate capacity for self-determination.[8] To do so responsibly, however, humans must see through the inchoate illusions that attach to the exercise of reason itself and have become manifest in history.

A third preliminary concern follows on the modernity issue. On the surface, there is little in Kant's perspective to distinguish him from the cautions of Montaigne or Pascal, the critical aspirations of d'Alembert or Condorcet, or the foundationalist interrogatories of Descartes, Spinoza, Leibniz, Locke, or Hume. But Kant thought they had not gone far enough, that they had not recognized the full implications of the critical thinking in which they were engaged. What is utterly novel in Kant, and what separates him from his forbears, is thus his view that critical self-determination is neither "made" nor "found"—to borrow Richard Rorty's distinction[9]—that is, neither invented nor discovered, but a *condition* for making any claims whatsoever about our world or our action. Because Kant's notion of critical self-determination cannot be derived from empiricist foundationalism nor inferred from rationalist speculative metaphysics (and their concomitant theological commitments), its status is neither natural 'fact' nor metaphysical claim.

The difficulties we thus encounter in clarifying the status of Kant's critical self-determination points up what is distinctive about his take on the modern unsettlement, or at least the unsettlement that Kant discerned in late-eighteenth-century Europe. The peculiarity of the age of criticism, Kant appears to be saying, is that while it can stand in awe of the heavens and of the earth, it cannot, as critically self-determining knowledge, enjoy the confidence that it is "suspended from anything in heaven or supported by anything on earth."[10] (Kant's own remark actually reads: "Here, then, we see philosophy put in fact in a precarious position, which is to be firm, even though there is nothing in heaven or on earth from which it depends or on which it is based."[11]) Such a concession is tantamount to the diagnosis that critically self-determining knowledge, belonging neither to heaven nor to earth, is 'homeless.' With the order of knowing so disturbed, the requirement that critically self-determining knowledge create a new domain for itself naturally follows.[12] And the first step in fulfilling this requirement, according to Kant, is introducing the language of 'the conditions of any possible experience.'

This language of conditions brings us to our final preliminary point. Both then and now, readers of Kant, from Solomon Maimon and Friedrich Heinrich Jacobi to Lewis White Beck and Robert Pippin, have blanched at the notion that by introducing the language of the conditions of possible experience, Kant managed to bypass the skeptical question of how we are related to what is 'out there,' to what 'really is the case,' be it the heavens or the earth.[13] For them, Kant does not so much overcome as delay the problem. True, he discards the Cartesian subject/object distinction as a misnomer, but he merely displaces it onto the relation between thought and sensation, which, though ostensibly yielding knowledge of external objects, does not extend to 'things in themselves.' I am proposing a somewhat different reading. The issue is not whether Kant failed to *resolve* the problem of skepticism, but rather whether he *dissolved* as nonsensical the grounds on which it previously had made sense. By reading Kant in this way, I depart from some aspects of mainstream Kantian interpretation, but this departure does permit me to say pointedly what Kant thinks is so unsettling about modernity and why the religion of conscience thus becomes so crucial.

The discussion will proceed in three steps: the first focuses narrowly on what Kant means by 'criticism'; the second, on what he means by self-determination before the tribunal of reason; and the third, what he means by the labor of critically self-determining knowledge. These steps will make clear, I hope, not only what kind of scaffolding Kant thinks must be collapsed but also what new backdrop comes into view against which the radicality of Kant's religion of conscience will stand out in sharp relief. That new background is the inextricable tie between freedom and evil that makes the threat of state-sponsored religious censorship inevitable.

The Role of Criticism

Criticism for Kant is self-knowledge, specifically the self-knowledge of reason. On first look, there is little in this definition to distinguish it from the Platonic tradition in philosophy or the Augustinian tradition in theology. But his motto, *"Recum habita, et noris quam sit tibi curta supellex"* ("Dwell in your own house and you will know how simple your possessions are"), drawn from the *Satires* of Persius, offers the first intimations that Kant's notion of criticism marks a departure from Platonism and Augustinianism. To be sure, the 'house' in which Kant desired to remain was reason, but on his own account the reason of his Platonic and Augustinian forbearers was beset with the peculiar fate of giving itself problems that it could not answer. So it was scarcely surprising that Kant deemed the history of the controversies over these unanswerable questions the "battle of metaphysics." He thought that these intellectual skirmishes had reduced metaphysics' once regal status to that of a contemptible outcast, and its articulations to "worm-eaten dogmatism."[14] But in the same breath in which he castigated metaphysics, Kant also vowed to take the only path left to solve the riddle of metaphysics. Thus if his efforts were not to be a fool's errand, he would have to propose a conception of rational criticism that lent a new meaning to the notion of "dwelling in your own house." However ironic it may seem, Kant's view was actually far from reviling metaphysics, and instead more committed to its centrality: "Metaphysics is the spirit of philosophy. It is related to philosophy as the spirit of wine (*spiritus veni*) is to wine. It purifies our elementary concepts and thereby makes us capable of comprehending all sciences. In short, it is the greatest culture of the human understanding."[15] So "solving the riddle of metaphysics" was not only roughly the equivalent of unraveling the Gordian knot of reason, of tracing out the lines of reason that had run ineluctably to a labyrinth of insoluble antinomies; but it was also a matter of stating afresh the historically 'true' course on which reason had been proceeding nonetheless all along.

From the vantage point of such a course, Kant thought, a purified comprehension of all the sciences would become possible. Implicit in this view, of course, was the claim that humanity had been dwelling in a mistaken conception of reason. Hence Kant's plan to rectify this problem by setting out reason's "origins, scope, and limits" inaugurated a course of inquiry that quickly would assume unwieldy proportions.[16] Kant himself recognized this unwieldiness, lamenting elsewhere that he had never been able to state to his own satisfaction what his program was about.[17] But it was not so much the scope of Kant's architectonic as the angle of his vision that has since proved so worrisome. By arguing from a perspective that he purported to be distinct from the frameworks in which the question had been raised earlier, Kant inadvertently positioned himself as the target of wide misunderstanding.

So let us proceed, tentatively. Criticism is the enlightenment of reason, by which reason may come, first, to understand that its speculative edifices have been finished before its grounds have been adequately prepared, thereby giving rise to many prized and beloved delusions.[18] Only then, second, can criticism function to abolish this semblance, in order that, third, what reason alone brings forth from itself can come into view through self-examination as an organon or system of pure reason. For Kant, then, criticism is a process. But whether it is individual or corporate, Kant's own voice or some sort of movement of reason that achieves social proportion, is ambiguous at this juncture.

Hints toward a resolution of this ambiguity appear in Kant's 'solution' to the problem of metaphysics, which he considered the ultimate vindication of his notion of criticism. On Kant's telling, rationalists and empiricists alike had misunderstood the nature of cognition. By sensualizing ideas, rationalists presumed that their concepts were telling us something about things as they are; by idealizing sensations, empiricists thought that they could preserve some original datum of experience upon which they could build their claims about knowledge. Neither camp, however, fully grasped the inchoate *combinatory* character of the mind that joins concepts and sensibility. Kant claims that concepts are mere forms of thought, containing nothing, whereas a manifold of sensory impression, or what Kant calls 'intuitions,' are themselves indiscriminate, and only come to count as discriminate by virtue of being in relation to a principle of discrimination. The crucial, albeit prickly, point in Kant's argument here is that we never have access to concepts or intuitions *apart from* their combination. Because we think *through* concepts, we can only represent them to ourselves in relation to or in combination with sensible intuitions. This is analogous to saying, as Kant does, that we can't think of a line without drawing it in thought, or of a circle without describing it.[19] Traditional metaphysics has run aground, Kant says, in its assumption that by abstracting forms of thought or sensations from experience, we can actually know something about either thought or sensation. By way of contrast, 'criticism' is a mode of thinking that attempts to delineate the conditions or presuppositions of representations that cannot themselves be represented.

How, and by what right, does criticism proceed as a distinct "ripened power of judgment" within what amounts to a pre-theoretical mode of awareness? How, in a word, can criticism delineate what is antecedent to representation? Despite his reticence to elaborate this in the first *Critique*, Kant does offer clues in his *Anthropological Didactic* when he alludes to an inchoate operation of reflection that *precedes* investigation.[20] By means of this operation, which is spontaneous and not intentional or deliberative, we are aware of diverse and presumably conflicting cognitions that serve as the source for an explicit investigation. Such investigation, in turn, is a correlate of this inchoate awareness. Proceeding with an eye toward the connections of coherence and unity of which reflection itself is not explicitly aware, investigation attempts to delineate the features that pertain to its domain. Kant's celebrated "transcendental unity of apperception"—"the supreme . . . principle . . . in the whole of human cognition"[21]—incorporates this correlation between awareness (the 'I as subject of thinking') emerging in spontaneous reflection *and* investigation (the 'I think' as a methodological

principle of unity). By restricting our spontaneous tendency to conceptualize our cognitive actions *to the domain alone in which they arise*, Kant emphasized the process of reflected control that he considered inherent to a system
of unified rationality that could be both consistent and avoid confusion.
Only a system of reason whose method of investigation has its origin in an
awareness central to reason, and that relies on this awareness to discern its
differences in application, can determine the true unity of reason despite its
apparently independent operations. This amounts to saying that the fundamental correlation between awareness and investigation is characteristic of
reason; or what is the same, that reason is inherently critical. So understood,
the method of criticism writes large its characteristic correlation: it proceeds
from an implicit, partial knowledge given in awareness *to* an investigatory
conceptual clarification. Criticism thus appears to be a matter of fierce intellectual integrity, with robust implications for individual responsibility.

But there is more to say about Kant's understanding of criticism as a
process. Conceiving of criticism as the correlation between awareness and
investigation implicitly entails the possibility of rejecting certain conceptu-
alizations of our cognitive capacities. Kant's determination to delineate the
conditions of representation therefore effectively raises a question: if reason
is charged with understanding its own form, which, by Kant's definition,
always eludes representation, then how is it to proceed? Kant's answer essentially amplifies his insight into the correlation of awareness and investigation: reason must look to *manifestations* of thinking. Criticism presupposes
the history of the manifestations of reason to understand its own workings.
It does not, therefore—at least in the way in which Kant presents the case—
simply turn 'inward' to discover its own form. Hence Descartes, Leibniz,
Spinoza, Locke, and Hume are not incidental characters making cameo appearances on the stage of Kant's *Critique*, but instead serve as concrete manifestations of reason through which the workings and illusions of reason
appear. This suggests, then, that for Kant criticism is not only an individual
but also a collective process, and that intellectual integrity cannot proceed
apart from the efforts of reasonable humanity.

Once criticism has discerned the form underlying the manifestations of
reason, or once it has understood the conditions under which alone representation is possible, but which themselves are unrepresentable, criticism
incurs the obligation to think in a way that departs from ordinary experience. Criticism should not assume that by conceiving of the conditions of

possible experience, it can thereby extend its knowledge beyond the boundaries of experience. To do so would surreptitiously introduce sensible content into concepts that do not by themselves possess any such content. Rather, criticism must embark on an entirely new way of thinking that relates only to the conditions that would have to apply in order for different kinds of experience to occur. Criticism is thus, in the deepest sense, *Ausgang*, which although literally means either "release" or "departure," can also convey the religious overtones of "exodus."[22] By treating the ideas of God, of freedom, and of the immortality of the soul merely as heuristic devices whose intelligibility derives entirely from their relation to the sensible, criticism begins its 'epistemological exodus' as it takes its first steps toward a system of pure reason or *organon*. But that these metaphysical ideas, long associated with religion, should also now acquire a new meaning, heralding the prospect of a new religious sensibility, marks a practical exodus, as well. Little wonder, then, that Kant exhorts courage—*Sapere aude!*—with respect to this dimension of criticism.[23] For *Ausgang* now implies not merely thinking these ideas in new ways, but also being guided by them in a new kind of conduct, both individual and corporate. And the call to new conduct, for Kant, means that criticism is also a religio-political process.

Self-determination Before the Tribunal of Reason

The significance of the religio-political process that issues from this call to new conduct comes clearly into view when we hold before our eyes Kant's metaphor of the 'tribunal.' To begin, on Kant's accounting, thinking freely affects the human disposition of mind, cultivating the capacity of *"freedom in acting."*[24] In turn, moral action will induce those who govern, or so Kant believes, to alter their principles as would befit and respect the dignity of such a moral citizenry. However much this may appear to qualify as wishful thinking, the underlying structure of Kant's claims makes it more radical than utopian. Indeed, the manner in which Kant envisions the link between thinking for oneself (reason determining itself) and freedom in acting (reason determining itself practically) points up this radicality. Kant thinks of 'tribunal' (*Richterstuhl*) as an apt metaphor to depict it.

One of the more arresting features of this metaphor, I think, is its capacity to help us pose the question of how we can adopt an epistemological

stance and an ethical stance simultaneously. On the face of it, Kant's epistemological strictures uphold the judging activity of the mind in a way that
effectively undercuts the beliefs that we may have held before entering into
critical reflection. Neither concepts nor intuitions alone offer us access to
the treasure trove of cherished belief; and concepts combined with intuitions in judgment limit our knowledge to the domain of empirical experience. To pursue this emphasis on judgment myopically, however, would
sabotage freedom in acting. So we have to think with Kant of the various
ways in which judging also unifies disparate elements of criticism and ethical
belief.

This is where the metaphor of the tribunal comes in. We may well think
of a tribunal as a judgment seat, with its connotations of the raised floor for
the magistrate's chair in the apse of the Roman basilica (the tribune). Or,
again, we may invoke the connotations of the apse of the basilica in the
Byzantine era that contained the bishop's throne. To think in this way of
the resonances that attach to the notion of tribunal would be to focus on its
structural features. But we should not overlook its connotation in Roman
history, where the term tribune also referred to those officers who were
chosen by the people to protect their liberties against the senate and the
consuls. This latter resonance of tribunal emphasizes its activity, not simply
its structure.

Kant weaves all these connotations of the metaphor into his account of
self-determination. Judgment, as the heart of Kant's thinking, is the elevated site of the mind's activity, apart from which concepts have no life.
And it is in the activity of judging that the rules announce themselves by
which freedom of thought may be secured against the encroachments of
dogmatism. In short, it is *in the course of the activity of reason* that judgment's
structure becomes manifest. It comes as no surprise, accordingly, that on
Kant's telling, reason does not enter the tribunal "to be instructed as a
student in appropriate recitation," but rather as "the appointed judge who
compels witnesses to answer whatever questions are put to them."[25]

This Baconian borrowing makes mischief for Kant. What he is actually
getting at is that judgment depends on a subjective contribution of the mind
rather than on some sort of principle of nature independent of the mind.
Such mischief notwithstanding, Kant's metaphor of the tribunal keeps before our eyes the notion of the correlation between a certain body of awareness and an investigation that delineates its aptness. Casting the issue in this

way helps us not only recall the correlative character of Kant's notion of the unity of the mind, but also prepares us for his conception of moral awareness. Just as a certain correlation arises between awareness and investigation that anchors theoretical reasoning, so also does another correlation arise between awareness and investigation that guides moral reasoning. In the midst of desiring, humans spontaneously become aware of a constraint upon natural inclinations. Implicit in this awareness is a distinction between a world of conceivable conduct motivated by the demands of sensibility and a world of conceivable conduct motivated by the demands of constraint. Correlated with this awareness is the investigation that reveals to us that such constraint frees us from any measure of sensible resistance. Kant calls the awareness of constraint "a fact of reason,"[26] and the investigation "respect for the moral law."[27] To pursue the insight of this correlation is to believe that the requirement of practical reason, or the moral law, is that freedom announces for itself the right to be active, and that the constitution of the world is susceptible to the effects of moral conduct that we pursue out of respect for the law.

The testimony of reason from which this insight emerges elevates the good will to the level of the unconditioned. Because reason, like the tribunal, is *both* structure *and* activity, it can reinforce the beliefs we already have by investigating their true nature, thus becoming, as it were, its own bishop. But this episcopacy of reason is efficacious only insofar as the referential relation between the facticity of the idea of the good and respect for the moral law remains in tact.

Moreover, in light of this correlation, we can understand why Kant thinks that reason determines the interests of all the powers of the mind— "the condition under which alone its exercise is promoted"—and that it can subordinate all its interests to that one without which reason succumbs: liberty.[28] Hence beliefs that pertain to the exercise of the liberty of reason can stand simultaneously with the strictures of speculative reason, because these beliefs have solely to do with the self-determination of reason. In this regard, reason is the tribune that, in the interests of liberty, declares everything subordinate to freedom.[29]

If, then, subordinating everything to freedom secures the domain of free thinking and acting, what does such self-determination undermine or 'unscaffold'? Much is at stake in this question, for a chief issue lingering behind it involves whether and how responsible autonomy is possible. Self-determination in the interest of responsible autonomy fundamentally undermines censorship in all its forms. It 'unscaffolds' both the religious trappings of the censors *and* their epistemological underpinnings. Accordingly, for Kant, the gravest impediment to responsible liberty is not so much dogmatism and cant as it is the pernicious practice of censorship. On Kant's reading, all are finally citizens of the domain of free thinking; thus all have both the moral right and obligation to resist the censorship of the Church or of governmental officials and to publish freely as scholars. When in 1784 Kant pointedly addresses this observation to clergy, subtly playing off *tribunal*'s connotation of 'bishop,' he is invoking the concrete circumstances that continually threatened responsible intellectual liberty not only in the Königsberg of his acquaintance, but elsewhere as well. "Subordinating everything to freedom" is, in the first instance, the sentinel's cry against the encroachments of censorship.

This cry was an especially timely one given Kant's theo-political environs. When Franz Albert Schulz assumed the leadership of the Pietist faction in Königsberg in 1731, he introduced a modified form, supporting Pietist convictions, of Christian Wolff's philosophy. Wolff attempted to synthesize Leibnizian rationalist metaphysics with Protestant doctrine in opposition to what he deemed the 'evils' of Spinoza's fatalism and atheism. As Frederick William I had eight years earlier removed Wolff from his professorship, banished him from all of Prussia, and banned the teaching of Wolffian philosophy at the behest of the Halle Pietists, Schulz's move was audacious. For it soon came to mean that students would be exposed to the Enlightenment thinking not only of numerous Wolffians, but also of Christian Thomasius, who had been influenced by the Pietists and warned his students against the dangers of Spinozistic sects. Within this climate, a version of Aristotelianism blended with Pietism also emerged. But the tenor at the school of theology remained tendentious, prompting Colestin Christian Flottwell to observe that "at this time, the Spanish inquisition is milder than it is."[30] By 1740, when Kant entered the University of Königsberg, the tone had begun to modulate. In that year, Frederick I died and Frederick II (Frederick the Great) ascended to the throne. More liberal in matters of religion, Frederick II was known to be interested in philosophy and literature. In 1744, by refusing to intervene, he allowed an anonymously published book advocating a Spinozistic point of view to be banned;

nonetheless, the king also thwarted efforts to have Christian Gabriel Fischer, who turned out to be the author, banished again. Such modification not withstanding, religious controversy and censorship persisted. Even when some years later (1755) Franz Albert Schulz served as rector of the university, something of this sentiment still remained prevalent: Schulz blocked Kant, who had studied dogmatic theology with him, from academic appointment until Kant would swear that he feared God with all his heart. Owing in part to general scruples over Kant's adherence to the rules of Pietist discourse, the professorial appointment did not materialize for Kant until 1770.[31]

For more than a decade after his *Inaugural Dissertation* (1770), Kant pursued and revised its trajectories in preparation of what would become the first *Critique*. Even with the more tolerant political climate of Frederick the Great, Kant grew restive over some emerging views that cast him as an atheist, worrying that they might cause him professional repercussions. His foreboding soon proved to be prescient. Shortly after his 1786 inauguration, Frederick William II (nephew of Frederick the Great), who had at first supported rational inquiry, reversed himself, supporting instead policies requiring strict conformity with the Augsburg Confession. Later in the year, the government forbade anyone at Marburg to lecture on Kant's philosophy until it could be determined whether Kant encouraged religious skepticism. By 1788, Frederick William II's policies included the Edict Concerning Religion and the Edict of Censorship. By December of the same year, philosopher Heinrich Würzer, who dedicated his *Remarks* to the king and enjoyed the king's initial favorable reception, suffered a reversal of fortunes and within a matter of days was imprisoned.

The reach of censorship once again overtook Kant in 1792. In what was primarily a political act, Kant published *Religion Within the Boundaries of Mere Reason* despite the censorship of the Gielsdorf preacher Johann Heinrich Schulz and others like him. Containing a series of four essays—some of which had previously been suppressed—*Religion* expressed allegiance to the efforts of the contributors to the radical journal *Berlinische Monatschrift* (most notable among whom, along with Kant, had been Lessing and Mendelssohn) to advance not only religious freedom, but also freedom from any kind of bondage. As had Wolff in 1723, and as did August Hermann Niemeyer and Johann August Rosselt at Halle and Johann Gustav Reinbeck at Frankfurt, Kant now faced the direct censure of the king: Frederick William II threatened "unpleasant measures . . . for continued obstinancy."[32] Only after the death of Frederick William II in 1797 did Kant again publish on religious issues.

With these events in mind, we can see that Kant's "subordination of everything to freedom" functioned, at least in part, to undermine the practices of censorship. There is much else about it that also comes to light. For Kant, the freedom to think is also opposed to any civil compulsion that would proscribe the arenas of *communication*.[33] Inasmuch as the freedom to think entails the responsibility to think clearly, true clarity in thinking depends entirely upon open, critical communication among persons. Policies that permit freedom of thought but restrict its communication therefore proceed at the wrong level; rather than promoting, they erode the very possibility of free thinking. Second, for Kant, freedom to think simultaneously opposes any form of compulsion over *conscience*, including the (implicit) prohibition of critical inquiry communicated subtly by prescribed formulas of religious belief.[34] In trying to set out the nature of religious beliefs, such formulas not only leave the internal structure of those attitudes unexamined, but also, in consequence, lend to such beliefs a static air, which cannot account for their motivational character in human conduct. Finally, if we think of subordinating everything to freedom as active resistance to the yoke of censorship, we can see that freedom must pursue a certain common course if it is to prevail. This means that free thinking engaged in an environment of other epistemological or ethical orderings could oppose those orderings and their encroachments successfully only if it subjects itself to a distinctive ordering characteristic of *all free thinking*. Kant's way of putting this point is to say that free thinking subjects itself to *"no laws except those it gives itself."*[35]

To recognize that the subordination of everything to freedom necessarily entails the self-giving of law—apart from which it would not be possible to account for human behaviors that are distinct from natural or sociocultural motivation—is to see that for Kant the issue of autonomy extends to the most elemental forms of mental activity. This, in turn, helps us to appreciate the depth of his insight that freedom or the self-giving of law always implies the capacity for doing evil. For we cannot make coherent sense of the human practice of giving law to ourselves if we overlook the human predisposition as living, rational, responsible beings to various goods. These goods include natural, rational, and moral ends, each of which is a variant of self-preservation. Accordingly, the self-giving law of self-preservation, *naturally* conceived, aims for the protection and maintenance of the species; the self-giving law of self-preservation conceived of as a *rational life-form*

implies equal worth in happiness; and the self-giving law of self-preservation conceived *morally* (unconditionally) incorporates the idea of humanity
considered as a whole.[36] Inasmuch as we are susceptible to all of these self-
given laws, each of which direct us to an end that is in itself a good, what
counts as moral is not some Manichean choice between good and evil, but
a choice among the most elemental motives of mental life. Although each
of these present themselves as justified, only one among them is unconditioned (the moral).

The reading I have presented thus far might tempt us to think that Kant's
solution to this dilemma of competing goods involves the claim that moral
choice consists in the right ordering of incentives, of the subordinating of
everything to freedom. To the extent that this description is true of Kant,
there is some justification to the complaint that his is too conceptual a solution. After all, the notion that we could solve the problem of the self-giving
of law merely by framing it correctly would amount to little more than a
sophisticated variant of the Socratic adage, "To know the good is to do the
good." And this variant, in principle, would be indistinguishable from the
moral utopianism of much Enlightenment thinking that omitted from consideration the vagaries of human motivation. But given what else Kant has
to say, it is more likely that this rather austere reading of Kant actually
suffers from a flattened sense of his conceptual structure, and consequently,
misses the radicality of the implications of Kant's structure for politico-
religious and epistemological processes. For Kant also seems to be saying
that in order to understand the concept of freedom in the context of the life
we live, we must amplify our sense of what freedom entails.

Moving, then, to a more elemental level, Kant adds to the idea of self-
giving law "a first subjective ground for the adoption of incentives (*Gesin-
nung*), that to us is inscrutable"[37]—what he describes in other words as the
"intelligible ground of the heart (the ground of all maxims of the power of
choice)."[38] So the problem is not, in Kant's view, merely one of the right
ordering of incentives, but also of the impossibility of retrieving that first
subjective motive for choosing, which we express through our choice of
self-given law. We express our humanity precisely in this dilemma of choosing. For what cannot be said by 'anyone' nonetheless informs the choices of
'everyone' in the ordering of their motives; to paraphrase Kant, "By [our]
maxims, [we] express at the same time the character of [our] species."[39] This
amounts to saying, in the parlance of Augustinian theology, that all our

willing articulates our fallenness, or that the fate of our freedom is its inextricable link to evil.

This is probably why Kant, in his *Groundwork of the Metaphysics of Morals*, observed that actual human behavior would likely *not* conform to the moral norms of his theory: "Even if there never have been actions arising from such pure sources, what is at stake is not whether this or that happened; that instead, reason by itself and independently of all appearances commands what is to happen; that, accordingly, actions of which the world so far has given no example, and whose very practicability might be very much doubted by one who bases everything on experience, are still inflexibly commanded by reason."[40] Here, in this tension between the limits of our knowing and the ends to which the moral norms of practical reason direct us, we encounter in full measure what Kant deemed the "precarious position" of self-determination before the tribunal of reason: it has "to be firm even though there is nothing in heaven or on earth from which it depends or on which it is based."[41] To be self-determined before the tribunal of reason, in essence, means that we can turn neither to anything in experience nor to any sense or intuition implanted from without to orient ourselves. Instead, we must subordinate everything to freedom, or resist every encroachment to free thinking and free acting, thereby becoming sustainers of our own law. But inasmuch as we are to be respecters solely of that law whose reach has now been revealed as fundamentally beyond our grasp, the greater price of freedom, haunted by evil, is that we live in the permanent possibility of falling apart.

The Labor of Self-critically Determined Knowledge

In 1765 Kant privately confessed Rousseau's impact on his thinking: "I am a scientist by inclination. I know the thirst for knowledge and the deep satisfaction of every advance of knowledge. There was a time when I believed all this knowledge could be the honor of mankind, and I despised all those who were bereft of such knowledge. Rousseau has corrected me. I learned to honor man, and I would consider myself less worthy than the average worker if I did not believe that all this [i.e., philosophy] could contribute to what really matters—the restoration of the rights of mankind."[42] Kant's contribution to 'what really matters' is often misunderstood, if not overlooked. When Kant claimed that "the critique of pure reason is the true tribunal for all controversies of pure reason," without which "reason is, as it were in the state of nature" and "cannot make its assertions and claims valid or secure them except through **war**," he was not merely speaking theoretically.[43] In support of his conviction that freedom of thought is "an original right . . . in which everyone has a voice," that "such a right is holy," and that such a right "must not be curtailed,"[44] Kant published numerous essays in the *Berlinische Monatschrift*.

This journal was the public face of a private society of senior officials in the administration of Frederick the Great who were committed to protecting the policies of enlightenment from the threat posed by Frederick's nephew and heir, Frederick William II.[45] At first influenced by, and then inducted into, the obscurantist Rosicrucian order by Johann Christolph Wöllner, Frederick William II had adopted the order's aim of bringing an end to the evils of rationalism. Wöllner had succeeded in taking the place of Prussia's minister for matters of church and education, Karl Abraham von Zedlitz (1771–88), to whom Kant had dedicated the first *Critique*; Wöllner had also obtained for himself the post of minister of ecclesiastical affairs. The Edicts Concerning Religion and Censorship swiftly followed; the editor of the *Berlinische Monatschrift*, Johann Erich Biester, was subjected to increasing police harassment; by 1792 the journal was forced to relocate from Berlin to Jena.[46]

It was thus no accident that Kant wrote about freedom of thought in the *Berlinische Monatschrift*. For what Kant discerned in his theoretical writings as the permanent possibility of disruption or of 'falling apart'—a possibility built into the notion of freedom itself—he also espied among the political and intellectual practices of Prussia not only the prospect of war, but also of 'fanaticism.' This *"declared* lawlessness in thinking," presenting itself as a "liberation from the limitations of reason," was for Kant an even more pernicious peril to free thinking than the looming threat of blatant governmental censorship such as that implemented by Frederick William II and Wöllner.[47] He argued that such "free flights of genius" undertaken in the name of free thinking valorize the privileged insights of the "genius," while tacitly subverting the validity of reason for everyone. The effect of such subversion is the repudiation of reason—or what is the same, *tacit* censorship. Furthermore, Kant feared the likely conjoining of such tacit censorship with its more virulent form. He worried that in the wake of such lawless 'illumination,' social arrangements aimed at curtailing the disruptions of spiritualists would come to be hammered out on the anvils of civil authorities, wherein what was previously a tacit and sectarian censorship of reason would give way to widespread constraints on freedom of thought in general.[48]

The immediate occasion for Kant's concern about fanatical religion was the so-called Spinoza controversy, which became public in 1785 when Friedrich Heinrich Jacobi published his correspondence with Moses Mendelssohn (*On the Doctrine of Spinoza in Letters to Mr. Moses Mendelssohn*), alleging that the venerated Enlightenment thinker Gotthold Ephraim Lessing was a confessed Spinozist.[49] Given the wider context in which a popular Pietist movement that claimed Spinoza as its saint had come to some measure of influence, Spinozistic pantheism, with the purported endorsement of Lessing, now appeared as a more formidable opponent than rationalist orthodoxy had surmised. The thought, however, that Lessing had embraced Spinozistic necessitarianism and atheism also quickened what was, for many, an even more overt suspicion: that Enlightenment rationalism might be more a force of moral and religious subversion than its public pronouncements professed. The exchanges between Jacobi and Mendelssohn became increasingly acrimonious; in 1785 Mendelssohn wrote to Kant that "all in all, this work of Herr Jacobi is an unusual admixture, an almost monstrous birth, with the head of *Goethe*, the body of *Spinoza*, and the feet of *Lavater*."[50] Not surprisingly, Mendelssohn's sudden death in 1786 prompted his editor, J. J. Engel, to place blame (erroneously) at Jacobi's feet.[51] In the ensuing furor, both Kant's own students, and friends mutual to Kant and Mendelssohn (Marcus Herz and Johann Erich Biester), urged Kant to weigh in on the matter, although there was not consensus among them as to which side he should support. (In point of fact, those representing each party to the dispute could justifiably cite Kant's own words in support of their views.)

Kant's initial response to the controversy seems to have been a telling ambivalence. Kant regarded Mendelssohn's *Morgenstunden* "in the main as a masterpiece of the self-deception of our reason"[52] and Jacobi's *On the Doctrine of Spinoza* "only an affection of *inspired fanaticism* trying to make a name for itself and is hardly worthy of a serious refutation."[53] But Kant also found much in each of them to admire, especially Mendelssohn's celebrated defense of reason and of religious tolerance and Jacobi's disaffection for metaphysics. So it was only when it became evident to him that their apparently shared penchant for the zealous defense of uncritical insight had the potential to invite press censorship that Kant at last forayed into the dispute. Although desiring to uphold the legacy of Lessing that Mendelssohn championed, Kant here sided neither with him nor Jacobi. Instead, he embraced the insights of his young correspondent Thomas Wizenmann to argue that Mendelssohn's conception of "healthy common sense" and Jacobi's principle of 'faith' were, at bottom, indistinguishable, because they claimed to be 'intuitive' and thereby antecedent to discursive reason.[54] In "What Does It Mean to Orient Oneself in Thinking?" Kant argued that to pursue the view that rational belief is based on anything other than *belief in reason itself* is, quite simply, to undermine reason.[55]

Two fundamental points underlie the course of Kant's defense in this essay of the self-given restraints of reason, or his insistence, borne out in his response to the Spinoza controversy, that reason must take only itself as its guide. The first concerns intuition. All intuition is, according to Kant, sensible intuition, owing to the essential correlation between sensibility and understanding. But sensibility and understanding, paradoxically enough, contribute to knowledge in essentially the same way: each provides principles of insight that are independent of experience. The a priori elements of sensibility are space and time, forms that contribute to the constitution of knowledge, just as do the concepts of the understanding. Hence the pure elements of sensibility are *both* sensation *and* a priori. Space and time are the modes of intuition through which any given sensation comes to the mind. For this reason, they constitute necessary conditions for our knowledge of possible objects. When, therefore, Kant speaks of a "need of reason" to orient itself (in a theoretical sense), he is invoking the necessary conditions of spatial and temporal ordering that reason needs in order to have knowledge of possible experience. As such rules are precisely what constitute the critical standpoint, it is, in Kant's view, just the opposite of what he takes Jacobi's 'mysticism' or 'intellectual intuition' to be. Jacobi's immediacy or 'faith' is unprincipled or, what is the same, 'declared lawlessness,' threatening the order of freedom.

The second, which is an elaboration of the first, has to do with the subjective conditions of reason's determination of objects in general. To presume that such conditions constitute the possibility of the object per se, as, in Kant's judgment, Mendelssohn assumes, opens the prospect that without a conception, no object really exists.[56] On such a reading, speculative reason can adduce the necessity of the existence of an infinite and active understanding as a *"keystone . . .* to support its freely floating arch" (emphasis mine).[57] Only in relation to this infinite and active understanding can 'possibility' or 'reality' become meaningful predicates of things. But Kant sees that Mendelssohn here confounds the critical *epistemological* concern over conditions under which alone knowledge of possible objects may be undertaken with the *ontological* concern over the existence of reality. And Mendelssohn accomplishes this by extending the applicability of the subjective determination of all possible objects from the domain of sensibility to that of the *supersensible.* By this move, Mendelssohn's 'healthy common sense' proves itself to be unprincipled, threatening, as does Jacobi's 'faith,' the order of freedom through its 'declared lawlessness.'

By way of contrast, Kant thinks that he has the deeper insight precisely where Mendelssohn in particular erred: the true *"keystone* of the whole structure of pure reason, even of speculative reason" would have to be lawful, indeed, *self-giving law*.[58] Kant finds such a law in the concept of freedom, but in its practical rather than theoretical sense. The pure practical use of reason consists in moral precepts that lead to the highest good in the world, which is possible only under the assumption that we are free. Insofar as the reality of freedom 'announces itself' through conscience as a law commanding us unconditionally to bring about the highest good possible in the world, it stands as the keystone of the vault of reason. For freedom, as an ordering of reason that is independent of the conditions of space and time, connects through human action an idea whose origin is in the intelligible world with an effect that is known in the sensible world. To make such an ordering intelligible to ourselves not as an ideal but as a reality, we must assume, according to Kant, an independent ground common to both the sensible and intelligible worlds—namely, God. But, to cast this in another way, the reality that attaches to the otherwise speculative conception of God derives solely from the reality of freedom.

Kant's tendency to privilege autonomous freedom over everything else means that orienting ourselves in reason both theoretically and practically is the outcome of the 'labor' (*Arbeit*) of critical thinking, not of the 'mysticism' (*Alchemie*) of 'genius' or the inspiration of fanaticism.[59] Late in his life, Kant declared that "the two hinges (*Angeln*) upon which the door of critical thinking swings are the ideality of space and time and the reality of free-dom."[60] Kant construed both the forms of intuition and the categorical imperative as kinds of mental activity that are rule-governed and, as such, strictly opposed to 'intellectual intuition' or 'mysticism.' To arrive at the insight that space and time are *forms* of intuition, or that the categorical imperative is the *universalizability* of rational maxims for human behavior, is more arduous than simply presuming uncritically the status of intellectual intuition or moral sense. But the slow ascent of such labor to insight is, even more, the only path to vouchsafe the authority—indeed the lawfulness—of reason from the irrationality, even madness, of complete intellectual freedom that destroys itself.

Unscaffolding Religious 'Madness'

I stated earlier that Kant's religion of conscience exposes a fundamental lacuna in the central shared epistemological tenets of Enlightenment thinking and historical religious dogmatism: the inextricable tie between freedom and evil. One of Kant's distinctive achievements is to have shown us that this tie comes into view only as we adopt a critical standpoint that is neither suspended from heaven nor anchored on earth. It is this feature of Kant's critical stance that, by and large, much of the philosophical tradition has ignored, or, if noting it, has dismissed as a variant of skepticism. Yet, as I suggested earlier, to understand—rather than to dismiss—the significance of this standpoint for Kant's desire to 'unscaffold' traditional thinking, we would need to take three steps: the first through 'criticism,' the second through the 'tribunal' wherein everything is subordinated to freedom, and the third through the 'labor' of self-determining criticism. With these steps behind us, I think we can begin to delineate the significance of this position for the religion of conscience by drawing together the chief themes of the steps we have undertaken.

First, more than anything else, criticism is, for Kant, the amplification of a fundamental correlation between awareness (reflection, *Überlegen*) and investigation (*Untersuchen*) that conceptually delineates connections implicit in reflection. So construed, criticism is a precondition for rationality or, what amounts to the same, the character of rationality. In precisely this sense, criticism constitutes both an exodus from inherited ways of thinking and a movement to an entirely new standpoint. One can now see why criticism is not metaphysics as traditionally understood. As Kant described his work in a letter to Christian Garve in 1783, criticism is "a whole new science, never before attempted, namely the critique of an *a priori judging* reason."[61] Because all judging proceeds under a rule of discrimination, Kant's critical search seeks the various kinds of laws under which distinct judgments are possible.

In an argument of consequence for Western philosophical and theological thought, Kant spelled out what he took to be the ramifications of a priori judging reason, which I have already touched on but can now review succinctly. Because what counts as the condition under which a judgment can be made is the rule by which a subject can discriminate one mental state from another, our experience of possible objects turns not on the question of how we are related to what is 'out there.' Instead, the condition of our experience of possible objects is a *prior* conception of objectivity that makes meaningful our questions about objects. And it is this conception of objectivity that functions as a rule governing the a priori combination of what is *given* to us (sensation) with the concepts that the understanding provides. The "work of judgment . . . is the fashioning of a concept by means of intuition into a cognition of the object; but . . . it is *not* . . . the reference of an intuition to an object in general . . . which is merely the *logical* use of representation" (emphasis mine).[62]

This claim, of course, warrants further explanation. In the transcendental sense in which Kant uses them, judgments are based on investigations of reflection. Such investigations attempt to expunge doubts about the conceptual delineation of the connections of the implicit knowledge of reflection, by validating and interpreting the connections in relation to the facts of the awareness and the operations that constitute it. This means that our valid principles of knowledge depend on an origin within our cognitive capacities to which we have access through the implicit knowledge of reflection. All our judgments, therefore, entail *rudiments* of this implicit knowledge. Specifically, as Kant formulates the structure of judgment, the distinctive feature of its unity—the "transcendental unity of apperception"—or the 'I think' that potentially "accompanies all of my representations"—signifies the presence of the implicit knowledge on which investigation and all subsequent judgments continuously rely. Judgments, however, also incorporate a *concept* of unity in the sense that is the explicit outcome of the investigation into reflective awareness. This is the unity of reason that is represented by the implications of the 'I think' and is made explicit in the categories. The unity of apperception in this respect is the principle in terms of which intuitions are combined into a coherent manifold that constitutes the cognition of an object.

Even though Kant invoked the same language of the unity of apperception to refer both to its sense as reflection and as investigation, he nonetheless preserved the distinction in his various assessments of identity. Among them, two in particular in the first *Critique* bear directly on this issue. One is the simplicity of self-consciousness, which appears in "The Paralogisms of Pure Reason"; the other is the identity of function, which appears in the "Deduction of the Pure Concepts of the Understanding."

The argument for the simplicity of self-consciousness advances the claim that the identity of the 'I' consists in its being related to all its thoughts in one and the same way. Inasmuch as the thinker cannot think anymore of itself in *mere awareness,* simplicity of self-consciousness, the 'I,' amounts to the consciousness that it both *relates to* and *distinguishes itself from* the contents of its awareness. Moreover, in a corollary argument, Kant maintains that the unity in the simplicity of the 'I' also manifests itself in the succession of states of awareness that it has, confirming the self-sameness or numerical identity of the subject. Indeed, Kant specifically claims that "what pertains to the thinking being in general" is that the identity of the 'I think' is "as identical subject in every state of my thinking."[63]

The argument for identity of function concerns the act by which the 'I' combines in the same way what is given to it through intuition. It postulates an a priori rule known to the subject to which all combination is subordinated, in order for the 'I' to recognize itself as being related to all its thoughts in one and the same way. Because the 'I' in mere awareness knows nothing beyond its being related to and distinguished from the contents of its awareness, the rules for combination must derive from this knowledge. Moreover, such rules must be *explicit*: "For the mind could not possibly think of the identity of itself in the manifoldness of its representations, and indeed think this *a priori,* if it did not *have before its eyes the identity of its action,* which subjects all synthesis of apprehension (which is empirical) to a transcendental unity, and first makes possible their connection in accordance with *a priori* rules" (emphasis mine).[64] Presumably the act of the subject, which guarantees the regularity of appearances, derives from the structure of self-consciousness and results in rules that relate the contents of what is given to it (empirical apprehension).

Taken together, these two arguments purport to establish central themes of the transcendental deduction: from the simple identity of the 'I,' one derives consciousness of rules that govern all apprehension. Whether the argument in the forms that Kant provides in the first *Critique* withstands scrutiny remains dubious; but certain considerations underlying them are not. Stated in terms of the distinction between reflection and investigation, it is evident that Kant thought that from the identity of the 'I' implicit in reflection, explicit principles could be delineated through investigation that demonstrate the connections already entailed in reflection. Recast in a more pointed way, the themes of Kant's arguments illustrate his attempts to establish the connection between the soul and its apprehension of sensible reality—given the strictures that we are neither suspended from heaven nor anchored on earth—by valorizing as pivotal the correlative character of the unity of self-consciousness.

Let me now point these considerations in a direction that leads to matters of religion. Because previous philosophy had misunderstood the nature of judgment, Kant thought that it had run amuck in metaphysical disputes or run aground in skepticism. In light of this philosophical disarray, Kant hoped that "critical philosophy would become . . . a promenade through a labyrinth . . . but with a reliable guidebook to help to find our way out as often as we get lost."[65] Insofar as Kant showed that the premises about judgment both of traditional metaphysics and of skepticism were misguided, his new 'critical' or correlative orientation appeared to have *dissolved* them.

Now if we are willing to follow Kant in thinking that he has dispensed with these premises, we begin to see just how radical his notion of criticism is, along with its attendant metaphor of 'tribunal.' Criticism, as reflection and investigation, and then again in its amplified form as both the structure *and* activity of judgment, is a process of clarification at once *theoretical* and *practical*. As both structure and activity, criticism has built into it the permanent possibility of falling apart as it assumes public, corporate dimensions. For apart from the premises of rationalism and empiricism, criticism is suspended from nothing above and anchored in nothing below. This is not, as some have surmised, the problem *with* Kant so as much as it is the problem *for* Kant, as his method of correlation confirms. So understood, the tribunal of criticism (the correlation of reflection and investigation in the unity of apperception), in Kant's view, can turn only to inner forms of mental activity—space and time and the categorical imperative—in order to guide and actualize itself. In effect, this turn means that the tribunal of criticism has no recourse other than to invoke belief in the lawfulness of reason as it pursues its course.

I am arguing that, for Kant, criticism *must* invoke this lawfulness of reason at every level of mental activity (which is merely another way of stating the methodological requirement to correlate reflection with investigation). Failing to do so leaves criticism vulnerable to attack from the flights of reason that insinuate themselves into the course of free thinking and free acting and function as insidious forms of censorship. Criticism may not be able to quell censorship in the 'real world,' but it has the obligation, in Kant's view, to monitor itself, lest it give succor to those outside forces that are given to the pursuit of such policies. Yet even as criticism seeks to discern the lawfulness of reason that has to govern every mental activity if freedom is to be protected, the ultimate subjective grounds for the adoption of self-given law (the correlation between the fact of reason and reverence for the law) remain inscrutable to criticism. Framing this peculiar tension as an antinomy is one way for us to capture what Kant finds so unsettling about the age of criticism: bound to the cause of freedom, yet beset by human radical evil, the 'age' cannot *know* what it truly advances in its promotion of freedom. Whereas 'criticism' must *believe* what it cannot know, it cannot, owing to its unknowing, escape entirely from the precarious possibility of unbelief. Despite its reason, then, the age remains fragile, owing to its unbelief in reason. To paraphrase Kant, to live in the age of criticism is not the same as living in a critical age.

However much, then, 'standing firm' in the face of this dilemma always means, for Kant, acting out of respect for the law, 'standing firm' is not limited to what we ordinarily take to be restricted to moral choice. 'Standing firm' is nothing less than the *labor* of eliminating all pretenders to the throne of free thinking in order that only self-given law of reason remains. By now it should be clear that for Kant, satisfying this need of reason is a process of opposing every form of lawlessness. And it should be just as clear that we may call this process, more or less precisely, 'criticism.' Extending beyond reason's review of its own historical manifestations and illusions to the individual and sociopolitical process of resisting censorship and promoting moral thinking and acting, criticism not only changes modes of thinking and acting, but also, according to Kant, upsets (at least potentially) fundamental assumptions of governance. But because lawlessness can creep into our highest aspirations without our noticing—the origins, for Kant, of radical evil—and can gradually establish itself through the choices we make in a way that flows into *our sense* of personhood, of community, and even of reason, no freedom can prevail until we have removed the edifices that house our most prized delusions.

Why, we may now well wonder, does Kant champion religion as the site of enlightenment when he so often reckons it to the account of the delusional? The answer depends on getting clear about what the question is not. Kant is notoriously impatient with historical religions, so the question is not about religion conceived of in this way. At the same time, he is arrested by the importance of what he takes to be 'the religious,' or "rational belief or faith," the reach of which extends to epistemological, moral, and political domains. So the question is really about Kant's reconfiguration of the religious.[66]

Answering this question entails an important, but potentially misleading, truth for Kant: faith is rational.[67] Kant is not simply stating theoretically that faith does not contradict reason. He also means the practical claim that faith is based *only* on unconditioned reason. Some might take this latter claim to allow Kant to smuggle back into consideration what he denied theoretically: that we have some knowledge of the unconditioned. But this is an unfair reading. Concerning the claim that faith is based only on reason, Kant is trying to say that reason can command us unconditionally to pursue the ideal ends for our conduct, and that faith in God is a *need* of reason, based on this rational command. What is more, by linking this claim together with the previous one of faith's rational consistency, Kant in effect prompts us to acknowledge that we must always regard rational faith only as belief, never as knowledge. And because everything we say about rational faith must conform to both of these claims, they serve together as a principle of judgment, or what could be called—not without irony—the 'rule of faith.' So, at the very least, 'religion' conceived of under the 'rule of faith,' is consistent with the tenets of enlightenment.

But this only takes us part of the way. As my use of quotation marks signals, we do not have a ready vocabulary to talk about the kinds of religious mental states that Kant envisions. The use of language that we have come to associate with Kant's theory of mental activity tends to overshadow the permanent possibility of criticism falling apart. Subscribing to this use would entail the loss of the importance of this 'rule of faith,' because such a use lends an air of stability to what remains inherently unstable. But if we bear in mind the instability that radical evil represents, the significance of the 'rule of faith' comes to this: because every principle that we embrace in the pursuit of our ideal ends has the potential to be regarded as a divine command, sorting out legitimate from illegitimate claims that are pretenders to the throne of religion thus depends on the adequacy of the rule governing judgment to bring into view what is at stake. Any rule other than the 'rule of faith'—whether it be one of rationalism, empiricism, mysticism, or common sense—conceals from view the problem of free thinking, thereby summoning delusion, if not, by virtue of such concealment, religious 'madness,' which cannibalizes free thought.

By way of contrast, the 'rule of faith' of a pure rational faith lays bare the inherent instability of critical free thinking—that in the end, criticism turns not on knowledge *of* reason, but belief *in* reason. So understood, the 'rule of faith' serves as no more than a "signpost" or "compass" by which we can "orient ourselves in rational excursions into the field of supersensible objects . . . which is fully in accord with the whole end of [freedom's] vocation."[68] And more than being consistent with the aims of enlightenment, orienting ourselves in freedom by means of faithful rationality is a process of *advancing* enlightenment. By keeping before our eyes the need of reason to stabilize its inherent instability, rational faith poses the question of whether it is ever legitimate to infer the existence of the object (God) that satisfies it.

Here, at last, we are in a position to encounter Kant's 'religion of conscience.' Criticism, in the end, is the work of a convicted conscience: the belief that no law other than self-given law ensures protection from the encroachments of censorship, and the faithful rationality that giving ourselves the law requires constant acknowledgment of what is inscrutable to us—our penchant for lawlessness, for evil. Unscaffolding religious 'madness' means more, for Kant, than countering religious dogmatism and fanaticism. At a more fundamental level, unscaffolding religious 'madness' also means excising any rule of judgment or mode of representation that occludes from view the crisis of free thinking and acting. No flight of reason, however grand, nor resonance of feeling, however deep, no chain-like coherence of rationality, however clear, nor the progress of common sense, however happy, can ever dispel from freedom the shadows of evil—or, failing that, escape their masterly self-deception.

But if we are to follow Kant's line of thinking, we may well ask whether reason would disregard its own laws in order to achieve only some kind of clarity about the crisis of free thought, or whether, in the face of such crisis, it would reconceive its own law, in order that freedom might prosper. However ambiguously, Kant seemed to favor the second option. Given that reason cannot, from the standpoint of conscience, deviate from the law that it gives to itself, and given that reason cannot conceive of any other law, heteronomy is the threat of the seduction of the inconceivable. So Kant inferred from the need of reason to steady its inherent instability the reality of an object (God) that satisfies it and holds out for it the prospect of finding a conceivable 'home.' Therein he espied a way to stand firm in the conviction that we might prevail in the crisis of free thinking and acting that emerges when we are no longer suspended from heaven nor anchored on earth.

TWO

Disenchantment and the Religion of Conscience

The fate of an epoch which has eaten of the tree of knowledge is that it must know that we cannot learn the *meaning* of the world from the results of its analysis, be it ever so perfect; it must rather be in a position to create this meaning itself.

— MAX WEBER, *Methodology*

To say that the modern subject is, as Hobbes and Rousseau hinted and Kant explicitly claimed, a citizen neither of the sensible realm nor of the intelligible realm, but finds itself somewhere 'in between,' seems harmless enough. But to go on to say that this is equivalent to the modern subject being 'homeless' poses more of a challenge. As the French phenomenologist Maurice Merleau-Ponty observed, the modern 'in between' means that perceptions and thoughts operate differently from what antecedent forms of intellectual life had claimed, and that neither subject nor object could be described in such traditional ways.[1] In other words, when we speak of the modern subject from the standpoint of the 'in between,' we are on the threshold of some perspicuous redescription, some new intellectual landscape. So if we want to understand the new mind-set, we will need to discern not only what is new in this construal of things—however obvious that might be to us, because it functions for us as a background assumption—but also, in order to grasp its full import, what it artfully eliminates from past: traditional descriptions of the subject.[2]

Such, in any event, is the task of this essay. In the prior essay, I argued that because Kant construed the modern subject as neither suspended from heaven nor anchored on earth, the religious import of the his philosophy was to secure belief against the encroachments of fanaticism and dogmatism by containing it within the limits of critical rationality. By exposing what he conceived of as religious 'madness,' Kant sought to excise any rule of judgment or mode of representation that obscured from view the crisis of free thinking and acting: the inextricable link between freedom and evil. In staving off the threat of such encroachments, Kant thought that it would be possible not only to curb the threat of state-sponsored religio-political censorship, but also to safeguard the prospect that the modern subject could stand firm in its freedom. Yet Kant's proviso that freedom implied the impossibility of eradicating evil tempered the ambitions of human self-assertion. It is upon this tempered sense of self-assertion that I now propose to build. I shall urge a reading of Max Weber's notion of 'disenchantment' that holds together both the claim that the modern subject's vocation is to assert itself against the world and the idea that the modern subject is steeped in loss. To help fill out this reading, I will ask what it means in this context to speak of 'loss,' especially in light of the subject's 'vocation.' I will argue that modern self-assertion is a medium through which the modern subject reinterprets its own rationality in a way that purloins the role that spirit once played.

Disenchantment

The particular state of things that nineteenth-century thinkers began to understand as modernity included the conviction that one can and should assert one's own truth against the world. This emblematic conviction sums up the idea that humans can grasp what is distinctive about themselves and galvanize their energies in a way that advances this distinctiveness. Early modern thinkers differed over how best to assert one's own truth. Descartes argued that reason could provide the means by which man could become 'master and possessor' of the natural world.[3] Spinoza claimed that when man is "prey to his emotions, he is not his own master, but lies at the mercy of fortune."[4] Hobbes observed that "good successe is Power . . . which makes men either feare [it] or rely upon [it]."[5] Thinking in these ways, however, amounted to more than the claim that everyone knows what they desire and can, according to its dictates, manipulate their environs. Such thinking assumed, further, that humans have a built-in affinity for truth, or—more radically—that they are already in possession of the truth that can set them free.

To insinuate a measure of certitude into these proposals, Hobbes, Rousseau, and others linked the notions of self-awareness and self-assertion under the broader concept of self-preservation, which legitimated self-assertion on the grounds that it was essential to the maintenance of life.[6] This was the reasoning: in order to know oneself, one had to preserve oneself; and in order to preserve oneself, one had to know oneself. The legitimacy of self-assertion here did not so much depend on a particular desire as it did on a heightened level of reasoning. Hence, the *dialectical formulation* of self-awareness and self-assertion—rather than a desire for life—became normative for the *concept* of self-preservation. Orienting thinking toward the abstract seemed to bear promise for openness, transparency, and objectivity in motives for action: reason in its purity would predominate as the life-force. And, given its affinities with the emergent physics of Descartes and Newton, the concept of self-preservation attained a kind of 'scientific' aura. Just as theories of inertia (or self-preservation) in Cartesian and Newtonian physics defined the laws governing the movement of bodies, so also did the broader theme of self-preservation appear to identify a universal law of human behavior. The strengthening of reason, through abstraction and through its identification with a scientific way of thinking, promoted a normative interpretation of self-preservation for many early modern thinkers.

Interpreters of many schools of thought agree—with varying enthusiasm—that the inward turn of modern thought is simultaneously a turning away from something else. For the most part, they concur in the view that as the subject achieves distance from what lies outside of it, rationality and freedom constitute the identity of its new position. By extension, they all concede that concomitant with the subject's position of detachment, a distinctive sense of happiness emerges. So they are of one mind in claiming that the subject, in pursuing conduct that satisfies the aims of *this* happiness, consolidates its new position of detachment, even if appearing manipulative toward others in the process. And they conclude, accordingly, with the observation that corporate identity for subjects who are so positioned can emerge only from free, contractual associations that confirm individual social and economic aims. Yet despite their apparent agreement, interpreters have diverged radically in their assessment of 'the something' from which the 'modern' subject is supposedly departing. Puzzling over this briefly will help to orient us toward the sense of disenchantment that figures in the thinking of Hobbes, Rousseau, and Kant.

The 'offense' from which moderns flee is, for some, the imperiling forces of nature. At one level, critical thinkers have interpreted the peril of nature to consist in the vicissitudes of climate and of geophysical processes.[7] Painful reminders of human limitations—little rains, searing summer winds, hailing out of crops, punishing winters—emphasize survival as the only blessing that the terrible angel of Nature can bestow. With somewhat different emphasis, other critics looked to the more erratic and dramatic forces of nature—hurricanes, tornadoes, earthquakes, and the like—as the deadly offense to humans.[8] At another level, critics have claimed that 'instinct' and 'intuition' link humans indissolubly to 'animality,' the preserve of nature, and so compromise the human prospects of empathy and understanding.[9] And at one further level, critics have lifted up the symbolic power of nature that the religious practices of animism, fetishism, and totemism articulate.[10]

Other interpreters have identified cultural practices as the source of the modern subject's difficulty. They designate narrative, history, and tradition as the culprits of culture that precipitated the modern subject's retreat. Narrative, in this view, functioned to illustrate important standards and examples worthy of imitation, as well as to provide a source from which law-like generalizations could be deduced. But such narratives were often far-fetched, exaggerated, or selective in their presentation of materials. So they seemed more to bring into view the vagaries of human experience than the certitudes that reason grants as the measure of human events.[11] In much the same way, history, as an amplification of narrative, proffered disclosures of some essential order that binds humans from the origin to the end of all things. Such 'epic' history attempts to coerce the motions of the sea of experience into an arbitrary form. Not only is such history reflective of an irrecoverable past, but also its form is frequently at disparity with law-like generalizations concerning human behavior.[12] Self-legitimating principles of reason, by way of contrast, appeared to afford the modern subject a safe preserve from the unpredictable diversity of historical actions and events. Eschewing narrative and history entailed, as well, the renunciation of tradition. Whatever norms or standards had flowed from narrative or history into the governance of cultural practices were now rendered suspect, if not meaningless, because they reflected little more than prejudice, dogma, and

cant. Tradition, in a word, seemed to embrace any sacred or secular paradigm whose origin and significance could be found in the past.[13]

By jettisoning tradition, the makers of the modern subject set into motion
anew the question of the subject's own beginnings or origins. For with the
deletions of narrative, history, and tradition from the lexicon of modern
subjectivity, the question of 'origins' achieved a new status. It would now
signify a 'presuppositionless' starting point. Indeed, the idea of 'origin' as
something that brings itself into being achieved wide currency in modernity. From its theoretical configuration—in which the modern subject
could, by delineating the formative powers of self-reflection alone, derive
the 'telos' of human existence—to its practical applications—in which moderns could discern the adaptive capacities of species in the natural struggle
for survival, or, in the meandering pathways of the Nile, define its
'source'—this new question of origins, cast in terms of the principles of
reason, exercised formidable influence.[14]

However much the rhetoric of 'overcoming'—be it of nature, history, or
tradition—or the rhetoric of 'origins' prevailed in certain preserves of
Western intellectual activity, it is misleading to think of them as encompassing the broadest reaches of modernity. Alongside, if not underlying, these
rhetorics is another: the rhetoric of irrevocable loss. This articulates the
fear that the world is disintegrating. Inherited from the Middle Ages, the
idea of the decay of the world figured prominently in the Renaissance cosmic order. According to this view, the universe (or macrocosm) and the
human being (or microcosm) correspond to one another as reflections.
Human disobedience to God, however, had disrupted the symmetry of the
world's pattern—a harmony ranging from God to the angels and extending
to human beings. Hence, natural disorder became coeval with the break-
down of social and emotional order. Shakespeare exploited this sensibility
in his depiction of King Lear, "minded like the weather, most unquietly,"
assailing nature's storm:

> Blow winds and crack your cheeks! Rage, blow!
>
> . . . .
>
> . . . And thou, all-shaking thunder
> Strike flat the thick rotundity o' the world,
> Crack nature's moulds, all germens spill at once
> That make ingrateful man![15]

Citing the Fall as a paradigm, sixteenth- and seventeenth-century European thinkers claimed that though the world had been created for human use, and humans, in turn, for the glory of God, the human violation of the natural order corrupted it. Wrote Samuel Purchas, seventeenth-century English compiler of travel and discovery writings, "All Arts are but the supply of Nature's defects, to patch up her ragged and worne rents, to cover rather than to cure or recover Mans fall."[16] The continuous and palpable decay of the world was reckoned as a sign of God's warning that the end was near: the six thousand years commonly allotted the creation were all but spent, and humans could both see and suffer the progressive and cumulative stages of disintegration. Indeed, the most expansive proponent of belief in the decay of the universe, Godfrey Goodman—the notorious Bishop of Gloucester who converted to Rome—maintained that the Fall both caused the corruption and was proved by it.[17]

Although the concept of world decay captured the imagination of encyclopedists, historians, and popularizers of science of this era and fueled the exhortations of countless preachers who were their contemporaries, it was not wholly their province. Alchemists, who often cast theological themes in terms derived from Hermetic and Neoplatonic traditions, also fastened on the idea. They proposed that the deterioration of nature is linked rhythmically with coagulations of nature, so that dissolution always prepares one for new formations. The aim of alchemy is thus to dissolve the imperfect coagulations of the soul, crystallizing them anew in a more perfect form. This work is accomplished in unison with Nature by virtue of a quickening of a natural vibration of the soul, which links the human and cosmic domains. Nature comes to the aid of this art of quickening, or prayer, which is the inward evocation of God through the pronouncement of a divine name. Because the word pronounced by the human in prayer is both a symbol of the eternal word and a remembering of God, it has the power of benediction, conferring change on the soul and a transmutation of the whole being into consciousness of the Absolute. This is an eschatological vision, one in which the chaos of the deteriorating world and the putrefying soul are transmuted through the mastery of art into the pure mirror of the Divine Word.[18]

So far, these ways of talking about the decay of the world harmonize with classical modes of thought. Yet the rhetoric of decay also took on 'modern' overtones. Within the languages of the 'new sciences,' the idea of fragmentation came to represent the loss of a unified cosmos. Copernicus, Galileo, and Kepler effectively extended the realm of mutability beyond Creation to the celestial circles of the sun and the stars. Admitting the possibility of other habitable worlds, the new astronomical calculations demonstrated the possibility of a universe without a fixed order. Not only did this proposal help upend the Aristotelian doctrine of the world's eternity, but also it intimated that the belief that human sin had taken root in nature paled before the evidence that the whole universe seemed to be involved in the fitful throes of mortality. English and French proponents of the belief in the decay of nature construed Copernican theory as evidence that deterioration is not limited to human moral failing, but extends to the material universe, heavens and all. For them, the new science and the teleological Christian vision of a moral universe appeared to overlap. But for opponents of this belief—notably the English clergymen George Hakewill and John Wilkins, the English philosophers Francis Bacon and Thomas Hobbes, and the French philosopher René Descartes—the two did not: nature, they claimed, has an order distinct and underivable from divine law.

On first glance, what is at stake in the seventeenth-century debates over the decay of the world is the viability of the notion of the human as microcosm: the human as the epitome of, and the end for, the world. On further reflection, it becomes clearer that the loss of the evidently palatable analogy of microcosm and macrocosm not only signaled the end of a way of thinking about harmony and metaphysical unity, but also heralded new ways of conceiving reason and faith, nature and the human, the natural and the supernatural. Sharper distinctions emerged, and with them, diverse laws applicable only to particular spheres; what counted as law in the domain of the supernatural had no power of purchase in the domain of nature. Francis Bacon, in his *Novum Organum* (1620), chided his age for the methods and ideas by which they justified common beliefs: "Again, men have been hindered from making progress in the sciences by the spell (I may say) of reverence for antiquity, and by the authority of men who have a great reputation in philosophy and by the consensus which derives from them. I have spoken above about consensus."[19] What needed to be lost, in other words, was that enchantment with the past that impeded the advance of the 'new science.'

If the modern rhetoric of loss has as one distinctive feature the surrender of one form of rationality for another, then John Donne's celebrated lament may be said to crystallize this particular sensibility:

'Tis all in peeces, all cohaerence gone;

All just supply, and all Relation:

Prince, Subject, Father, Sonne are things forgot.[20]

Indeed, by the middle of the seventeenth century, what Donne foresaw had come to pass: the philosophy of the whole had been displaced by various philosophies of the parts. Increasingly, the solutions to "Philosophicall secrets" were sought through "humane reason" rather than by use of the Scriptures.[21] What set in was a certain rationality reluctant to characterize the whole world in terms of its parts, or of the end for which it was designed, or of some ideal that it no longer approximated.

Within a generation, this rationality assumed new proportions. In his drawing *The Artist Moved to Despair by the Grandeur of Antique Fragments* (Figure 4), Henri Fuseli depicts a figure so blinded by grief that he covers his eyes with one hand and with the other, reaches toward and reads by his touch the giant foot resting on the pedestal adjacent to him. Just behind the foot, elevated on another pedestal, rests a hand pointing in the manner of imperial gesture; at the edge of this pedestal, a plant pushes its way through the cracks. What is lost is the sight of wholeness, and the heroic proportions and authority of the past. What remains intact is the slight figure scarcely able to support itself (presumably representing modernity) in mourning, if not melancholia, before these fragments.[22]

Just as the rhetoric of loss, configured in the trope of the fragment, denoted the negative, so also did it embody positive connotations. These include the deliberate winnowing of political and religious convictions, and in its most extreme case, the French Revolution, the deliberate destruction of what were claimed to be repressive traditions. In much the same spirit, Friedrich Schlegel and his intimate associates (August Schlegel, Caroline Michaelis, Dorothea Mendelssohn-Veit, F. D. E. Schleiermacher, L. Tiek, Novalis, W. Wachenroder, and F. Schelling) valorized the fragment of what had been lost as a "miniature work of art."[23] For them, fragmentation became a matter not merely of loss, but a wellspring of creative opportunity. The rhetoric of loss here signified both a separation from the past and an ambition to create a new future.

Perhaps the most suggestive attempt to integrate the rhetorics of overcoming, origins, and loss into a paradigm for the interpretation of modernity appeared in the late-nineteenth-century work of Max Weber.[24] Borrowing from Friedrich Schiller's phrase, the "disenchantment of the

Figure 4: Fuseli, *The Artist Moved to Despair by the Grandeur of Antique Fragments* (1778–79). (Bridgeman-Giraudon / Art Resource, NY.)

world," he employed the term 'disenchantment' (*Entzauberung*)[25] to describe the historical process that gave rise to the rationality he considered to be characteristic of modernity. In this process (which Weber claims to have existed in Occidental culture for millennia), the principle that one can master all things by calculation supplants the notion that there are incalculable, mysterious forces to which one must have recourse in order to implore or master them.[26] In its bald form, Weber's thesis about 'disenchantment' can be read as a simple, albeit far-reaching, shift in outlook from a prescientific and 'religious' view to a scientific one.[27] In his lecture "Science as Vocation," Weber might begin with the material conditions under which science is learned in the university system (the regimen of training and expectations), but he does not address the theme of disenchantment until well into his second topic: the inner conditions of scientific thinking. These he takes to be hard work and the recognition that the outcomes of such work will, in time, become outdated. To think scientifically, he seems to be saying, is to adopt the inner presupposition that one is linked to a chain of infinite progress, in which the motive for accomplishment also precipitates the surpassing of every accomplishment. But adopting this presupposition entails, simultaneously, surrendering the presupposition that life is an organic cycle that provides its own terms of fulfillment. In other words, if one adopts the viewpoint of an infinite march of progress, one abandons the hope of a final resting place in which one is, in some way or other, reconciled to the mysterious forces of the world. Under the presupposition of infinite progress, accordingly, the world becomes disenchanted. Intercessory practices give way to technical calculation. So scientific thinking can never be the provenance of meaning or prescribe for us what world of meaning or values we should embrace. Instead, it serves to help achieve principled clarity about the decisions regarding values that we are bound to make. Because clarity is on the side of scientific thinking, Weber concludes that one can only act with intellectual integrity by accepting the "rationalization . . . intellectualization, and above all the disenchantment of the world" with dignity, or by making an intellectual sacrifice to unconditional religious devotion on ethical grounds. On this reading, the gap between religion and science, between values and principles, between the holy and clear thinking is unbridgeable: the chasm between them is disenchantment.[28]

But the end of Weber's lecture seems to contradict this reading. There we are told that

> we live as did the ancients when their world was not yet disenchanted of its gods
> and demons, only we live in a different sense. As Hellenic man at times sacrificed
> to Aphrodite and at other times to Apollo, and above all, as everybody sacrificed
> to the gods of his city, so do we still nowadays, only the bearing of man has been
> disenchanted and denuded of its mystical but inwardly genuine plasticity. Fate,
> and certainly not 'science,' holds sway over these gods and their struggles. One
> can only understand what the godhead is for the one order or for the other, or
> better, what godhead is in the one or in the other order.[29]

This seems to mean that 'chasm' as a metaphor for disenchantment is hardly satisfying, precisely because the boundaries between differing modes of thought are more permeable than 'chasm' and 'unbridgeable' suggest. But to rebel against the metaphors of chasm and of unbridgeable and their intimations of stasis and death is to insist on the notion that disenchantment is a creative process of more subtlety and complexity than the previous reading would have us believe.

I think Weber's lecture owes its interest and its strength to this reminder of the quarrel between religion and science, the tension between an effort to achieve fulfillment in life and an effort to promote the continuous enrichment of culture by ideas, knowledge, and problems. If Weber is correct, this tension perdured under numerous forms, and for this reason may be said to be characteristic of the way in which modernity confronted its contingency. But to see Weber in this way would be to acknowledge that we have merely blinked at the way in which many moderns viewed the polymorphous character of the relation between science and religion. Rather than construe the modern as the site of a contest between science and religion over the one true way to describe the world, here we might begin to see it as a resumption of the eternal struggle among the gods as to who would have power over a world of selves that had become de-divinized.

Weber's lecture does lend itself to such a reading. Again, we can take our bearings by Weber's decision to examine the material conditions that affect "science as vocation." These might also be called the practical rationalities under which aspiring American and German scholars function and that affect their prospects. In the German system, a scholar, on the basis of a book and formal examinations before the faculty, begins as a *Privatdozent*, lecturing on topics of his own choosing, and receiving no salary other than student lecture fees. The German scholar must therefore rely on his own funds, without anything other than the moral right to expect consideration for the prospect of advancement to *Habilitationsarbeit*. Generally teaching fewer courses than might be desired, although enjoying more time for research, the *Privatdozent* operates under something of an involuntary set of restrictions. By way of contrast, a young scholar in the American system begins as an assistant with a modest salary. Overburdened with teaching requirements and the expectation of significant enrollments, the young American scholar's course of teaching and research is dependent on the curricular demands of the institution, precisely because it employs him. But whether either the German or American scholar will advance is, in Weber's view, more often than not driven by economic considerations and by what he calls 'the fact of hazard.'[30] By 'hazard,' Weber does not mean "the human, all too human, factors" that occur in the academic process of selection, but instead "the laws of human co-operation, especially of the co-operation of several bodies."[31] This, he contends, is especially clear as German universities drift more toward the American model of capitalist enterprise—which separates the worker from his means of production, and alters the laws of selection by a collective will: scientific training, once the province of the intellectual aristocracy and its modes of selection, now falls under the sway of capitalist democracy and its principles of selection.

When looked at in just this way, Weber's account is not so much a comparison as it is a sketch of the way that different rationalities intersect and precipitate alterations: the introduction of American capitalist enterprise into German plutocratic intellectual aristocracy precipitates alterations in modes of selection by a collective will, which Weber claims to issue in the predominance of mediocrity. Here, in other words, in embryonic form, is the process of disenchantment. It has not so much to do with one kind of description of rationality supplanting another as it has to do with one kind or description of rationality altering how one sees another kind or description of rationality, and so how one sees oneself.

To pursue this way of reading Weber would be to discover the way in which he becomes mired in the tension between the search for the one right description and the appreciation for a multiplicity of descriptions. On the one hand, Weber sees scientific thinking as the legitimate heir to Plato's discovery of the concept as the key to the apprehension of true being and the Renaissance elevation of the experiment to the level of the rational principle of research. This is the heritage of knowing and acting rightly, with the aim of being a good citizen of the state. On the other hand, there are numerous and indispensable descriptions of science as, for example, the way to true being (Plato), to true art (Galileo), to true nature (da Vinci), to true God (Swammerdam), or to true happiness (Bacon). Each of these descriptions altered the way in which science understood itself and contributed to the viewpoint that the worth of science is not intrinsic, but vested in its relation to whatever field of values practitioners of science ultimately embrace. Physicians, aestheticians, jurists, historical and cultural scientists, and cultural philosophers, accordingly, differ in their presuppositions and their interpretations of the value of their work. Weber is caught between his desire to defend scientific thinking as the clear, rational elucidation of principles, and his intellectual obligation not only to represent other descriptions of thinking, but also to show how their intersection with each other has culminated in the recognition that the ultimate possible attitudes toward life are irreconcilable. To the extent that he pushes in the direction of science as the one true description, Weber incurs the risk of replicating the 'grandiose' claims of the other great tradition of intellectual rationalization to flow from the Hellenic spirit: Christian theology. But in recoiling from the grandiosity of Christian rationality's claim to be "the one thing that is needful," Weber, circumspectly invoking John Stuart Mill, flirts with the prospect of polytheism.[32] His solution to this dilemma is to thread his way between the opposing poles by ceding absolute authority to neither. To put this another way, Weber is neither willing to surrender the idea that science is the one right description, nor is he disposed to honor an expanding repertoire of alternative descriptions. But he is prepared to acknowledge that both have power over us.

This acknowledgment amounts to another qualification of Weber's notion of disenchantment—the shift in outlook from the 'religious' to the 'scientific'—with which we began. Surfacing in the last part of the lecture, the acknowledgment emerges in the context of Weber's increasingly frequent references to fate. Here he alludes to the brute fact of contingency, the way in which the world can overwhelm us and blot us out. It is not clear to him that religious interpretations, any more than scientific interpretations, can avail in the preservation of the dignity of humans so confronted. Hence, the idealism of the wish that one could overcome the mysterious incalculable forces that befall us by mastering the world by calculation wanes. The only power we have over the world is neither calculation nor intercession, but *recognition* of our contingency. Weber specifies the contingency of his time to consist in the retreat of the "ultimate and most sublime values" from public life, in the loss of great monumental art, and in the dissipation of prophetic spirit such that it is no longer the common weal of the body politic. To such an age, the lines from the fifty-third chapter of the Book of Isaiah are true, precisely because they are read in a way that distinguishes the sacred from the beautiful, the holy, and the good:

> And to whom has the arm of the Lord been revealed?
> For he grew up before him like a young plant,
> And like a root out of dry ground;
> He has no form or comeliness that we should look at him,
> And no beauty that we should desire him.[33]

According to Weber, such a reading becomes possible only in the wake of the recognition of contingency, which precipitates a shift in the "bearing of man," denuding him of his "mystical but inwardly genuine plasticity."[34] Bereft of a divinized portion of his soul, the reader encounters not the poetic voice of God issuing through the word of the prophet and quickening the pathos of our finitude, but instead the impersonal formulation of a principle: the true is not the good. Disenchantment is linked to the particular contingency in which one finds one's self. And it achieves its particular configuration in the peculiar rationalities one employs to articulate one's fate.

In the absence of any prospect to discover some ultimate reconciling principle to adjudicate among the competing claims of value spheres, the individual can do no other than to create his or her own ways of construing fate, and so, figuratively, of deciding which god will be served and which offended. Whether or not others will embrace such figures of disenchantment, or whether, indeed, they will become a part of the stockpile of images by which humans take their bearings, is beyond our ken. In this, Weber thinks that we find ourselves in the situation of the Edomite watchman's song of the period of exile—Watchman what of the night? The watchman said, The morning cometh and also the night—invoked in Isaiah's oracles. So from those whose figures of disenchantment have become woven into our cultural tapestry we can learn much. When Weber urges us to find and obey the demons who "hold the fibers of our life," he may be interpreted

to mean understanding the ways of speaking and symbolizing that our culture has found useful, as well as idiosyncratic figures of speech that do not
catch on. Only against such a backdrop can we understand how peculiar
figures of speech serve to crystallize and set the tone for a life. And only
against such a backdrop can we pursue his counsel that we see the "devil's
ways to the end in order to realize his power and his limitations."[35]

Another way of making this point is to say that the social process of
disenchantment always begins with an idiosyncratic figure of speech that
expresses something novel about contingency that may capture the imagination of a wider public. And it is captivating precisely because of its relation to other figures of speech that are already the coin of the realm. The
newly minted figure of speech, if it is to become emblematic for an era,
must become common for a particular historical community. The point to
be made, accordingly, is not that this or that disenchantment existed, but
rather that *this*—instead of that—*way of giving voice* to disenchantment came
to enjoy public succor. But this amounts to the paradoxical claim that 'disenchantment' is not so much a 'result' as it is an ongoing stage-setting by
which one takes one's creative bearings. So Weber's notion that disenchantment is the replacement of a religious view with a scientific one falls flat if
it is read reductively, as referring to a certain state of affairs in the world,
rather than being read as one among numerous creative expressions of
disenchantment.

Let me now try to draw out the implications of this reading of Weber for
the question with which I began: what is the nature of the modern subject's
detachment that permits it to consolidate rationality and freedom as characteristic of its new position? I have suggested that the best way to understand
the pathos of Weber's notion of disenchantment is not as a modern discovery of the actual nature of the world and of the self—a depiction of forces
'out there' or 'inside of us' that have to be overcome through mastery—but
as the recognition of the contingency of any figure of speech that we elevate
to the level of paradigm for the interpretation of life. Because disenchantment, in principle, upends the staying power, if not, indeed, the very notion,
of paradigm, it disturbs the absolute criteria of rationality and fuels the
driving forces of creativity. Owing in part to his Nietzschean sympathies,
Weber took this to mean that the process of disenchantment precipitated
the need for decision. But it is possible to be more playful than Weber
apparently was willing to be. We can take the import of his unwillingness
to cede absolute authority to any position, to entail the willingness to juggle

several descriptions of the same event without having to claim that one is essentially right. To do this, of course, would be to surrender the notion of 'the modern subject' as some sort of identifiable entity, and to replace it with the more modest one of a particular subjectivity in a specific discourse. This substitution, in turn, would oblige us to recast the question about the nature of the modern subject's detachment in a way that no longer takes for granted, and therefore restricts, the privileging of Enlightenment rationality. We would ask, instead, about a particular subjectivity within a particular form of rationality.

To show what this revised question would look like, we need first to remember what Enlightenment rationality privileges: the view that human reason and conscience, as innate faculties that grasp what is true and right, are powerful enough to abjure the intellectual darkness of superstition and prejudice, and to end the stupidities and cruelties of evil. Isaiah Berlin has observed that this commitment rests on the assumption that all truths are compatible with one another and require a kind of omniscience to solve "the cosmic jigsaw puzzle."[36] In Enlightenment rationality, in effect, reason and conscience are divinized. And a further effect of this commitment is to require us to divide our personalities into two distinct parts: the one, God-like, the other, fallen, and in need of redemption.[37] Berlin's observations help us to see why the core commitment of Enlightenment rationality could be said to be both squarely opposed to, and rife with the prospects for, the processes of disenchantment. To the extent that Enlightenment rationality commits us to the view that the divinized portion of the soul is an organ of eternal truth, we are to the same measure committed to a hymn of enchantment. Francis Bacon, in a quotation cited earlier, observes that "men have been hindered from making progress in the sciences by the spell (I may say) of reverence for antiquity, and by the authority of men who have a great reputation in philosophy and by the consensus which derives from them."[38] Prima facie, such a spell or enchantment would seem to thwart the encroachments of disenchantment. But in whatever measure the 'lower' portion of the soul—the animality and the passions—challenges the hegemony of enchanted rationality, proffering competing descriptions or rationalities that are irreconcilable with the dominant rationality, and so do not fit with other rationalities as pieces of one coherent cosmic jigsaw puzzle, the prospects for disenchantment soar. No less a thinker than David Hume confirmed this outcome when he noted that "reason is, and ought only to be the slave of the passions."[39]

This seeming standoff of Enlightenment rationality with itself, and also with the notion of disenchantment, is chimerical. It begins to vanish as soon as we drop the Enlightenment standpoint that there is some overarching framework, some final, ultimate perspective (think Hegel) within which we can ask, "How do these things go together?" And we can shed this standpoint, without fear of compromising our intellectual integrity toward the period, because we can cite this assumption as part of a particular description of rationality. What we give up is its commitment to an intrinsic character of reason. Once we see that a description of Enlightenment rationality is merely a heuristic device, that it is not inviolate, and that it cannot escape its historicity, we can begin to appreciate it as but one of many descriptions that express Enlightenment disenchantment.

In light of this point, we might begin to suspect that we are ill-served by our conventions of speech that invoke 'the modern subject' or 'the subject of modernity.' For despite our best intellectual efforts, we find that our habits of thought, the force of the way in which we associate ideas, repeatedly dispose us to think of 'subjectivity' as something intrinsic and of 'the modern subject' as a representation of that subjectivity, which perdured through a particular historical epoch. Indeed, the intellectual interest in the 'something' from which the modern subject 'turned away' might be read as yet another in a long series of attempts to give a more perfect picture of what that intrinsic subjectivity really was. So it behooves us to ask instead a more modest question: What figures of speech in a particular modern discourse contributed to the social formation of specific notions of subjectivity? When asked in just this way, the question is restricted to interesting and important shifts within language itself. By focusing our attention on the historical role of linguistic innovation, this question helps us to see that what has been spoken of as 'a turning away by the modern subject' bespeaks a belief in a largest possible framework, a kind of melting pot of ideas about subjectivity that transcends the contingencies of history, within which the 'modern subject' comes into view. But to accept the premise of our question—that there are no standpoints outside particular historically conditioned and temporary vocabularies—is to reckon such a belief, and the questions that arise from it, misguided. Instead, our question, emphasizing as it does particular innovation in specific, contingent discourses, presses us to acknowledge the disenchantments peculiar to specific discourses. This difference means that we are now asking our question in such a way that we cannot answer it by producing paradigm cases of what disenchantment is per se. We can only answer it by discovering how the innovation in the Hobbes-Rousseau-Kant discourse on religion simultaneously expresses a peculiar disenchantment. It is to this discourse, which I call 'the modern religion of conscience,' that we now turn.

The Religion of Conscience

Linking Hobbes, Rousseau, and Kant together is, at the very least, contra-canonical. The English philosophical canon would link Descartes, Locke, Berkeley, Hume, and Kant; the French canon, Descartes, Geulincx, Malebranche, Rousseau, and Kant; the German canon, Leibniz, Wolff, and Kant; the American canon, Locke, Hume, and Kant, with Descartes, Spinoza, Leibniz, and Berkeley often added for good measure.[40] Each of these philosophical canons reflects certain ways of reading and the contingencies of certain philosophical problems that gripped the minds of particular philosophical communities. Each also carries its own presuppositions about what in the past constitutes error or illusion. But to the extent that these canons have become institutionalized, and have informed our reception of the Kantian corpus and of the crucial problems with which he was dealing, they become constrictive. However invaluable their role in transmitting ways in which past thinkers attempted to articulate enduring problems by grouping together—for a host of reasons—their intellectual heroes, such canons also predispose us to miss a great deal. If, for example, such canons school us in the tropes of rationalism versus empiricism, monism versus pluralism, or skepticism versus mysticism as ways of figuring the issues of modernity, we will be less likely to notice other philosophical developments. Or if one thinker or another fails to achieve full canonical elevation—again, for any number of reasons, not the least of which are nonintellectual—the canons do not dispose us to be ardently inquisitive about the relationship such lesser saints had to whatever canonical thinker or problem that we are considering. Omissions of this kind that proceed from canonical thinking contribute to our puzzlement over the linkage of Hobbes, Rousseau, and Kant.

For our purposes, I propose that we set such canonical thinking aside, substituting instead something more nearly like a genetic approach in which

we recover previous formulations—even if lost in the canon—that are necessary to understanding subsequent redescriptions. Specifically, this would
mean for us that we would take into account the historical evidence of both
Rousseau's reliance on and revisionist stance toward Hobbes, as well as
Kant's celebrated dependence on Rousseau and subtle recasting of Hobbes.
It would also mean departing from modes of conceptualization with which
we ordinarily have to do, in order to entertain a way of conceptualizing in
which Hobbes, Rousseau, and Kant are joined: the attempt to develop a
philosophy based on ordinary consciousness. And this mode of conceptualization is precisely the kind of formulation that we need to follow if we want
to pinpoint what Hobbes, Rousseau, and Kant thought was distinctive about
their understanding of religion.

What is a philosophy of ordinary consciousness? It attends to natural
questions that we ask about life—questions of survival and security, of fear
and hope—rather than being preoccupied with 'pure' theory. After all,
everyone is embroiled in some one or another state of consciousness, as well
as the felt need to justify it, but few are given to theorizing about it. What
is self-evident to anyone, even if not a philosopher, is that states of conflict
and disharmony seem intrinsic to the human situation. And in short order
it also becomes evident to anyone that such conflict and disharmony will
only give way if we find some resolution for it. The search for some resolution in unity, for some clarification of the final ends toward which we might
best move, extends beyond life as we know it in this world. For recourse to
knowledge of the natural world provides no knowledge of such ends, and
so is of no avail. Inevitably, some kind of metaphysic that aims at the whole
of human life must arise in order to amplify our self-understanding that
derives from the natural world. The ideas that issue from such speculative
thinking need not be conceived of as explanatory. Instead, they serve a *heuristic* role, providing guidance toward the unity that reason seeks. Within
this rubric, the idea of religion is conceived of as no more than one such
heuristic device. Even so, religion is construed as continuous with the strivings of ordinary life. And religion is also thought to embody the potential
of unmasking the falsifications and reductions of subjectivity that arise when
subjectivity is interpreted solely through the language of the natural world.
So conceived, religion is indissolubly linked with the interests of ongoing
self-interpretation to resolve disharmony and conflict.

Hobbes, Rousseau, and Kant could agree in principle to the summary I have just sketched. Each accords to self-preservation a central role in their interpretations, and each deploys the basic building blocks of the notion of self-preservation—a force, a guiding principle, and a capacity for self-awareness that issues in conscience. But their emphases fall differently on these elemental features of self-preservation.

To begin, let us look at Hobbes. He argued that all persons are possessed of the power of self-preservation, as well as the contemplative powers by which to derive the precepts that govern it. Put differently, everyone not only endeavors to secure themselves against the forces that may imperil them and to procure the good they desire, but they also remain aware of themselves as acting in this manner. Now to persist in seeking a contented life requires certain wariness toward the future. For one never knows what the future will bring. So all persons, Hobbes argues, live in a Promethean-like state, besieged daily by the eagle of anxiety that gnaws on their hearts.[41] Seeking relief from the assaults of this anxiety, some humans attempt to harmonize the present with their own aims by learning the natural chain of connections among events; others, fearing the powers that may either do them harm or be of help, imagine what the ordering of life might be. Those who pursue the course of causal explanation arrive at the idea of the un-caused cause, which they call 'God,' even though they have no innate idea or image of such a God. Forgoing recourse to such reasoning leaves others to fancy for themselves "Powers Invisible," to which, in times of distress, they make supplications or, in times of good tidings, give thanks. Hence, the anxiety, and its concomitant fear of things invisible, that is coeval with self-preservation is the seed of religion.

Hobbes goes on to argue that humans have cultivated this seed of religion for the purpose of cultivating civil society. What is more, they have done so in two ways. One is the development of religion by following human invention, advancing the aim of humane politics to found a peaceable and charitable commonwealth.[42] The other is the development of religion according to God's commandment and direction, with the aim of advancing divine politics by delivering to human beings the laws of the Kingdom of God.[43] Both ways of linking religion with the cultivation of civil society might appear to be no more than a product of time and chance. But in the Hobbesian account of things, these ways of linking religion and civil society are necessary: both are coeval ideas whose wellspring is self-preservation.

Why is this the case for Hobbes? Self-preservation provides one explanation. For Hobbes, self-preservation is a complex notion, whose parts are not reducible to each other. Principal among these is force or power, which is essentially unimpeded motion. Hobbes calls this force a 'Right of Nature,' and refers to its unimpeded state as 'Liberty.' Alongside this force is a precept that guides it. Calling this a 'Law of Nature,' Hobbes claims that the precept obliges one to eschew that which is self-destructive. From the outset, then, there is disharmony or conflict between force and precept, *right* and *law*, of which everyone is aware. This disharmony, in theory, is especially evident when the exercise of force occurs under the aegis of widely differing and highly individualized precepts of what is self-perpetuating. For if each individual makes use of her powers as she sees fit to preserve herself, no one is free from the encroachments of others on their property, their bodies, or even their lives. Such a state of disharmony and conflict Hobbes denotes as "Warre," and is the basis for his infamous indictment of the race:

> Whatsoever is consequent to a time of Warre, where every man is Enemy to every man; the same is consequent to the time, wherein men live without other security, than that what their own strength, and their own invention shall furnish them withall. In such condition, there is no place for Industry; because the fruit thereof is uncertain: and consequently no Culture of the Earth; no Navigation, nor use of the commodities that may be imported by Sea; no commodious Building; no Instruments of moving, and removing such things as require much force; no Knowledge of the face of the Earth; no account of Time; no Arts; no Letters; no Society; and which is worst of all, continuall feare, and danger of violent death; And the life of man, solitary, poore, nasty, brutish, and short.[44]

Part of the resolution to this state of conflict, Hobbes argues, is for all individuals to adhere to the same precept governing their powers of self-preservation. To do so, individuals voluntarily enter into a social contract. The object of their decision to enter the social contract is a good for the individual: by ceding the option of exercising their powers in any way they choose, and obliging themselves to embrace one precept that is binding on all, individuals win for themselves the benefit of peaceful relations. For the one precept for self-preservation, and the person who embodies it, represents a common will for harmonious self-preservation. In other words, the common precept for self-preservation incorporates a *modification* or *particular determination* of the power of self-preservation that enhances—rather than sunders—this inalienable right of nature.

But the establishment of a commonwealth is only *part* of the resolution of the conflict and disharmony that is intrinsic to the awareness of self-preservation: it addresses primarily the *precept* governing self-preservation. Precepts, by themselves, however, are no more than words. If the words are truly to rule—if, that is, the peaceful resolution, of which the commonwealth is a part, is to stand—they must captivate the understanding by their compelling power. Knowledge of what finally makes power compelling or sovereign is not to be found in the workings of nature, but in its eternal first cause. So to fill in what is missing from the resolution of the conflict and disharmony—an interpretation of the *power* of self-preservation—will press us ineluctably toward a religious metaphysic. Hobbes' argument bears out this implication. He explains that power is the force of motion that remains in motion unless impediments hinder it. The power that suffers the least impediments will be greater, if not irresistible. In turn, the most irresistible power will exercise the most dominion. The most excellent power, exercising the most dominion, is omnipotence. It is precisely this thought of power without impediment that we invoke when speaking of the eternal first cause or when imagining invisible forces that may imperil us. Because such omnipotence is incomprehensible, Hobbes suggests, we call it 'God.' Moreover, it is from such omnipotence that we derive the idea that God has sovereignty over all humans. In consequence of this, humans are to honor God, thinking as highly as possible of this power. But how are we to think of God, insofar as all of our thinking is finite and renders us incapable of conceiving or imagining the Infinite? Such thinking must follow the course of negative, superlative, or indefinite attributes, such as "Infinite," "Eternall," or "Just." Now although "there be many things in Gods Word above Reason . . . there is nothing contrary to it."[45] So for Hobbes we may speak analogously from the power of nature, noting that God is its eternal cause, just as we may speak analogously from the laws of nature, designating God as eternal law.

To say that God is eternal power and eternal law is to strike a distinction between God and nature: God is not nature, but the *Author* of nature. The importance of this distinction lies in its implied corollary: sovereign power (omnipotence) is *not* natural power (limited). In other words, the distinction functions as a critical principal ("Soveraign of all Soveraigns") by which to assess abridgments of power and law (by "earthly Potentates") in the human sphere.[46] By virtue of such a principle, Hobbes thinks that we are able to ask whether some directive from civil authority is contrary to God or whether our religious practices might prompt us to believe erroneously that we are exempt from civil law. So the critical principle functions as a guide between the Scylla of civil zealotry and the Charybdis of religious fanaticism.

If we are to follow the logic of Hobbes' argument, we see that keeping the distinction between sovereign power and natural power before our eyes requires first that we know what the divine laws are, and second that we dispatch our duty to express the honor of God through public worship. We learn of the divine laws not only from the natural world of God, but also from Scripture. The laws of the natural world do not contradict God, but they do not exhaust the laws of God either. Scripture, God's word to humans, supplements natural law, for it teaches the obedience necessary for reception into the Kingdom of God.[47] Repentance—a turning away from transgressions toward the will to obedience—and faith in Christ (that Christ's reign as king is eternal) are all that is required for salvation. Both requirements reinforce the prospects that a peaceable commonwealth may flourish, insofar as the laws of the sovereign power and those of civil authority are commensurable. Moreover, both requirements also militate against private inspiration or private revelation, inasmuch as neither of the latter carries the authority of (public) law, which could subvert the commonwealth. These requirements, then, are the equivalent of saying that sovereign power constrains us to be faithful to a conception of religion that enhances the public interests of the commonwealth. Consistent with this view of religion, the role of worship is both to articulate a fear or confession of the power of God, and to establish as its end the quickening of our obedience to this power that directs us to conceive of the law of nature as the law of God.

Such a conception of religion, applying as it does in principle to every commonwealth, establishes a court of conscience in which the omnipotent God reigns and to which all citizens as well as civil authorities are subject. By such conscience, we have a means to acknowledge our own darkness, our own spiritual errors, whereby we advance interests that are contrary to the law of nature, and so, to the eternal law of God. At first blush, it appears for Hobbes that conscience has to do with matters pertaining to religious practices or doctrines, notably excesses in scriptural interpretation or ecclesiastical authority pronounced in the name of the (Roman) Church.[48] But upon closer reflection, it becomes evident that conscience pertains to *all* matters in which any interpretative discourse—be it a religious or speculative metaphysic, a tradition, or a natural philosophy—bears adversely on the operations of the commonwealth. So conscience functions ultimately as a way of unmasking falsifications of subjective life that subvert the prospects of a moral commonwealth and for this reason comes to bear most forcibly on civil authority.

This Hobbesian way of looking at religion makes vivid the distinction between self-interpretation based on a preestablished teleology, as for example, is evident in Aristotle or Thomas Aquinas, and self-interpretation based solely on self-reflective assessment of the basic motion of life, the "continual relinquishing of one place and acquiring of another."[49] It makes clear that we have neither an innate nor an empirical notion of how we are related to nature, even though we are aware of the natural impetus to preserve ourselves. This obscurity, which manifests itself in a tension between power and governing precept in self-preservation, and again in the tension between our individual and social modes of being, forestalls resolution of these conflicts through natural reason alone. So in the absence of some preestablished interpretive framework, and in the face of the limitations of our natural reason, we have only our awareness of our own self-preserving efforts to which to turn for criteria to guide a speculative interpretation. This amounts to saying that in the Hobbesian account, the obscurity in our awareness prompts metaphysical questioning. By drawing on the basic components of self-preservation—especially force, but also precept, and self-awareness—as guides for interpretation, Hobbesian metaphysical questioning proceeds. The outcome of such speculation is a religion of conscience that aims at galvanizing human fear around the specific interests of obedience that preserve a secure and peaceable commonwealth.

But Hobbes' view of religion breaks down whenever the interests of obedience to maintain the commonwealth no longer define conscience. Such, at least, was Rousseau's criticism. He thinks that if we are to avoid the idea that conscience is the internalized voice of society, that it is a product of reflection on the structure of the commonwealth and its prejudices whose purpose is to hold individual anarchical penchants in tow, we have to say that humans are fundamentally order-loving, and that conscience, an "inner light," guides this love.[50] In support of this aim, Rousseau extols conscience as a "divine instinct," an "immortal voice," and a "sure guide."[51] Rousseau has something more in mind than simply according honorific titles. He thinks that the individual exercise of conscience is the expression of freedom.

Rousseau argues his case in the following way. He begins with the contention that all of us are able to direct our reflection inward and to attend only to that which is of immediate interest. Recognizing that we are readily led astray by speculative arguments that exceed our capacity to know, we can resolve to limit our reflections only to that which appears intuitively true. Our first care must be with our well-being, which we watch over by loving ourselves and whatever contributes to our own welfare and preservation.[52] We are able to exercise self-love through the recognition that even though we are passive, sentient beings, we are, as well, active, intelligent beings who compare and judge our feelings. Through the exercise of our intellect, we are able to distinguish between those things that enhance our well-being and those that hurt us. Further reflection on this distinction leads us to acknowledge that we often measure our own well-being by comparing ourselves with others, and at times we wish that they preferred our interests above their own. Wishes such as these implicitly embody the assumption that just as when we wish to move our bodies and they move, so also when we elect to direct our attention in a particular way and it is subsequently so directed, we exhibit spontaneous, willful acts. Self-preservation, then, in some way that is not yet clear, appears intuitively to be a spontaneous willful act.

Of course, the spontaneous act in which we wish that others preferred our interests above their own is the equivalent of preferring ourselves to others. Self-preference, for Rousseau, is a perversion of self-love or selfishness.[53] It is never satisfied, nor can it ever be, because it is the well-spring of ever-escalating needs. But if selfishness undermines our self-preservation by perverting self-love, we must strive to avert its certain destruction of ourselves. Rousseau argues that some patterns or laws doubtless exist that govern self-preservation. Doubtless, too, we must be aware of them in order not only to align our wills in a self-loving way, but also to recognize selfishness as a perversion of self-love. Indeed, love of self, fear of pain, revulsion toward death, and desire of well-being are all innate *feelings* of which we are aware that are suitable to the preservation of our nature.[54] So self-preservation appears, again in a way that is not fully clear, to incorporate some ordering principle that may govern the spontaneous, willful act.

For Rousseau, the conviction that self-preservation is a spontaneous willful act governed by innate feelings that may govern in a suitable way prompts a restricted kind of metaphysical questioning. This questioning is not concerned with general and abstract ideas such as blind forces, movement, or uniform motion. It is concerned instead with experiences intuitively true to us. These include our awareness of being active intellects, of being spontaneous willful actors, and of being possessed of feelings that enhance our well-being and preservation. From such awareness, we discern in the workings of the world around us both the movement of matter and a harmony of order that bespeak a will that moves the universe and an intelligence that guides such movements by certain laws.[55] We *feel* this intuitively to be true, although it grants us no further knowledge about the being of such an intelligent will, who remains hidden from our senses, confounds our understanding, and escapes our rash efforts to determine where or what this one is whom we call God.[56]

Guided, then, solely by our *feeling* of God's relation with us, Rousseau argues, we turn again to ourselves to discover our place in the order of things that God governs. Given our capacities to act upon our environs and to contemplate the whole universe, we find within our hearts gratitude for the one who has so positioned us within the order of life. Given, further, our relationships to other humans, in which we both act and are acted upon, we find that our willing can proceed, independent of being acted upon, even though we do not always have the strength to persevere. This discovery deepens our love for God because it shows that we have been created to be free and good. We know that we are free because our wills can depend only upon the power of our judgments, and we are able to choose what is suitable for ourselves without anything outside of ourselves determining our actions. In a word, when our judgments alone determine our wills, we are free in our actions.[57]

Rousseau does not end here. Inasmuch as we are aware of the ordering of God in our feelings of self-love that are suitable to our preservation, he argues, we are *not free* to desire our own destruction or hurt. Instead, our freedom consists in willing our own good, but without external compulsion. So although the love of good and the revulsion toward evil or destructiveness are just as natural as our feelings of self-love, inasmuch as they are a part of our awareness of the ordering of God within us, these feelings do not preclude temptation or the abuse of our liberty. But such feeling can constrain us. For although a feeling, it constitutes an innate principle or criterion by which we may judge our own actions and the actions of others. And when this feeling constrains us, we call it 'conscience.'[58]

To put the matter more sharply, then, Rousseau holds that our freedom consists precisely in the exercise of conscience, or in those acts in which conscience alone determines our wills. Every endeavor to preserve ourselves is potentially conscience-driven, and so an expression of freedom in the ordering of God. Now to say that conscience-driven endeavors of self-preservation issue in our own well-being is the equivalent of saying that to be just will lead to happiness.[59] After all, just as the goodness of God is the powerful and loving ordering that maintains and links together all that exists, so also our goodness is the conscience-driven use of our power and love to serve and to take pleasure in this ordering.

However much this may be evident in our hearts, it does not appear to be born out by our experience. Indeed, just the contrary seems to be true, and Rousseau readily concedes this. It is more nearly the case that everywhere the wicked prosper and the just remain oppressed. Either conscience deceives us and there is no God, or the casuistry of selfish reason blinds our hearts to the God who is the source of our conscience. This conflict between conscience and selfishness, between a life that serves the whole and a life that makes use of the whole to serve itself, requires resolution. But little in the world affords solace. Indeed, in the hubbub of the world, prejudice and fanaticism militate against the resolution of this conflict and shroud it with obscurity. So the hope for its resolution must lie beyond this world and beyond our knowledge. Accordingly, the search for this hope prompts further, modest metaphysical conjecture, based on those feelings that are self-evident to us.

With respect to our feelings, we know not only that we are passive receptors of sensations that affect us, but also active intellects that compare and judge. The active intellect, which is immaterial, is the seat of self-preservation. When the material body dies, the active and living substance is preserved, retaining all the force it has used in moving passive and inert substances. Freed of the illusions with which the body and the senses hamper it, the active and living substance can contemplate the beauty of the eternal order of God.[60] Quickened by this beauty, the voice of conscience regains its strength and power, precipitating feelings of delight or remorse for the lives that we have lived, and for the fate for which we have prepared ourselves. In this way the laws of God that govern the ordering of life are carried out. For life ordered in relationship to the whole of life, the common center of which is God, is the triumph of conscience. By way of contrast, Rousseau explains that life ordered in a way that makes the individual the center is the triumph of wickedness: "If the Divinity does not exist, only the wicked man is reasonable; the good man is but a fool."[61] The resolution to the conflict between conscience and selfishness lies in the harmonization through the law of conscience of the interests of the glory of God, the good of society, and our well-being. This resolution derives from the application of the tenets of the religion of conscience as a heuristic guide to reason. We find the seeds of the religion of conscience in the feeling of gratitude that issues from the experience of self-preservation in which we honor what protects us and seeks our good. The ideas we have of God arise from our feelings of our relationship with the divine. We affirm that God is a cause outside the physical universe that produces the latter's movement, that divine intelligence governs the universe, and that God is the being who governs all things. We further affirm that God has made us free in order that we might do the good by choice and has endowed us with an inborn principle of virtue and justice, a divine instinct, that we call conscience. For these gifts, accordingly, we owe God worship. For Rousseau, such worship proceeds from the heart in gladful adoration of the order of the universe that the wisdom of God has established and the providence of God maintains. Insofar as the veneration of God is uniform, it reinforces and enhances the purposes of good order and contributes to sound public policy. In sum, Rousseau argues that we overcome the conflict between conscience and selfishness through the maintenance of a personal freedom that depends on the performance of public services guided by the religion of conscience and its practices of worship.

To see the endeavors of self-preservation in the Rousseauian way—as spontaneous acts in which conscience alone may determine the will—is to drop the fatalistic pictures of the self either as a marionette or as a material automaton. Once the causal tie between the self and God has been severed, the theodicy link between moral disorder and providence breaks, as well. In the breach, an assumption comes into view that has lurked behind many uses of theodicy. This is the idea that moral disorder contests providence. Now this idea makes sense only if humans can comprehend the being of God. But if we have already surrendered the scholastic rationality of external causality, its idea of the comprehensibility of God has gone with it. We need not be left empty-handed, however. For we can substitute for this idea the certain feeling of our relationship to God, which seems to cancel out the absurdities we want to avoid that issue from abstract metaphysical speculation.

Here Rousseau seems to be saying that by renouncing the idea that we can comprehend God, we can set the stage for the freedom of conscience and the religion that celebrates it. The religion of conscience he envisions nurtures the aims of a just and harmonious society, even as it provides an intellectual bulwark against the cynical encroachments of fanaticism and atheism. At the same time, it affords a way for persons to pursue the practice of their own religious traditions without compromising their personal integrity, provided that they were willing to align such traditions with the embrace of the dictates of their consciences. Above all, Rousseau wants us to believe that there is something deeply human—conscience—that resists the constraints of culture. But Rousseau also cautions us that conscience is timid. Experience supports the view that the temerity of prejudice and selfish interests can overrun conscience. For him, in short, a budding conscience left untended is a conscience that the cultural weeds of disdain and dismissal overgrow and eventually choke out.

Kant thought that this concern about the timidity of conscience was a mistake. We cannot believe that the announcement of conscience is true, that there is a just order in which the good rather than the wicked prevail, if we are simultaneously willing to admit that some countervailing force—be it cultural or otherwise—can efface it. This would be tantamount to a nihilism in which the honest and dishonest are "engulfed in one wide grave . . . and thrown back into the abyss of purposelessness."[62] Even as Rousseau's notion of conscience completely fascinated him, Kant became convinced that it was inadequately conceived. Kant did not like Rousseau's identification of conscience with the order of nature. This identification provided no assurance that the dictate of conscience—namely that the just life will lead to happiness—is not illusory. In order to achieve this assurance, conscience has to take recourse to supplemental reasoning that allies itself with, and supports the interests of, conscience. The argument that if the deity does not exist, only the wicked reason rationally, and the just are fools is an illustration of such supplemental reasoning. However compelling the argument, it nonetheless entails the tacit admission that conscience does not, by itself, give rise to a moral image of the world in which the just prevail. This image appears, instead, to be the strategic outcome of some secondary reasoning to defend the integrity of conscience at its point of vulnerability. It is precisely this need that leaves the dictates of conscience open to attack from a skeptical culture.

Where Rousseau erred, Kant proposed what he took to be a better idea. He thought that we had to think of conscience as lying, in part, outside nature. This would open a prospect, independent of experience, for linking the dictates of conscience and the moral order. In other words, Kant was persuaded that once we think of conscience alone as requiring a particular kind of conduct, we become bound to think of a cluster of related ideas. These include both the idea that our obedience consists in pursuing purposes that derive only from conscience, and the idea of a world that is amenable to, rather than hostile toward, the fulfillment of these purposes. Taken together, these ideas—regardless of what we might actually do or of what enervating forces culture might bring to bear on us—issue in the insight that the moral order is not a helpful fiction that bolsters belief in the validity of conscience, but rather an awareness that arises spontaneously because it is linked indissolubly with conscience.[63] To spell this out is to see that Kant thinks of morality as the voice of what might be seen as the divine part of us. Put another way, for him, the notion of conscience centers around the search for righteousness deep within us. He conceives its seat to be in the unconditioned character of the moral self, in that part of us not subject to the conditions of space and time, which is not phenomenal, and which escapes, thereby, chance and natural causes. This means that our moral awareness, although making itself manifest, cannot be put into words. Articulating our belief in the validity of moral awareness would therefore require of us that we proceed indirectly. We would want to open up a space in our thinking that would be respectful not only of the limitations of our thought, but also of the "great revelation" that we experience but cannot comprehend; and we would then have to be willing to venture the thought that this is evidence of the "God within."[64]

Of course, thinking in this manner would require us to part company with Rousseau and his order of nature. It would oblige us to say, instead, that the starry heavens above *cannot* be the order of which conscience is a part. Indeed, such thinking would lead us to observe that the starry heavens *symbolize* for us an order of which we are aware, but for which we can have no rational justification: the order of the moral law within. Moreover, thinking in this way would help us to see that what we accomplish by this symbolization is an initial connecting of our belief in moral awareness with another conviction for which we *can* provide rational justification. And it would open a way for us to fill out our picture of moral awareness. For as we draw other connections, this manner of thinking eventually brings into view an interpretation of the role that moral awareness plays within the complex interaction of various mental activities. To follow this path, as thinking of this stripe does, leads us to respect *both* the integrity and limits of relatively independent domains of discourse *and* their connections. It is precisely this respect that enables us to develop a defense of our belief that moral consciousness is inexplicably our point of contact with a power not ourselves, our encounter with a conscience that announces itself, our brush with the sublime.

How would we have to argue in order to adopt this Kantian point of view? In brief compass, the steps Kant advances in *Religion Within the Boundaries of Mere Reason* are these. All of us are self-loving creatures of desire. We seek to maintain and advance our lives by way of the factors that determine our desires. Purely mechanical self-love or the instinct for self-preservation may govern them. This natural impulse propels self-protection, assures the natural propagation of the species, and provides for the nurture of children. It promotes as well the social impulse for community.[65] Comparative self-love or the instinct for self-preservation that reason supplements with the desire for equality with others may also govern desires. This rationally informed impulse prompts us to acquire worth in the eyes of others, but it may also incite us to attain for ourselves superiority over others as a precaution and for the sake of safety. Even so, the rivalry that can issue from this impulse, which need not exclude mutual love, may spur the development of culture.[66] And rational self-love or the renunciation of all that is instinctual in self-preservation, thereby ensuring the preservation of conscience-driven personality, is a third factor that also may govern desires. Purely rational self-preservation promotes respect for conscience or the moral law as in itself a sufficient incentive for our wills. This amounts to saying that purely rational self-preservation is the preservation of what is most deeply essential to humanity, namely, freedom.[67]

Inasmuch as each of these factors has the potential to govern human desire, they are constitutive of what is necessary to be a human being. Indeed, each of them is good in themselves and predisposes us toward good.[68] But how these factors come to be combined in particular human lives is the critical issue that marks, *in principle*, the sort of human that any of us might become. What therefore makes the issue of combination critical, for Kant, is the manner in which we *think* of it. We would not want to take recourse to the idea that such combination is a matter of contingency, any more than we would want to cast it in terms of the conflict between reason and the passions. For to think in these ways would compromise the prospect that conscience *alone* can determine the will.

We move from fatalism to freedom when we realize that a theory of the will must be a theory not just of environmentally conditioned sensible actions, but also of sensible actions *and atemporal intelligible actions that guide them.*[69] An intelligible action is an idea that is a necessary condition for moral purity. To privilege the intelligible actions of the will over its less privileged sensible actions is to embrace the idea that there is something more important than anything empirical observation might offer. It is to delineate scrupulously the limits of reason and to make room for faith. It is to believe so deeply in our freedom that we brook no excuses for our moral shortcomings. In a word, it is to envision ourselves as radically and fully accountable for our choices. In support of this commitment, we say that the will itself must contain the possibility for deviation from conscience *antecedent to* any particular choice. Whether the will is too weak to follow the incentives of conscience, or requires further reasoning to supplement the incentives of conscience, or simply neglects conscience makes little difference in spirit.[70] All possible deviation from conscience, all dereliction of the duty to subordinate the incentives of self-love to moral self-love, flows alone from our own intelligible actions. But how we actually order the incentives to self-love that govern our conduct is a secret of our hearts.[71]

This way of thinking about how we combine the factors that may govern our self-preservation enjoys a certain virtue. It charges the perversion of the rightful ordering of the incentives to self-love against the account of the

will. But this way of thinking suffers from a certain penury, as well. At the
end of the day, the moral balance sheet doesn't tally: "But the rational
origin of this perversion of our will whereby it makes lower incentives supreme among its maxims, that is, of the propensity to evil, remains inscrutable to us."[72] What is more startling, still, is that this deficit extends to
conscience, as well, despite its otherwise august character: "Yet there is one
thing in our soul which we cannot cease from regarding with the highest
wonder, when we view it properly, and for which admiration is not only
legitimate, but even exalting, and that is the original moral predisposition
within us . . . *and the very incomprehensibility of this predisposition*, which announces a divine origin, acts perforce upon the spirit even to the point of
exaltation, and strengthens it for whatever sacrifice a man's respect for his
duty may demand of him" (emphasis mine).[73] So to think about good and
evil in this way is to be thwarted in our desire to know the origin of conscience. It requires us to drop the assumption that our beliefs about what
matters most will lend themselves readily to the same kind of intellectual
scrutiny that we direct toward the natural world and its objects. It compels
us to admit that we have no way to verify conscience. In sum, it forces on
us the recognition that our own awareness of the immediately compelling
character of conscience is not something that we can explain. All we can
do is acknowledge it.

But if despite its unverifiability, conscience is something we are prepared
to acknowledge, a new point of departure opens to us. The acknowledgment permits us, even as children, to estimate the worth of other persons.[74]
It provides us with a standpoint from which to value what in ourselves and
in other persons counts as decency: unflinching devotion to and dutiful exe-
cution of the bidding of conscience. And it bolsters our conviction that
conscience alone can govern conduct that appears within the situations and
circumstances of the natural world. So while we cannot explain conscience,
our acknowledgment of its validity can precipitate *respect* for it. Respect,
literally, is the act of looking back. To look back to conscience is, figuratively speaking, to discern not only the beliefs about the conduct it requires,
but also the inseparably linked beliefs about the constitution of the world
as amenable to such conduct. We can derive this insight from conceptual
analysis by saying that respect for conscience is at once awareness of conscience *and* of a moral image of the world. Both develop simultaneously as
a single, indivisible complex.

To see how this redescription links conscience and the moral image of the world, we would need to continue down this path. Now we would take our bearings with the claim that conscience commands us unconditionally to act according to duty. Strictly speaking, this means that conscience needs nothing beyond itself as an incentive to duty and so does not need religion at all.[75] To adopt this mandate of conscience would lead us to ask what the consequences of our actions might be: we would wonder, perhaps, to what end or purpose we must direct our activities.[76] Or, more simply, we would wonder what we are to desire. Now if conscience alone, by presenting a purpose, responded to these questions, its answer would be that the unavoidable condition of fulfilling its directives would be the highest good. The highest good would represent the final end in which all duty-governed actions co-inhere.[77] Such an answer rightly would give us pause. For we would recognize that one cannot derive the idea of the highest good from duty alone. Duty commands unconditionally, requiring strict adherence without regard for consequences. Deriving the idea of the highest good would therefore require an *extension* of the idea of duty so that it could include the idea of the 'final end' of action.[78] Accordingly, the proposition, "Make the Highest good possible in the world your final end," would have to be a synthesis of the ideas of duty and of action, of conscience and of the final end.[79] Put another way, we would conceive of the highest good as a complex unity that arises independent of experience. And we would note, further, that just as duty precipitates within us a feeling—respect, which alone is to motivate our conduct—so also does the final end. It provides us with something we can love, indeed, crave to possess. But our desire to possess the highest good (which is an extension of duty) can never supplant respect as our motive for moral conduct. Instead, it must remain subordinate to respect. So the moral image that arises simultaneously with this notion of conscience is one of a world in which duty and the fulfillment of this craving for the good—our happiness—are proportional.[80] Kant's outlook, in turn, underscores our implicit belief that there must be an omnipotent moral ruler of the world under whose care the balance between duty and the fulfillment of the love—between justice and happiness—occurs. And it brings into view our conviction that the conditions of time cannot prevail over the commandment of conscience to be virtuous: to subscribe to the validity of the commandments of conscience is to subscribe implicitly to the belief in the immortality of the soul. Taken together, these assumptions amount to the claim that awareness of conscience entails a religion of conscience, or that the ordinary person already possesses a kind of metaphysics in which, because conscience and the final end are linked, as Kant famously says, "morality leads ineluctably to religion."[81]

Whatever misgivings we might harbor toward this Kantian way of looking at things, it is hard to deny its merits. It sketches a plausible way to understand that virtuous conduct can prevail despite the inchoate character of radical evil. Wrong willing eviscerates neither the voice of conscience nor the image of the moral world. In addition, it proffers correctives to both the Hobbesian and Rousseauian accounts of the religion of conscience. Conscience is no more the internalization of societal prejudice (Hobbes) than it is the illusory artifice, albeit helpful, of a visionary (Rousseau). The connection between conscience and the moral image of the world takes place independent of experience and manifests itself in the experience of moral awareness. It therefore stands in need neither of societal warrant nor of supplemental reasoning to defend its integrity from skeptical attack. Moreover, this Kantian account of conscience helps us to evade the 'choice' between Hobbes and Rousseau, between the incentives of mechanical self-love and those of comparative self-love. Each of these incentives is good in itself, and leads to ruin only if it claims more for itself than lies within its rightful domain. On the one hand, although preserving ourselves and our species, or seeking equality with others and worth in their eyes is assuredly good, such incentives can scarcely claim to be disinterested. They therefore exceed their rightful domain when they purport to account for the kind of motive that is selfless and yet sufficiently compelling to lead us to act in a moral way. On the other, promoting the social impulse for community, and spurring the development of culture in the service of preserving what is most deeply essential to humanity—respect for conscience—entails no such trespass. These incentives, when subordinate to the incentive to duty, are wholly consistent with conscience-governed, rational self-preservation.

Where the Kantian account of conscience and its religion most deepens lines of conception already present in the Hobbesian and Rousseauian accounts is in the strictures that apply to theological thinking. Whereas Hobbes and Rousseau were reluctant to say anything directly of God that did not supplement their thinking about self-preservation, Kant refused to speak directly of God. He claimed instead that we can only speak of God indirectly, and that only from the context of our awareness of conscience—although we might not be able to articulate our beliefs or even know that we hold them. By driving thoughts about God and immortality deeply into the domain of conscience, between the ordering of duty and love on the one side, and the ordering of incentives to self-preservation on the other, Kant effectively subordinated God to freedom: rational belief in God derives entirely from the rational belief in freedom.[82]

Seen from this angle, the theological strictures of the Kantian outlook are just facilitators. They promote the inner coherence of the religion of conscience, and they safeguard common decency from the zealotry and pretensions of revealed religions. Because the moral image of the world incorporates a notion of God, it becomes permissible to view duty (from the point of view of the highest good) as divine command. Conscience, therefore, serves as the tribunal before which we are to measure all claims of revealed religions.[83] We can speak of the Son of Man as the personification of the principle of the good and of sin as a transgression of duty understood as a divine command. But of the works and means of grace, of miracle, or of mystery, we can say nothing more than that these matters border on the religion of conscience, as they are incomprehensible to a moral perspective. In a word, when in our thinking we translate all religions into the vocabulary of rational religion, and so construe all persons as rational beings, the prospect opens before us that in acting from duty alone (and not merely in accord with duty), we can advance the cause of democratic institutions and cosmopolitan political consciousness. In this particular take, facilitating this complex cause is tantamount to creating the Kingdom of God on earth.

The Kantian way of looking at things thus appears to divinize conscience in order to achieve moral intelligibility. But it also appears to vouchsafe the integrity of conscience by limiting God to the status of *parergon* to obligation. This is a different way of understanding the Kantian claim to limit reason in order to make room for faith. In place of the idea that Kant curbed the appetite of a rationality that wants to run riot in the transcendent, we would say instead that Kant redescribed rationality in a way that precluded the possibility of attributing a reason or will to God that differed from our own, and therefore rendered faith in God unimaginable—apart from a cooperative role that this otherwise divergent idea could play in the service of a moral end. In a word, Kant's rational belief refuses to brook the notion of the alterity of God's will.

Up to now, I have been trying to make a positive case for what I have been calling the religion of conscience. By taking up the views of Hobbes, Rousseau, and Kant, I have tried to shed some light on how and why this way of speaking about religion came about. The attempt to develop a philosophy based on the primal experiences of ordinary consciousness represented a radical critique of interpretive frameworks that assumed preestablished goals of life. Such self-validating theological and philosophical programs, while once purporting to be impervious to criticism, were clearly faltering in the modern Western intellectual world. However novel the focus on the basic experience of self-preservation as a way of understanding our relation to the world seemed to be, it nonetheless presented conceptual difficulties of its own. Because the experience of self-preservation in some way gives us the world, it cannot simultaneously be the medium through which we comment on the relation of self-preservation *to* the world. This would be the equivalent of jumping over our own shadows or lifting the rock on which we stand.

Hobbes made recourse to a limited, speculative metaphysic to resolve these conceptual difficulties. His excursus into metaphysical thinking occurs at the point of his reflections on power: irresistible power draws us into obedience to the prospects of moral commonwealth, and conscience unmasks potential subversions of it. Rousseau engaged metaphysical speculation when he became convinced that self-preservation is a spontaneous, willful act, and that innate feelings can determine how we relate to the world. His speculation gave way to fevered embrace once he invoked the existence of God to ensure that dictates of conscience would prevail and that the just would triumph.

Just as Hobbes and Rousseau thought of the religion of conscience as an indispensable element to the establishment and maintenance of a moral commonwealth, so also did Kant. Unlike his counterparts, Kant did not think of the ethical commonwealth as a comment on the way in which we are, by way of self-preservation, related to the world. Instead, he thought of the ethical commonwealth as an implication of the way in which a free, conscience-governed mind relates to itself. The mind that subordinates to the dictates of conscience its incentives to act is a mind that proposes a way of life with certain foundational assumptions. To act according to conscience is to imagine a world in which humans relate to each other in a conscience-bound way. The assumptions of the immortality of the soul and the existence of God that help to spell out what that world would look like are not some sort of metaphysical gloss—Kant was too circumspect for that. Rather, they are no more than discreet borrowings from Christian thought that, when rationalized, help elaborate conceptually the mystery of our inner freedom and its relation to moral community.

The religion of conscience, revolutionary in its day, suggested that ordinary consciousness could cast light on the seeds of religion implicit in moral conviction. Despite its influence, however, the religion of conscience never enjoyed secure moorings. The subject that it portrayed belonged neither to the domain of ideas nor to the domain of nature. Positioned somewhere 'in between,' in its free self-assertion, the subject tends to wrench itself ever further from history, the natural world, and God. For this reason, the euphoria of the religion of conscience—that its free subject can transform the world—bespeaks a certain sense of being conflicted by the traditional rationalities of history, of nature, of God. The subject is beset with disenchantments. At bottom, the subject of the religion of conscience is rooted in nothing more solid than itself, compelled in its solitude to dizzying legislation of endless duties to perform. Perhaps this vertigo of the subject is what prompted some of the later Romantics to discern in the euphoria of the religion of conscience a measure of disquietude.

Disenchantment and the Religion of Conscience

It is tempting to suggest that the disenchantment peculiar to the religion of conscience manifests itself in the de-divinization of God. This suggestion seems to flow from the observation that as the process of self-preservation became increasingly rationalized, the significance of God narrowed. And it appears to find further confirmation in the fact that the succession of rational life-forms that arose from this austere notion of self-preservation relegated more and more of what could be said of God to their *parerga*. So with this diminution of God, conscience came to be lionized, if not divinized.

The apparent virtue of this suggestion lies, doubtless, in its conformity to the bald form of Weber's thesis about disenchantment. To reprise that form: disenchantment is a shift in outlook, stemming from the substitution of one rationality ('religious') with another ('scientific'). The disenchantment thesis and the suggestion about the religion of conscience concur in the notion that the modern subject surrenders the mode of thinking that reckons God as the preserver of life. In its place, they adopt another, which portrays the subject as having the power to preserve life. It seems to follow from this that by asserting this power, the modern subject is usurping for itself the role that God once played. We are left with a portrait of Promethean theft, of the modern subject heralding its own purely rational, ahistorical motives as the new seat of the divine.

On my reading of the Weberian thesis, the claim that disenchantment manifests itself in the de-divinization of God is misguided. By valorizing the self-assertion of the modern subject, this claim minimizes the sense of loss. What is the import of this minimization? At one level, something important that Hobbes, Rousseau, and Kant have in common does not figure in this claim. Hobbes despaired over the decay of civil order and, for a time, dreaded that ecclesial reactionaries might have him prosecuted. Rousseau lamented the erosion of the natural order of freedom and, for much longer than Hobbes, lived in terror as he fled from the Inquisition for fear of death. Kant decried the belief that we belong to any preestablished order at all, and anxiously endured the threat of "unpleasant consequences" that accompanied the royal censure for his public statements urging the establishment of a rational religious order.

It is alluring to think that their commonality consists in the entrenched and dangerous resistance that they encountered in their attempts to substitute one rationality (the 'scientific') for another (the 'religious'). We would then characterize what they had in common as a shared political fate, in which the old regime attempted to consolidate its position by silencing the intellectual spokespersons for a new order. But this characterization is unconvincing. It turns on the idea of two competing orders, in which one triumphs and replaces the other, the last-ditch repressive efforts of the vanquished to overrun the insurgents, notwithstanding. Whatever else we may know of that time, it is clear that this assumption is unwarranted: the competing rationalities and the social orders that they undergird persist, in one form or another, to this day.

But if, instead, we were to think of this commonality not so much as a political problem but as an existential intellectual crisis, we will have taken a long step toward understanding the 'loss' of which these thinkers were speaking. In asking what precipitated the crisis, we would readily answer that it was a conflict between rationalities. Saying this might lead us to puzzle more deeply about the conflict. We might begin to notice how one rationality alters another, and how it simultaneously qualifies the other's warrants for authority. It would not be long before we discerned the reciprocal nature of this qualification: each rationality in the encounter modifies the other. And this would help us to recognize that the point at which conflict erupts is where the intersecting rationalities actually undercut the absolute authority of each other. So we would then be prepared to say that what Hobbes, Rousseau, and Kant held in common was the existential intellectual crisis that the intersection of scientific and religious rationalities precipitated. And this is the point at which the greatest losses were incurred. Seen from this angle, the crisis amounted to this: scientific rationality confronts religious rationality with a reality of which it cannot speak—an order wholly apart from God. Religious rationality confronts scientific rationality with a reality of which it cannot speak—the order of God and liberty. Both alter the other. In consequence of this, neither rationality can claim absolute authority; each rationality sustains a loss.

If this was the existential, intellectual crisis and moral malaise that confronted Hobbes, Rousseau, and Kant, then the way in which they tried to see their way through it was the religion of conscience. To take this possibility seriously is to see the integrity with which they recorded the losses. *Both* God *and* the modern subject are de-divinized in their discourse on the religion of conscience: this is its disenchantment.

To help us conclude this account, let us first return to the opening theme of this essay. There I said that the modern 'in between' means that perceptions and thoughts operate differently from what antecedent forms of intellectual life had claimed. What I had in mind when I referred to earlier forms of intellectual life were those that claimed that we belong to the order of God, that we are located somewhere in the 'great chain of being.' By way of contrast, the modern 'in between,' conceived of as now independent of this chain, introduced new conceptual requirements. Among these was the necessity of casting the modern subject in an altogether different light. Specifically, this meant developing discourses that conceived of God and the modern subject in a way that did not depend on an ontological relationship. Hobbes staunchly maintained the distinction between God and nature; Rousseau severed the causal tie between God and the self; and Kant maintained that there was no theoretical link between God and the self other than what we invent for heuristic purposes of understanding. At the same time, there was some urgency to purport that an important connection perdured.

Glimpsing some of how this connection was secured, second, becomes possible once we compare the basic structure of the modern religion of conscience with its antecedent intellectual form of classical Stoicism. We have learned of the aptness of this comparison from Wilhelm Dilthey, Max Weber, Ernst Troeltsch, and Dieter Henrich.[84] In their view, we are able to trace the manifold perspectives of modern philosophy to the elemental structure of Stoicism and its pivotal element of self-preservation. My reading of the religion of conscience lends itself to this interpretive tradition. But now I want to draw out the *difference* between classical and modern thoughts and perceptions. This contrast will help bring into view something of what was lost in severing the ontological tie with God. We will then be better prepared to assess the attempt to secure a new connection with God.

Both the Stoics and the framers of the modern religion of conscience take their bearings with the notion of self-preservation. Both embrace a similar kind of reasoning that sees our first impulse as to preserve ourselves. From the outset, or so this reasoning asserts, we are in a state of being both familiar with and well-disposed toward ourselves. Moreover, only insofar as we are so disposed toward, and familiar with, ourselves, can we preserve ourselves. Now if we are not on good terms with ourselves, we become alienated from ourselves. But becoming alienated from ourselves imperils our ability to preserve ourselves. And the less able we are to preserve ourselves, the more alienated we become. So we are all aware, at least in principle, not only of what is distinctive about, and alien to, ourselves, but also of our innate capacity for resisting this alienation. The cumulative significance of these points comes to this: because we are familiar with ourselves, we know something of our nature before entering into relationships with others and before reflecting on, and abstracting from, the world that is manifest to us. Precisely because this is so, our self-acquaintance and self-preservation can serve as the basis for the goals we set in life. Such a conclusion differs widely from those (Thomistic) views that construe self-knowledge to be dependent on a preestablished goal.

The Stoics thought that aiming at this sort of self-established goal bespoke an imperative that we regulate our constitutions. They meant by this that the requirement that we need both to cultivate an ever-deepening awareness of the significance of our original impulse to self-preservation and to stabilize it: how we relate to ourselves over time becomes the definition of who we are, and how we thematize our relating becomes the definition of our rationality. The modern framers of the religion of conscience, too, had views about self-regulation, pretty much the same as those of the Stoics. Both thought that to be appropriate in the way in which we relate to ourselves is simultaneously to be appropriate in the way in which we relate to the world. What they had in mind was that the distinction between what is one's own and what is alien is a governing feature in perception and action. They often differed in details. The Stoics wanted to remain at home in the world, and thought that by repelling contrary impulses they could attain to the status of the sage who is in harmonious repose with all the elements. Hobbes wanted a world without anarchy, and thought our desire to enhance our lives could subdue our destructive penchants, thereby issuing in a well-ordered commonwealth. Rousseau wanted to escape the fetters of culture and thought that our sense of appropriate love could triumph over selfish love, facilitating a return to the common ordering of nature. And Kant wanted to avoid skepticism and fanaticism, and thought that critical rational thought could dissolve our illusions, permitting duty alone to forge the way to a universal, ethical commonwealth.

Not only did the modern framers of the religion of conscience thus echo the Stoic way of thinking, but they also emphasized the Stoic doctrine that sustained introspection is basic to insight. Hobbes, Rousseau, and Kant all thought that such insight leads not to disparagement, but to appreciation of and active involvement in the world. Moreover, they all conceived of such insight as progressive. Because such a course of reflection dissolves viewpoints incapable of preserving us, the promise opens that we will discover something more than the self-generating powers of our egos. Neither the Stoics nor the moderns were disappointed in their belief. Their reflections led them to discover that the principle of unity of the world is at once the principle of unity of the individual.

Discoveries of this order are more like mirrors than they are like windows. They tell us more about the talents and beliefs of the writers than they offer us some transparency to plain fact. Because they wrote in just the way and time that they did, the Stoics could conceive of the original unity as creative fire (*pyr technikon*) or spirit (*pneuma* or fiery breath), whose binding force prevents everything from disintegrating. They saw nothing roundabout in their claim that something of this original spirit resides in all living beings, disposing them to regulate their own constitutions and manifesting itself as reason (*logos*). Nor did they think that it was anything less than obvious to conclude that self-knowledge—wherein we discover through reason what our distinctive value is—had to be the first and dominant motive of living beings. To the modern makers of the religion of conscience, claims of this sort fell short of the obvious. For them, the reach of reason beyond the compass of human experience was suspect. It seemed axiomatic that the unity they discovered by abstracting from their endeavors to preserve themselves also had to be the unity of the world. But they knew little of spirit-laden reason, and still less of an original creative fire. They eschewed the Greek idea that the divine and the soul were of the same fiery substance, and thereby connected. Indeed, they so distrusted fiery reason that they campaigned against it. By branding fiery reason, variously, as zealotry, fanaticism, or mysticism, they succeeded, to the minds of many, in denigrating it.

This account of intellectual history turns on the *difference* between the Stoics and the modern makers of the religion of conscience in their conceptions of reason. The moderns neglect, or are wary of, spirit. Such forgetfulness is the result of the natural desire to consolidate the position of the modern subject by minimizing its loss of connection to the divine order of being, its loss of the sense of being possessed. But beyond the loss of ontological connection, this forgetfulness signals, as well, a loss of intellectual connection with the Christian tradition of St. Paul and St. Augustine, through which the Stoic way of thinking had been mediated. With this loss, it was no longer possible to speak of the soul as the *imago dei*, and in this sense connected with God, any more than it was practicable to conceive of resting in the tranquility that one receives from the God. Instead, the language of the self and its assertion absorbs most of the metaphysical musings once accorded the soul. And the unrest of the human heart (as the modern religion of conscience portrays it) redirects its search for solace toward the tranquility it makes for itself. Tranquility comes into being only within and through human self-regulation. Audaciously, the religion of conscience asserts that without human self-preservation, the prospect of tranquility would disappear. This is the acknowledgment of a certain terror that if *we* do not preserve ourselves, that if *we* do not know who we are, all will collapse into helplessness.

The disenchantment peculiar to the modern religion of conscience is thus its forgetfulness of spirit that issues in the de-divinization both of God and of the modern subject. Arising out of the crisis precipitated by the intersection of religious rationality with scientific rationality, the disenchantment of the religion of conscience faithfully attested to the losses that both rationalities incurred. It could no longer allow asylum to those who wanted to keep God an independent complement to our weaknesses and needs, and assigned much of what tradition has said about God to the *parerga* of its own discourse. Nor, with the same indefatigable integrity, would it brook either religious fanaticism or scientific dogmatism. Yet, dispirited, the religion of conscience acknowledged that the cost of the crisis of the modern 'in between'—of the conflict between nature and ideas, between science and religion—was that the new intellectual landscape in which its authors and their peers had to work required them to think less of themselves and of God, both at the same time.

The religion of conscience was not some sort of theoretical mistake. It was an ambitious undertaking in the face of far-reaching loss to discern a religious metaphysic intrinsic to the workings of ordinary mental activity. It was a rationality that attempted to express that which the traditional rationalities were ill-suited to address: the emergence of individual freedom and the burgeoning of science. And it did so with scrupulous attention, as a matter of conscience, to the limits of each discourse of human inquiry, in order to safeguard the integrity and well-being of the individual. This, clearly, is the most precious achievement of the religion of conscience. From their inception, however, the new discourses encountered phantasms of past rationalities hovering at the very boundaries that they labored to establish.

It has become a convention to be chary of universal rationality, and for this reason there is reluctance to try on the thinking of the religion of conscience. Or, better, it has become a reason to dismiss it out of hand. I think that such dismissals cause us to miss the enduring pathos of the religion of conscience. To look at the religion of conscience as a project of triumphalist self-assertion is to miss the losses from which it sprang. Should we turn to Fuseli's *The Artist Moved to Despair by the Grandeur of Antique Fragments* (Figure 4) as evocative of the spirit of the time in which the religion of conscience developed, we encounter poignant regret for lost totality, irrevocable loss, and a vanished wholeness. The figure, which we may take as emblematic of modernity, bows with grief in the face of the fragments of history, cosmos, and culture. No longer enchanted by the past, the figure is still in some sense bound to it in mourning. Indeed, the figure appears to be caught between his mourning for the fragments of the past and his own faltering attempts to find his own footing. Against such a backdrop, we can more clearly understand the costs of the de-divinization of God and the de-divinization of the self in the modern religion of conscience.

THREE

Disfiguring the Soul

The glass chose to reflect only what he saw
Which was enough for his purpose: his image
Glazed, embalmed, projected at a 180-degree angle.
The time of day or the density of the light
Adhering to the face keeps it
Lively and intact in a recurring wave
Of arrival. The soul establishes itself.
But how far can it swim out through the eyes
And still return safely to its nest? The surface
Of the mirror being convex, the distance increases
Significantly; that is, enough to make the point
That the soul is a captive, treated humanely, kept
In suspension, unable to advance much farther
Than your look as it intercepts the picture.

. . . .

The soul has to stay where it is,
Even though restless, hearing raindrops at the pane,
The sighing of autumn leaves thrashed by the wind,
Longing to be free, outside, but it must stay
Posing in this place. It must move
As little as possible. This is what the portrait says.
But there is in that gaze a combination
Of tenderness, amusement and regret, so powerful
In its restraint that one cannot look for long.
The secret is too plain. The pity of it smarts,
Makes hot tears spurt: that the soul is not a soul,
Has no secret, is small, and it fits
Its hollow perfectly: its room, our moment of attention.

    —JOHN ASHBERY, "Self-portrait in a Convex Mirror"

Parmigianino's sixteenth-century painting *Self-portrait in a Convex Mirror*
(Figure 5) is the subject of John Ashbery's poem. In this portion, Ashbery

Figure 5: Parmigianino, *Self-portrait in a Convex Mirror* (ca. 1524). (Erich Lessing / Art Resource, NY.)

portrays vividly the sequestering effect of reflection. To the mirrored gaze, he notes, everything is surface. Just as nothing exists for this gaze that is not surface, so also there are no words that adequately depict this surface. Hence, the dilemma: there is only the peculiar slant of language to affirm what this surface is or is not. If we transpose Ashbery's observation about the portrait to the unhoused intellect in the modern religion of conscience, it helps us to take note of a peculiar feature of this particular subject. Like Parmigianino's painted reflection, this subject's fate is to be a captive of its own form of attending. I am going to argue that there is a distinctive sense in which this is so. To reach this end, however, I will need to do some provisional conceptual spadework. To locate the point I want to discuss, we need to take three steps. The first narrows the scope of my remarks to the necessity of some form of self-knowledge in reflection; the second narrows it even further to the way in which this form functions as a rule of figuration. The third step leads to the recognition that the rule of figuration performs as an agent of disfiguration, which effaces the soul.

The Form of Attending

I begin by noting that my point—that the subject's fate is to be captive of its own form of attending—could amount to little more than the truism that we all see things from our own perspective. To make my point something other than vacuous, I need to fill in the details about the form of attending that holds the subject of the modern religion of conscience. In this form of attending, the subject claims to derive its identity directly from its spontaneous self-awareness. Standing behind the subject's claim is the formal assumption that the 'I' gives itself to the other (the object) and then encounters itself in the objectified form (as specular other). It is not difficult to visualize this. We can readily imagine ourselves looking into a mirror and encountering an image that reflects to us our identity as attenders. But this way of conceptualizing what we see is misleading. The identity of the subject comes not directly from itself, but from its reflection (its specular other). Moreover, we could scarcely know that what we see is ourselves unless we already knew who we are.

Chasing down this well-known circularity is not, however, what I have in mind. I propose instead to focus on the (unacknowledged) intervening form in this model of reflection that makes self-recognition possible. By this I mean simply acknowledging the necessity of introducing some form of self-knowledge into the act of reflection that the subject of the modern religion of conscience claims to experience. This amounts to invoking—to recur to Ashbery's poetic observation—a peculiar slant of language to speak of that for which there are no words. By means of this invocation, the subject of reflection endows consciousness with a determinate form. The quandary is over what that form might commit us to. For what the 'I' deploys in the interpretation of reflection is a particular form of objectification that delimits the notion of subjectivity.

In the preceding essay, I tried to suggest a way of thinking that will help us to delineate what kind of hostage the subject of the modern religion of conscience is. I argued that the mind portrayed by the modern religion of conscience is in search of mooring. It belongs neither to the realm of nature nor the domain of ideas. Duty becomes the safe port. Only as the mind attends to duty can it secure and preserve itself in freedom. Everything depends, therefore, on our attention. It is, of course, not so much what we attend to as how we attend to it that determines our dutifulness. So the way in which we think about ourselves, our souls, makes all the difference.

The modern religion of conscience requires thinking of ourselves as an empty, rational form of interiority. All that is available to us are the rules of rational activity that we apply when we think of any sensible object. Inasmuch as we have no sensible intuitions of our souls, we are bound to think of them merely through the form of our rational mental activity, which we learn through our knowledge of objects. This means that when we reflect on ourselves, the path from the image of ourselves as reflected to ourselves as the ones reflecting is not immediate and direct, but requires the introduction of a rational form (the concept of an objectified self) in order for us to know that it is ourselves that we encounter in reflection and not something else.

This brings us again to Ashbery's poem. What he portrays, in part, is the outcome of looking at the soul through concepts when there are no words to say what it really is. His take on this is that we restrain the soul when we think that it must conform to the manner of our attending. In effect, Ashbery is claiming that our attention holds the soul hostage.

It is in this Ashberian spirit that I embark on my exploration of the captive soul in the modern religion of conscience. Soul-talk, of course, is a slippery business with a checkered history. Its role in the grand narratives of modernity differs significantly from those it played in classical theology and philosophy. Once seen as the animating force of life inextricably linked to the body, the soul in modern discourses instead represented the non-self-identical character of the human body with other material objects in the world that did not possess souls. What this seemed to suggest was the need to think about immateriality as a way to designate the uniqueness of the human body as a distinctive kind of force in the world. To pursue soul talk was to lend oneself to the supposition that some dimension of bodily creativity set it apart from other objects. But this supposition, if literalized, could and did give rise to the idea of some spectral entity or invisible surplus that inhabited bodies. While this way of speaking offered a way to account for the kind of distinction that set human bodies apart from other bodies, it also created insurmountable problems of picturing the soul as a ghostly kind of body whose reality and whose connection to the material body were at best questionable.

Some modern thinkers, cognizant of these issues, grouped them under what we now call the 'subject-object' problem. They pored tirelessly over the way in which the activity of the thinking subject constitutes its identity.[1] What they meant by identity was the constant relationship of the subject to itself, which made it possible for the subject at any moment to be aware of its own awareness. Many of these thinkers claimed, following Descartes, that this self-awareness is the result of the subject objectifying itself. Just as the subject could represent objects to itself, so also could it turn this activity of representing back on itself. What followed from this reflexive activity, they argued, was a unique kind of self-relation. Self-relation, on this under-standing, was unique precisely because it was an identity between an activity and the result of that activity. And this identity, in turn, made it the point of absolute certitude, freed from all skepticism about the sensible world.

But arguing in this Cartesian fashion posed difficulties. It was not clear how the spontaneous activity by which the subject came into relation to itself also related to the objective world of knowledge. Both Hobbes and Rousseau implicitly avoided the Cartesian problem by linking self-consciousness to the natural instinct for self-preservation. For them, the subject becomes the lord over internal and external nature by preserving itself against what would deprive it of its existence. The upshot of this link-ing was that some form of objective knowledge is constitutive of subjectiv-ity. It remained for Kant to delve more deeply into the correlation between self-consciousness and self-preservation and to spell out explicitly how the Cartesian chasm between the spontaneous activity of the subject and the objective world of knowledge could be overcome. He showed that an object becomes determinate by way of its relation to the subject, and the subject becomes aware of its own unique identity only by way of its relation to objects. Thereby, Kant opened the way for conceiving of self-preservation as the maintenance of the subject's unique rational identity as the conceptu-alizer of objects. At the very least, this meant that the concept of an object played an indispensable role in the self-knowledge of the subject.

The Rule of Figuration

I said earlier that to understand the distinctive sense in which the subject of the modern religion of conscience is captive of its own form of attending, we would have to take a number of steps. The first of these was through the reflection model of consciousness to the intervening form of self-knowledge (the concept of an object). The second step follows: the concept of an object functions as a rule of figuration. We need to get a clearer idea of the role figuration plays in determining the gaze of the subject.

I begin by noting that the way in which Hobbes, Rousseau, and Kant linked the spontaneous activity of the subject to objective knowledge appears to have facilitated shifts in certain descriptions. As they developed what I have called the 'religion of conscience,' object discourse and its corresponding subject tended to overshadow traditional soul discourse; scientific rationality displaced much of Augustinian theological rationality; and morality superseded biblical religion. It is tempting to think of redescriptions of this order as akin to a Rortian instance of one vocabulary replacing another. On this way of looking at things, one way of speaking, which gives promise of great things and helps us to achieve certain of our purposes, supplants another, which has become entrenched and no longer seems useful. But this interpretation is unconvincing. It is more nearly the case, historically speaking, that each of these vocabularies has survived, albeit often with altered significance. To see the shifts in these vocabularies historically and developmentally prompts a certain modesty regarding purposes and ends. The makers of the modern religion of conscience could no more foresee the ways in which their arguments would profoundly affect the development of the modern study of religion than Moore or Russell could foretell the resurgence of interest in Romantic theories of subjectivity (which they thought they had upended) at the end of the twentieth century.[2] But if we are willing to be more circumspect, a different reading emerges: the ends that a new way of construing an issue serve only come into view *over time*. The implications of speaking in that particular way become evident only by *using that way of speaking*. Precisely by virtue of this way of speaking, it becomes possible to envisage something that otherwise would be unimaginable and so to dream up novel purposes.

This last point permits me to redirect our present discussion about shifts in descriptions away from ends or purposes and toward the distinctive features of a way of speaking. Viewed from this angle, construing the subject as indissolubly linked to the object becomes a matter of distinctive speech. To put the matter formulaically, we might say that the makers of the modern religion of conscience—by linking the concepts of subject and object in just the way that they did—were effectively drawing up some linguistic battle lines. By means of such lines, these moderns proposed to separate those forms of distinctive speech that could legitimately count as taking on a power of meaning more than themselves from those that could not.

What does it mean to describe "forms of speech taking on a power of meaning more than themselves"? It is a commonplace that words become figurative when we wrench them from their ordinary use and place them in a sentence as a substitute for a more obvious word. What becomes distinctive about this substitution is the new significance of the word in relation to others. So, for example, by substituting 'plows' for 'sails' in the sentence "The ship sails the sea," I introduce new significance by saying, "The ship plows the sea." At the very least, this significance grows out of a certain cooperation and interaction of meanings among words that intimate a pattern or scheme: 'plows' invokes images of a blade cutting furrows into a surface and turning it up. It is this pattern, whose meaning differs from any single word or from the sum of the words that constitute it, which is the figure of speech. Put another way, a figure of speech is an assumption of ordering by which we make sense of the world.

The makers of the modern religion of conscience wanted to draw a line between those configurations of words that would count and those that would not count in making sense of their world. So Hobbes, for example, was content to speak of a Christian commonwealth but shrank from talking of the universal church.[3] Rousseau would happily invoke the image of a wise and powerful will that governed the universe but eschewed the image of a single source of all things.[4] And as is well-known, Kant spurned talk of works of grace while often invoking the imagery of satanic guile.[5] These distinctions that the makers of the modern religion of conscience struck seem to support the notion that pursuing some figures of speech and casting off others is essential to portraying their religious outlook on the world. I think we can sharpen this point by saying that the distinctions rest on the assumption that a command of 'figure' is a major skill necessary in the interpretation of narratives of religious self-identity.

I am trying to say that figuration remains central to the way in which the modern religion of conscience links the spontaneous activity of the subject to objective knowledge of the world. Simply put, figuration refers to the practice of using words to constitute a pattern or design that intimates some new significance that differs from their ordinary meaning. What often escapes our notice is the role of figuration in the modern religion of conscience, although I suspect that any reader of Hobbes, Rousseau, and Kant develops a sense that familiar turns of phrase—especially religious phrases —acquire a distinctive, if not outright strange, turn. I think that we can trace those distinctive turns of speech to the conception of objective knowledge in the modern religion of conscience. To be more precise, I want to suggest that the concept of an object functions in their thought as a rule of figuration.

To appreciate this suggestion is to begin to see how Ashbery's poetic lament over the captivity of the soul casts light on the modern religion of conscience. As Kant made explicit, to say that the subject is related to the objective world of knowledge is to say that the concept of what an object is governs all configuration. How one represents the figure of the subject is thus dependent on what the concept of an object is. In turn, the figure of the reflecting subject rules what we mean by attending. So the more the concept of an object limits the ways in which we configure the subject, the more narrow our attending becomes. This is why we may begin to suspect that the peculiar slant of language in the modern religion of conscience not only narrows our reflective gaze, but also pre-commits us to an impoverished knowledge of what the soul might be.

How Figuration Performs

The kind of account that I have begun to develop lends itself to questions about what sort of figuration the concept of an object might prompt. To arrive at this point is to begin to take the third step that I introduced at the outset: to note how figuration performs. Is our paltry gaze the reason that the soul recedes into the background? Or is this recession due to something else somehow running amiss? As Ashbery has it, the portrait says that the soul must move as little as possible in the room that we have made for it. I take this to be tantamount to saying that the modern soul's captivity is due to the way in which the concept of an object narrows our reflective gaze. The reason "that the soul is not the soul . . . and . . . fits its hollow perfectly" in the troping of the religion of conscience is, presumably, that the concept of an object functions to bring us ultimately to disillusioned knowledge.[6] This seems to answer the first question, rendering the second superfluous. But I think this judgment too hasty. Perhaps "the soul is not the soul" because the concept of an object functions as an agent of *disfiguration*.

By disfiguration, I mean limiting the basis for substituting properties in patterns of speech. As an expression of skeptical disbelief, such limitation can upend a trope. In this sense, disfiguration appears as the use of one figure to discredit other figures in which we have, at some time or other, placed our confidence. Giovanni Bernadonne's (St. Francis) 1223 Christmas crib in a natural grotto in Greccio is an infamous example. He drew on Isaiah's images of the ox and the ass (Isaiah 1:3: "The ox knows his master, and the ass his master's crib, but Israel does not know, my people does not consider") and the Lucan account of the shepherds visiting the Christ child, emphasizing the low estate of the birth of the god-child and connecting it to the Eucharistic death of the Christ. Therein he implicitly discredited a competing liturgical emphasis on the visitation of the Magi, which underscored the regal status of the child and his eternal reign. (Caravaggio's *Adoration of St. Francis of Assisi and St. Lawrence* emphasizes St. Francis's role in this new configuration. See Figure 6.) Similarly, but in less dramatic fashion, Hobbes' figure of the Christian commonwealth discredited the figure of the universal church, just as Rousseau's figure of the governing moral will discredited the figure of the single source of all creation. Naturally enough, such disfiguring carries with it, at some level, the overtones of defacing, of marring the external appearance or significant details of something. We probably are inclined to imagine this as an act of vandals who damage a statue or painting. But we might also imagine it as the expression of a kind of moral or religious fervor, as in the sweeping iconoclastic programs of some of the Swiss Protestant reformers. Far from being a random act of violence, this latter image intimates some kind of design: some configurations are valid and some are not; one can distinguish reliable figures from unreliable ones. It means, as well, that someone, somewhere, is busy drawing up battle lines over what counts and what does not.

There is another level of marring by which disfiguring, more than upending, actually decimates a tropological system. This is the level at which disfiguring functions to render an entire system suspect by disabling pivotal tropes within it. To look at the Swiss reformers from this angle would be to see their removing religious icons and stained glass windows as rendering

Figure 6: Caravaggio, *Adoration of St. Francis of Assisi and St. Lawrence* (1609). (Scala / Art Resource, NY.)

suspect the Roman veneration of the lives of Christ and his mother. In later decades, Hobbes substituted the mechanics of force to interpret the workings of the human mind, rather than projecting a human face or personality into it. His substitution disabled the trope of *prosopopoeia* or the rhetorical practice of introducing personification to an abstract thing. Let's get clear about what this claim is by getting clear about what it is not. The claim is not that the meaning or emotions of a personality that ordinarily get tacked on to what would otherwise be meaningless mental activity now find themselves suspended. On the contrary, there are many levels and textures of mental activity that go into the business of meaning-making to which we want to call attention. Many of them have to do with the complex relation of consciousness and language that is the condition of our thinking. But these are distinct from a rationalizing orientation to the world that attempts to name that for which, because antecedent to our thinking, there are no words. In so naming, such rationalizing orientations cover over what they name as much as they reveal it. So when the operation of disfiguration suspends a particular way of configuring and rationalizing mental activity— such as Hobbes' suspension of prosopopoeia—it can decimate an entire tropological system. This Hobbes did to the metaphysical tropes of his contemporaries, which derived from Aristotle and the Schoolmen, rendering them suspect. His suspension was due, in part, to the conviction that there are some places that can neither be faced nor named directly. And it was owed, in part, to his conviction that "Fairies" and "Ecclesiastiques" were "crafty ambitious persons" who used superstition, ghosts, false prophecies, and prognostications "to abuse the simple people."[7]

Just as in the previous one, this level of disfiguration may serve our need to strike distinctions between those figures that count and those that do not. But unlike the other, this level of disfiguration helps us to make such distinctions by proffering an assumption of epistemological certainty. This assumption may cut in one of two directions. In the first, the assumption manifests itself in the notion that some figures are more apt than others, and that to employ those that are apt is to bring a certain truth into view that otherwise would not be evident. In the second, the assumption surfaces in the conviction that we can come to certain knowledge that no figures grant epistemological certainty, although some are more reliable than others in helping us to arrive at this knowledge.

It seems to me that in the tropes of disfiguration in the modern religion of conscience, both directions of the assumption of epistemological certainty are at work. Indeed, I think they play off each other to achieve a particular effect, although I suspect that, in the end, the second direction gets the upper hand, especially in Kant's version. I will here only sketch the outlines of two examples—one each from Hobbes and Rousseau—to illustrate how certain disfiguring tropes in playing off one another achieve the effect of effacing the soul.

What Can One Say of the Soul?

Consider, as our first example, Hobbes' celebrated denunciation of theologians' metaphorical assertions regarding the Kingdom of God. To speak of it as "Eternall Felicity after this life in the Highest Heaven" or as the "Kingdom of Glory" or as "Sanctification" or the "Kingdom of Grace" was no different in principle for Hobbes than to conjecture in the manner of the barbarous, attributing animate characteristics to invisible powers. "There was nothing," Hobbes writes, "which a Poet could introduce as a person in his Poem, which they did not make either a *God*, or a *Divel*."[8] So as Hobbes sees it, the problem is the introduction of metaphor to personify invisible powers and thereby, implicitly, to distinguish the spiritual from the temporal.[9]

But Hobbes won't brook this distinction. He holds, instead, that the 'Kingdom of God' signifies nothing more than a way of understanding the political body that people constitute with their votes. It maintains the distinction between omnipotence and limited natural power, and in doing so, provides a critical principle by which to assess abridgments that earthly potentates may make of power and law in the earthly sphere. Hobbes' opposition to metaphor (or more exactly, to prosopopoeia) disables the tropological system of his contemporary Christian divines. His opposition takes the form of displacing prosopopoeia with analogical thinking. Rejecting any projection of human characteristics of happiness onto a spiritual space, Hobbes instead focuses on of the figure of 'kingdom' as an analogue to the Leviathan. The Leviathan, as we will recall Hobbes' construal of it, is an elaboration of the basic building blocks of the notion of self-preservation—a force, a guiding principle, and a capacity for self-awareness that issues in conscience. Inasmuch as this is the foundation of certitude in Hobbes' outlook, the figure of the Kingdom of God, as an analogue of this foundation, extends it. Replacing (by disabling) figures that are not a reliable means of certitude with the figure of the Kingdom of God is a way in which Hobbes advances what he thinks counts as a sound precept of experience. So in this movement of disfiguration, the epistemological assumption is that at least this figure is a reliable means of reaching epistemological certitude.

At the same time, the name of God that Hobbes cobbles together with the figure of kingdom serves to remind us that here we encounter, in part, omnipotence or sovereign power. For Hobbes, this means that we face the incomprehensible, and so, that which we cannot configure. He flatly asserts that no figure can tell us anything of "the many things in God's Word" that are "above reason." So what we name by the word 'God' can be nothing more than the way in which this omnipotent power is related to us. When, accordingly, we join the word 'God' to the word 'kingdom,' the ensuing figure serves as a way of configuring omnipotence as it relates to us. But it in no way declares what God is or circumscribes God within the limits of our imagination. Interpreted from this perspective, the figure of the Kingdom of God helps us to know with certainty that no figure grants ultimate epistemological certitude.[10]

It seems pretty clear that these two directions—the claim that the Kingdom of God is nothing more than a way of speaking of the political body that humans constitute, and the claim that 'God' affixed to 'kingdom' signifies the incomprehensible and non-configurable—conflict with one another. A better way to see this entails different modes of disfiguration whose interplay functions to guard against over-conceptualization. That is, their interplay impedes our tendency to fill in more information than we have by providing too cogent an interpretation. We see this in how Hobbes configures the soul. Adamantly opposing the view that the soul is a separate substance, which by nature "hath Eternity of Life,"[11] Hobbes holds that the "*Soule* . . . signifieth . . . either . . . Life, or the Living Creature . . . the Body alive."[12] So understood, the soul is an animating power or material life force. Far from being assured of immortality, life endeavors to preserve itself by defending itself against whatever would deprive it of existence. Once we see soul as self-preserving embodied life, there is much else about it that can come to light. It becomes possible through reflection on this embodied self-preserving endeavor to abstract from it a rational orientation toward the world. By means of this rational orientation, one can say that the principled governance of this endeavor preserves life. Abstracted principles of self-preservation, of course, assure nothing—life is not by nature immortal. But to the extent that they lay claim to our desire to act, and so become incorporated into our conduct, they function as conscience. And as bodied forth in conscience, they can affect the outcomes of our activity.[13]

To move from animating power through its rationalization, by way of reflective abstraction, into orienting principles of self-preservation is to move from seeing the soul as life force to seeing it as conscience. By developing a figure of the soul in this way, Hobbes is proposing, in effect, that at its most rudimentary levels, the soul's role in meaning-making issues in a rational orientation within which it becomes possible to speak of it as conscience. The moves he makes follows his linking the spontaneous activity of the subject with the world of objective knowledge—the link between self-consciousness and self-preservation. These are the lines he pursues repeatedly to ascertain certitude, as in his development of the figure of the Kingdom of God. And just as in the development of that figure, Hobbes develops this figure in a way that displaces another: the configuration of the soul as substance.

Hobbes thinks that configuring the soul as substance assumes that, from the outset, the soul has been taken up into a rationalizing structure of consciousness. He has in mind the particular orientation of the medieval Schoolmen's conception of the rationalizing structure in which no soul is hindered from its immortality, regardless of its conduct. What Hobbes is opposing, I think, is that any soul could understand itself at the outset in terms of an organized structure of propositions. That these, independent of engagement with the objective world, should proffer certitude, and lay out the tracks along which the soul's life is being directed to run, strikes Hobbes as ludicrous.

By contrast, Hobbes thinks that the tracks along which the soul's life may run are beyond our ken. He states clearly that we can only configure the soul as having eternal life if we conceive of this as an act of God's grace, bestowed on the faithful.[14] To link the soul to God is, as we have seen in the linking of kingdom to God, a way in which Hobbes signifies the incomprehensible. Put another way, this figure of the eternal soul not only effaces the figure of the soul as naturally eternal, but also, in disabling the tropological system within which it functions, emphatically points us to the certainty that no figure can grant ultimate epistemological certitude. Indeed, we begin to suspect that figures only give back what we have put into them.

So what we can say in the end with Hobbes is that the soul is a life force whose own rational self-articulation may issue in the conception of conscience, which is the principle for governing and preserving life. This is the peculiar slant of language by which Hobbes tries to articulate that for which there are no words, his moment of attention that holds the soul captive. Or as Ashbery has it in another place in his poem:

> Today enough of a cover burnishes
> To keep the supposition of promises together
> In one piece of surface, letting one ramble
> Back home from them so that these
> Even stronger possibilities can remain
> Whole without being tested.[15]

How Does the Soul Show?

Matters do not fare much differently for Rousseau. Like Hobbes, Rousseau entered into festive combat with speculative metaphysicians. "Never," he wrote in 1762, "has the jargon of metaphysics led to the discovery of a single truth, and it has filled philosophy with absurdities of which one is ashamed as soon as one has stripped them of their high-sounding words."[16] The reach of his vituperation extended as well to the Church, whose dogmatics he lampooned as little more than the instruction that the faithful believe everything that the Church decided, including the most absurd doctrines. This dogmatism prevented him—or so he claimed—from believing anything at all. But Rousseau saved his most derisive invective for the materialists. He scoffed that their reasoning resembled that of a deaf man who, because never having heard, denied the existence of sound. More than a clever riposte, this quip bore within it the makings of a claim that Rousseau would attempt to exploit. For he thought that to those who have ears to hear, there is "the inner voice that calls out to them in a tone that can scarcely be ignored."[17]

Rousseau's is a more elusive point to make than might first appear. In effect, he is attempting to call attention to something in our experience that shows, but about which difficulties accrue regarding how to say what it is. For however we might try to say what this aspect in our experience might consist in, our saying would tend to cover up or conceal what is showing. I think we may more readily grasp what Rousseau is trying to point up if we bring into view that with which he is at odds. Rousseau opposes the Hobbesian configuration of conscience. That configuration turns on the propositional claim that a certain course of conduct governs and preserves life. Both to rationalize it and to provide the structure within which it has the particular content, Hobbes locates this proposition in a web of other beliefs. Now if the web of beliefs that rationalize it should shift, the proposition of conscience would shift, as well. This potential troubled Rousseau. He thought that it could render conscience a variable feast, subject to whatever whims of rationalization or mind-like structures of belief might be operative at a given time. Instead, he proposed a notion of conscience as a tendency inherent within the mind. Bearing its own intelligibility, this tendency both resists the encroachments of rationalizing orientations and can disrupt any system of rationality.

To attempt to make this point, Rousseau embarks on a course of argumentation in "The Creed of the Savoyard Vicar" (*Emile*, 1762) that he anchors in effects. From such effects as he thinks are self-evident, Rousseau draws only the minimal inference that these effects show some cause. From the self-evident effects of sensation, for example, Rousseau concludes that something else has caused them. Or again, from the effects of judging and comparing, Rousseau infers that they show active thinking as their cause. Hence the rule of thinking to which Rousseau subscribes is that he will trust feeling or the awareness of effects more than reason. To cast this in terms of the language I am attempting to develop here, Rousseau trusts what shows more than what is said. As is no doubt evident from this way of putting the matter, Rousseau's strategy is to draw our attention to mental activity that is antecedent to any particular rational orientation.

Rousseau presses this strategy in two directions. By correlating sensations with the external objects that give rise to them, on the one hand, and sensations with internal self-awareness, on the other, Rousseau links objective knowledge with mental activity. Initially, this enables him to develop an analysis of mental life on the basis of our experience of objects. We are not only sentient beings that objects affect, but also active, thinking beings who compare, judge, and reflect on the affections. Subsequently, Rousseau moves from an analysis of the experienced properties of objects to the force that gives rise to them. From the movement of inanimate bodies that we perceive, Rousseau infers a cause that we do not perceive, but to whose existence we nonetheless feel keenly that we can attest. And as a spontaneous first cause of motion, this force must, according to Rousseau, be conceived of as a will.

Now it is tempting to claim that Rousseau is pursuing an analogy between the human mind and the divine mind. To interpret Rousseau in this way would be to suppose that just as spontaneous acts of the human will effect action, so also spontaneous acts of the divine will effect motion in inanimate bodies. But this would be to misread Rousseau. He claims that analogy no more than indicates an affirmative answer. Our knowledge of the spontaneous acts of will, be it human or divine, arises from an immediate awareness or intuition. It is precisely this immediate awareness or intuition that shows, but about which we have difficulty speaking. Clearly, analogy misguides us by saying too much and so doesn't do the job. To guard against overinterpretation, Rousseau disables Hobbes' system of analogical tropes by deploying a system of *metonymy*.

A metonymous figure of speech substitutes an attribute of a thing for the thing itself. In respect of this substitution, metonymy is fundamentally a negation. To speak of 'the bench' for the judiciary or 'the crown' for the monarchy is both the substitution of an attribute for something in its entirety and the negation of all but that attribute. Such negation is especially evident in a particular form of metonymy called *metalepsis*. In metalepsis, the augmented negation in the substituted attribute removes so much particular detail that it becomes generalized, thereby heightening the effect. Thus, for example, Shakespeare's *Henry VIII* substitutes the figure of 'the end' for the figure of 'sacrifice': "Go with me like good angels to my end." In a way that similarly heightens the effect, Rousseau substitutes the figure of 'feeling' for the figure of immediate self-awareness or intuition. 'Feeling' points up a dimension of elemental mental activity that encompasses immediate awareness of an affect that shows the correlation of subject and object, but avoids (or, better, effectively negates) particular details.

Rousseau's use of metonymous figures to draw attention to an elemental form of mental life suggests that if we are to understand conscience, we have to have some sense of how the activity of the mind effects transformations on the inner contents of propositional attitudes. To take this suggestion seriously is to begin to see the strategic role that his system of metonymous (and metaleptic) tropes plays in his argument. It is to see that metonymy makes manifest how intuition becomes a conceptual requirement to account for this inner transformation. And to have accepted this is to have taken a long step toward recognizing how Rousseau develops intuition under its metaleptic designation as 'feeling' and integrates it into moral thinking and practice.

'Feeling' and 'Showing'

What does such 'feeling' show? For Rousseau, it shows the various features of mental life that together go into building up a world-intuition (*Weltanschauung*). Let me trace rapidly the steps through which this answer seems to unfold. In a condensed passage in "The Creed of the Savoyard Vicar," he claims: "For us, to exist is to feel; our sensitivity incontestably comes before our intelligence, and we have feelings before we have ideas."[18] He then goes on to say, in an aside, that by feeling he has in mind both a received impression that affects us, exciting our attention, and the object that causes it. So to be aware of feeling is to be aware, at some level, of this correlation. And it is precisely from this awareness (correlating affection and object) that Rousseau discerns the activity of the mind. What first shows in this awareness, then, is a kind of active attending that requires both comparison and recognition.

This felt correlation discloses a second feature. The mind alone produces the activities of comparing, which means that these activities are spontaneous. From this felt awareness of spontaneity, in turn, the mind is able to discern spontaneity in the movements of objects around it, and to distinguish such spontaneity from communicated movement (i.e., movement from a cause other than itself). Indeed, by dint of this awareness, the mind recognizes such spontaneous movement as the cause behind the movements of inanimate bodies within the universe. Again, such a spontaneous movement entails acting, comparing, and choosing, all of which are components of recognition.

It is a matter of conviction for Rousseau that a spontaneous willful act that moves the universe has to be the act of an intelligence. He derives this conviction from what he calls an 'involuntary feeling,' a recognition of ordering with which he is already familiar. Hence, when he says that he believes that a powerful and wise will governs the world, he is saying that these are the notions he brings together—reflections upon the 'object' that causes the 'feeling'—to extrapolate the components of feeling he already has. In a word, what feeling shows, third, is the ordering of God. This is why Rousseau says that he feels God within him and "perceives God every-where in his works," but as soon as he attempts "to contemplate God as he is in himself," God escapes him.[19]

Nonetheless, because we are at least aware of this ordering, we are also aware, at some level, that it disposes us toward that which is suitable for our nature. This is Rousseau's fourth point. He is confident that our feeling shows self-love and desire for well-being, fear of pain and inclination to flee what is harmful to us. Put differently, by showing an ordering that serves our common interests, our feeling manifests both love of what is good and aversion to the deprivation of good. In this way, or so Rousseau leads us to believe, our feeling exhibits the double relation we have to ourselves. Either we may honor our feeling and serve the order that it bodies forth or we may disregard our feeling and subvert its order. To disregard our feeling is to prefer to serve our own selfish interests, which deprive the good.

With all appropriate parrying concluded, Rousseau now takes aim at his principal point. He proclaims that to the extent that our feeling of common ordering prompts us to hold our selfish interests at bay, it simultaneously shows itself, fifth, as conscience, as a sure guide, as an infallible judge of good and evil.[20] It is as conscience that our feeling prompts us to love the good. Rousseau's point is telling once we understand that this power of conscience is manifest not merely in terms of its representational content, but also—and especially—as a motivated form of mental activity. In this form, conscience both resists the encroachments of rationalizing orienta-tions and disrupts any system of rationality.

I think that once we have grasped Rousseau's model of extrapolation from what shows in feeling—from attending to spontaneous activity, from ordering to the double relation we have to ourselves, from sure guide as conscience to the inherent tendency to disrupt any system of rationality—as an exhibition of a form of mental activity that issues in a world intuition, a certain mystery evaporates. This is Rousseau's puzzling claim that it is possible to explain the immediate source of conscience independent of reason itself. This claim is puzzling when one thinks of conscience only in terms of its rational content. How, we might ask, could conscience be anything without rational content, without specific propositions regarding our conduct? So long as we cling to the notion that content alone matters, there seems to be no good answer to our question. But once we follow Rousseau in freeing ourselves from the notion that we capture conscience fully by its rational content, a beautifully simple answer emerges: the ordering of conscience appears wherever there is feeling and intelligence.

It should not be difficult for us to see at this point in the argument that Rousseau takes his figure of feeling as conscience to be a reliable means of reaching epistemological certitude. He thinks that this figure not only shifts us away from Hobbes' ideologically favored system of tropes, but also, thereby, leads to knowledge shed of illusion. But there is, as well, another sense in which even the figure of feeling as conscience does not grant epistemological certainty. To round out my comments on Rousseau, I want now to take up this second disabling sense of the figure of conscience.

Accounting for the Incomprehensible

The lure of Rousseau's figure of 'feeling' as conscience is that it purports to offer an account of an inherent mental activity that on the surface appears incomprehensible. So, for example, the Savoyard vicar's admonition to limit ourselves to the inner light of our first feelings seems unfathomable on its own, but becomes intelligible when linked to the sequence of feelings that, considered severally, manifest a sense of ordering. Such consideration seems to be a kind of intuitional explanation, whose point is to impart a particular type of intelligibility. To introduce this kind of explanation is to invite us to broaden our conception of what we include in mental life, to think of feeling on a par with rationality as a motivational force of truth.

Only thus, Rousseau seems to be saying, can we speak of the soul. Unless we can see the soul as linked to an inner light antecedent to ideas—however much it is prone to be hidden from us—there would be nothing of significance that we could say about any sure guide in the immense labyrinth of human opinion. But this account runs into difficulties insofar as it tries to explain feeling by appealing to an objective reality that plays a *causal* role in bringing those feelings about. It is only because there is a common ordering (God) that affects my soul, exciting feeling of which I become aware, that I can speak of what Rousseau is calling the self-evident truth of feeling. The search for links to external objective reality, to be sure, while safeguarding him from the more dubious 'subjective' claims of Cartesianism, nonetheless commits Rousseau to some external point from which the subject is in some way removed. Despite this remove—or, perhaps, precisely because of it— the external point remains determinative of what the subject is. Inasmuch as Rousseau was never able to wean himself from his profound distrust of reason as an agent of corruption, he seems to have maintained an aversion to its imaginative role in structuring experience, thereby making more stark the determinative role of the external point in the identity of the subject.

How does this peculiar constraint play out in Rousseau's configuring of the soul? The basic phenomena Rousseau wants to explain is the human capacity to initiate action. "I want to act," he writes, "and I act; I want to move my body and my body moves."[21] But Rousseau has reminded us that we know nothing more than the effects of the human capacity to initiate acts, which is to say that we know nothing of the nature of this capacity. This caveat points to the difficulty with which we have seen Rousseau to be dealing all along: offering an account of something that appears to be incomprehensible.

In particular, we lack an understanding of what the soul is. Rousseau, in effect, has smuggled the notion of the soul into his discourse, without any account of how he arrived at it. He appears to know that his claim that the soul is an active, willing immaterial force, whose essence we do not know, does not fit the bill. And he suspects that his claim that the 'voice' of the soul is conscience or the feeling of the common order fares no better at filling in the lacuna. We are, after all, just as confused with the idea of an immaterial force as we are with the idea of an infinity of relationships. But when, in turn, Rousseau comes to speak of that common order as 'the divine order,' as an established order "manifesting a unity of intention in its rela- tionships that contribute to the preservation of the whole," he seems to have made some sighting shot that will help lend intelligibility to soul-talk.[22] For what moves and governs this order is a cause that Rousseau calls God.

Once he has added the idea of an external point, God, Rousseau thinks that we are in a position to begin lending intelligibility to what we have been saying. To the claim that the soul feels this common order, we may now add that this is tantamount to feeling the effect of God. And to have said this means that when we claim that the soul feels harmony and proportion, we may also claim that the soul feels virtue, beauty, and goodness. This is why when Rousseau says that the soul feels gratitude and benediction toward the Creator, he has in mind not so much that the idea of God he invokes is something new (others had said much the same of God before him), as that the idea of God makes intelligible something that is new, albeit unfamiliar: the soul as the impulse to freedom.

On my reading of Rousseau, to equate the soul with the impulse to liberty is to say that the soul is the force by which we try to remain in connection with objective reality. In Rousseau's lexicon, objective reality is not equivalent to material reality. He abhors that sort of equation, which he maligns the materialists for making. Objective reality is rather the ordering of the universe. Only by remaining in relation to this ordering, he argues, does it become possible for the soul to experience itself as a subject set within this ordering of objects. Naturally enough, as the soul sees itself as subject, there is, simultaneously, a sense in which it is differentiated from the established ordering. So choosing to remain in connection with this ordering becomes for the soul a defensive maneuver, an act of self-preservation, against the loss of reality. Thus, the feeling the soul has of this ordering can function as a prompt to maintain the connection with objective reality.

By adopting this perspective, we might begin to see the soul in a new light. It would be more precise to say that *only* in this light, cast by the notion of the established ordering, can Rousseau configure the soul. For in this light the soul first sees itself as subject among other objects; and in this light, the soul sees its 'feeling' functioning as a guide (conscience) for its actions. This feeling of regard for universal harmony provides the soul with a way to construe both its feeling of subjectivity *and* its feeling of conscience.

It does not seem too much of a stretch, therefore, to link this reading to Rousseau's view of the immortality of the soul. His argument that the soul survives the death of the body turns on the assumption that the established order is just; given the oppression of the just in this world, universal harmony must prevail in the next.[23] It follows from this, or so Rousseau thinks, that the soul must survive the body sufficiently to assure the divine order.

Beyond this, however, we know nothing. We do not know what the life of the soul is after the death of the body; we do not know if the soul is by its nature immortal; indeed, we have no idea of the soul apart from the "beauty of the order which strikes all the faculties of our soul."[24]

I can summarize all this by saying that Rousseau's use of metonymic and metaleptic tropes of feeling to configure the soul brings it to its apogee so long as we speak of it from the external determinative point of the established (divine) ordering. But to the extent that we can say nothing of it apart from the determinative characteristics of this ordering, these tropes efface the soul. Thus we know nothing of how the soul takes up the feeling of this ordering into its imaginative life or how it metabolizes the feeling into a world-intuition. In short, what meaning this encounter has for a subject is a mystery, just as is the matter of how the subject weaves the memory of this encounter into its self-interpretation. So when Rousseau imputes responsibility to the soul, after the body's death, for maintaining its self-identity through the memory of what it has felt, we have no way to demystify these mystifications. This is the disabling sense that comes from configuring the soul as feeling. It leads the reader to epistemological and theological uncertainty. This is the point at which 'feeling' falters. The promising lure of Rousseau's figure of feeling (conscience) to provide intelligibility rests on the premise that the meaning of objective reality is simply given or simply invoked. It is as if the soul has received an oracle, a communication from the author of the established order, which, despite its chain of transfers—from feeling to willing, from conscience to world-intuition—survives intact, unelaborated. But this is to disregard the extent to which metonymic (and metaleptic) tropes are, in Rousseau's telling, the way in which soul elaborates its feeling en route to discovering its task of recreating cosmic unity.

Rousseau's system of tropes leaves us, accordingly, with these aporiae: either the soul receives an oracle to which it cannot attend or the soul subverts by its attending the oracle it receives. This is a variant of the problem of offering an account of the incomprehensible, which metamorphoses it into the comprehensible. And it is akin to the Ashberian query about the soul's captivity, now cast as the question of what it is that the soul encounters in reflection. To see that the soul mirrors its blindness as it distorts its object of reflection helps us to make sense of Ashbery's provocative observation:

Whose curved hand controls,
Francesco, the turning seasons and the thoughts
That peel off and fly away at breathless speeds
Like the last stubborn leaves ripped
From wet branches? I see in this only the chaos
Of your round mirror which organizes everything
Around the polestar of your eyes which are empty,
Know nothing, dream but reveal nothing.[25]

What Is Conceiving of Objectivity?

At the beginning of this essay, I observed, following Ashbery, that the fate of the soul is to be a captive of its own form of attending—and I added that this is especially true of the subject featured in the modern religion of conscience. The soul's captivity to its own form of attending has gone missing in Western philosophical and theological accounts. To be sure, recent thinkers have made much of the so-called self-presence of the subject to itself, which is a variant of older complaints about the circularity of the "reflection model of consciousness."[26] But even these more recent observations have tended to overlook the peculiar linking of self-awareness to self-preservation that characterizes the subject of the modern religion of conscience. So the question of the 'unacknowledged' role that 'objective knowledge' plays in the self-knowledge of this particular subject—a role to which Rousseau called our attention—has also tended to go unanswered. By contrast, to take that role seriously is to see that it informs which figures of speech the makers of the modern religion of conscience thought counted toward self-knowledge. It follows that when we talk about the role played by figures of speech in this sort of self-knowledge, ambiguity arises. Figuration in the modern religion of conscience leads both to epistemological certitude—certain figures are more reliable than others—and to the certitude that figures do not grant epistemological knowledge. By bearing this ambiguity in mind, we become clear about how figuration in the modern religion of conscience works to disfigure.

To frame matters in the way that I have pushes hard at the question of what sort of objectivity we are talking about in the modern religion of conscience. It is clear enough that what Hobbes had in mind differs from what Rousseau thought. Beyond saying that Hobbes ties objectivity to propositional forms and Rousseau to intuitional, talk about objectivity quickly devolves into the opaque. This is why, I think, Kant accorded such centrality to the question, "How do we conceive of objectivity?" To propose one way of answering this question, I will draw on the sketches of Hobbes and Rousseau that I have just completed. Both think that we can speak of God only as God relates to us; both think that we must speak figuratively of the aspect of God that is in relation to us; and both think that our talk of the soul reflects that part of God about which we speak figuratively. When thinking about these matters, Hobbes and Rousseau believe that they have in mind the same awareness that ordinary people possess. But each of them approaches this 'ordinary consciousness' from different directions.

For our purposes, it suffices to characterize the difference roughly as an *empirical approach* (Hobbes) versus an *intuitional approach* (Rousseau). In the empirical approach, Hobbes views the soul, by way of analogy, in the context of self-preservation, its practices (compacts that ensure the well-being of the community and public religion that reinforces obedience to the compacts) and its institutions (the Leviathan and the Christian Commonwealth or the Kingdom of God on earth). Thus the meaning of the soul (conscience), because it depends on the natural customs and practices of self-preservation, is subject to revision as such practices and their institutional arrangements change. In the intuitional approach, Rousseau attempts to step outside customs, practices, and their attendant beliefs to arrive at an enduring perspective: the established ordering of God. When reflected in the soul (conscience), this ordering reveals custom, practice, and belief alike as illusory. Whether we can understand the general, perduring framework of objective thought that Rousseau's metonymic and metaleptic figures imply is debatable. But few would dispute that he believed the experience of conscience to be partially and continuously constitutive of the common ordering, rather than, as Hobbes had thought, the internalization of a socially determined outlook.

By bearing in mind this tension between the empirical and the intuitional approaches, we can see Kant's accomplishment more clearly: he seeks to dissolve the tension by linking the approaches to answer the question, "How do we conceive of objectivity?" This amounts to the requirement that Kant demonstrate how, instead of being at odds, empirical thought and intuition are actually harmonious. Kant's well-known allusion to the tree of knowledge signals the way that he proposes to meet this requirement: "There are two stems of knowledge, namely sensibility and understanding, which perhaps spring from a common, but to us unknown, root. Through the former objects are given to us, through the latter they are thought."[27]

When Kant speaks of sensibility and understanding, it seems as if they are clearly distinct, neither being reducible to the other. In point of fact, they are always combined. What Kant is doing when he strikes such distinctions is 'transcendental reasoning' or a preoccupation with the modes of our knowing that are independent of our experience or sense impressions, but that, nonetheless, contribute to empirical thought. Sensibility or intuition is one such mode of knowing. Simply put, intuition is the capacity for receiving impressions. Understanding is the other mode of knowing. By virtue of understanding, we know objects through representations. In a certain sense, intuition precedes the capacity of understanding to know objects. Kant never tires of emphasizing the import of this 'certain sense.' What we experience is always given to us through intuition, never through understanding. Hence, Kant's celebrated dictum: "Concepts without intuitions are empty, intuitions without concepts are blind."[28] Apart from the givenness of sensation, the structure of the mind would remain hidden from us, as it only becomes manifest in the activity of experiential knowing. This experiential knowing may assume two forms. The first he calls 'formal intuition,' which is a unified manifold of intuition. In this form of knowing, we intuit an object, but have not yet rendered an explicit judgment about what sort of object it is. I might, for example, be making my way in the early hours of the morning across a foggy lake and suddenly be aware of something just ahead of me, even though I don't know exactly what it is. Just as suddenly, I become aware that it is a derelict skiff, and veer away from it. This is the second form of experiential knowing, which Kant calls 'perception.' In it, I bring the object that I have intuited under a concept, thereby making an explicit judgment of what it is possible.

But are these forms of knowing harmonious? And if so, what makes them that way? After all, one is merely intuitional, whereas the other is, because overtly conceptual, a determinate perception. Kant thinks that he can show that they are harmonious by establishing that subjective conditions of thought can furnish the possibility of all knowledge of objects. Principal among these is the formal condition that the mind combine the manifold of intuitions into a unitary consciousness. This is simply a way of noting that the intuitions we receive do not bear with them unity, but receive such unity from the mind as it combines them. The rules that govern this combinatory activity Kant calls 'categories.' Because they govern the way in which the mind combines intuitions, these categories are the concepts that constitute what objectivity is.[29] To put this another way, when the mind unites intuitions and categories, it can then make a judgment about the intuitions, and experiential knowledge of an object becomes possible for us. While this seems to settle the question of how to account for determinate perceptions, it doesn't appear, at first glance, to offer a way to fill in what we might mean by intuitive experience of objects where there is no such explicit judgment. So we still lack a way to speak of the harmony between these forms of knowing.

I said at "first glance," because it is easy for us to confound what Kant means by a concept of an object with an empirical concept. We readily assume that what is under discussion is a particular object whose contents we organize. Whatever we could say about the concept, accordingly, would pertain solely to the particular one that we see. Even if we insist that the mind does have a role in organizing the contents, it would, at most, be contingent on the particular experience or appearance. This would amount to little more than empirical concepts of objects. But such is not what Kant has in mind. By 'concept of an object' Kant means the concept of an object *in general,* or that in terms of which the mind unifies any manifold of intuition into a unitary consciousness.[30] To see the concept of an object in this way is to see it as both as a rule of combination (the mind unifies the manifold of intuition) and as a rule of unity (the form of the unitary consciousness). We are now able to discern that the concept of an object defines both the ordering of the contents of an object and its relation to other objects. Precisely because the rule is the same in both instances, they apply not only to any particular manifold of intuition, but also to the relationships among diverse manifolds of intuition. This is why, in part, Kant can maintain that there is a harmonious relation underlying intuitional and perceptual experiential knowing.

More remains to say, for we have yet to see fully what constitutes the relation of mental representations to an object. This is the role of Kant's infamous 'I think' that he claims must accompany all our representations. Although it is certainly implicit in the idea of mental representations, be they concepts or intuitions, that someone thinks them, this notion is not analytically entailed in them. So a separate notion, 'thought,' needs always to stand in relation to representations. Enter the 'I think.' By itself, this thought is empty. I was about to say that by itself this thought teaches us nothing, but that would not be quite right. The 'I think' has, so to speak, an 'internal accusative,' requiring an x for it to think. So it teaches us that whatever 'I think' means is manifest only in the activity of thinking some x. For Kant, this means that the act of thinking unites a manifold of given representations in one consciousness, and in so doing shows that the function of combining them presupposes a principle of combination that remains the same through change (i.e., that the principle of unity that governs combination is numerically identical). This is equivalent to saying that thinking implies both a unity of consciousness (the combined manifold of representations) and a unitary consciousness (the consciousness that has combined various representations in the same way). Or as Kant makes the argument, it is the 'I think' that confers unity to consciousness and so to all our knowledge.[31]

Here we have carried out within a transcendental perspective an activity of combination that is both a principle of identity and the condition in terms of which thinking identity is possible. So conceived, combination is a way of ordering, presupposing the potential of relations. At the same time, combination as a way of ordering implies analytically rules by which this order goes on. From this perspective, the numerical identity of combination is the (a priori) foundation for the rules by which the mind "has before its eyes the identity of its act."[32] Kant's truncated way of putting the point is this: "The analytic unity of apperception is possible only under the presupposition of a certain synthetic unity."[33]

To play this out is to see the deeper sense in which Kant thinks that the intuitional and perceptual modes of experiential knowing of objects are harmoniously related. It is to see that although only the synthetic unity of consciousness constitutes the thought that relates representations to an object, the analytic unity of consciousness (i.e., its numerical identity) comes into view only in the context of the manifold of intuitions that is already unified under the same principle of numerical identity. Only as I constitute objects of experience am I then able, so to speak, to 'constitute' myself. Or again, I can think myself only under the terms of the concept of an object. This suggests first that combination, transcendentally conceived, by presupposing both modes of relating and rules that govern that relating, gives rise to the distinction between intuition and concept (or, what is the same, between sensibility and understanding), as well as to their necessary relationship. Second, it makes clear that our intuition is conceptually saturated. Our awareness of our intuitions is never independent from a conceptual framework that determines the range of distinctions we strike. Finally, it helps us to see that the twofold sense of unity—pertaining both to the contents of an object and relations among objects—holds equally for the way in which we represent ourselves to ourselves, and so, Kant claims, to the original synthetic unity of apperception.

Kant can thus affirm the empirical approach of Hobbes and the intuitional approach of Rousseau, but claim to dissolve the dilemma between them by arguing that they have misunderstood the nature of objectivity. Objectivity is not something 'out there.' It is simply the mind's rule-governed activity, which combines the manifold of our intuitions into the unity of thought. So it is only in relation to an intelligence that there is such a concept of objectivity.

Sophistry and Figures of Speech

To say with Kant that the subject must create the world in order to create itself may seem to return us to an empirical approach, or to the idea that the subject is indissolubly linked to the customs, institutions, and practices of its world. Specifically, it may seem to return us to the Hobbesian view that the social construction of reality is an analogue of the natural process of self-preservation. But it does not. The social construction of reality, for Hobbes, forms a defense against anarchy, a proof that life need not be nasty, brutish, and short. It expresses the human capacity to co-opt nature, as it were, and to elevate the natural laws of self-preservation into a rational life-form. But what Kant thinks we share is not the ability to co-opt the laws of nature, but the capacity to create the laws of nature themselves. Because we think *through* rules (the concept of an object) that unify both the contents *of* and the relations *among* objects, *the unity of the mind implies the unity of nature.*

The upshot of this is not some Rousseauian intuitional approach to the soul. In marked contrast, Kant says, "The thinking I (the soul) . . . does not know itself through the categories, but knows the categories and though them all objects, in the absolute unity of apperception, and so through it-self."[34] Because they confounded the transcendental nature of objectivity with experiential objectivity, both Hobbes and Rousseau mistakenly pre-sumed that they could speak figuratively, either analogically or metonymi-cally, of the soul. But this amounts to no more than what Kant calls the *sophisma figurae dictionis*—the sophistry of figures of speech.[35] In exposing this sophistry, Kant upended the ambivalence that Hobbes and Rousseau had managed to maintain toward figures of speech and epistemic certitude. In his view, figures of speech never grant certitude.

The remaining situation—that there is no empirical explanation of the soul, of the 'thinking I'—leads to a sobering sorrow that we are blind to our own souls. Our poetic guide throughout this thought experiment, John Ashbery, gives voice to the modern subject's emergent grieving in this way:

> I go on consulting
> This mirror that is no longer mine
> For as much brisk vacancy as is to be
> My portion this time.[36]

If we think ourselves only as we do any object in general, there can be no getting a glimpse of what the soul might be like beyond the bounds of objectivity that does not lapse into the nonsensical. Despite this restriction, or perhaps precisely because of it, Kant thinks that the soul as a 'pure,' unconditioned form of thought (i.e., pure reason) is distinct not only from sensibility but also from human desires and passions. Moreover, he thinks that he has learned from his rapt encounter with Rousseau that this uncon-ditioned reason often contravenes in human affairs. So he wants to say that something about our inner experience can endow our practical conduct with a 'norm' that shows what we cannot say. He then argues, in effect, that even though we may not be able to legitimate talk of the soul in isolation, we may speak of it implicitly in relation to the 'norm' governing our practical ability to act in a particular way.

For our purposes here, it is not necessary to grapple in depth with Kant's ethical theory. Suffice it to say that for Kant, conscience announces itself within the context of empirical awareness. By conscience, he means our consciousness of duty that occurs whenever we propose to ourselves a course of action. Ordinarily assuming the form of an imperative—"Do your duty!"—conscience's announcement of itself may also assume an interroga-tive form (reason querying itself)—"Have you done your duty?"—and in this way expresses its diligence.[37] Clearly, awareness of this stripe is distinctive. It somehow incorporates a kind of spontaneity that is not empirically conditioned. And Kant thinks it imperative that we not compromise the integrity of this awareness by interpreting it as we would any other empirical awareness. Instead we have to devise a way to conceive of an unconditioned spontaneity that nonetheless has an effect on empirically conditioned consciousness. This amounts to the hope that we might be able to gain insight into what our souls are by considering more than the states of empirical consciousness to which we have been attending. We do so by extending our purview to images of moral awareness to which we are willing, or feel obliged, to append the notion of 'soul.' By stating what Kant hopes to devise in this way, we see more readily the path that he wants to pursue. He has both to observe the theoretical strictures he has placed on what we might mean when we speak of the soul and consider some 'image' of the unconditioned.

To accomplish this, Kant reprises the insight that the soul (as the unifying form 'I think')—because 'empty'—is parasitic on the objects of experience that it constitutes for its own meaning. He then applies this insight to the interpretation of the unconditioned (moral awareness). For him, this means, in effect, thinking of the soul (as the unifying form of dutiful willing) by way of analogy with the rules of theoretical reason. Kant thinks that we are justified in pursuing this analogy; it gives us a discreet yet consistent way to observe that the unconditioned will (pure reason relating to itself) is 'empty' apart from the manifold of conditioned, 'empirical' desire given to it. In turn, this prompts us to see that only in the context of given, conditioned desires does the form of the will (unconditioned autonomy) become manifest. So we arrive at the insight that we know the 'unconditioned' by virtue of its effect on the conditioned.[38]

To round out the analogy with theoretical reason, we would need a 'concept of an object,' albeit one whose domain is moral awareness. As in theoretical reason, such a 'concept' presumably would entail two senses of relation: the unity of the object is the same as the unity among objects. In a word, a moral object would be that in the concept of which the manifold of desire is unified; or again, the good is both the unity of moral awareness and the unity of the moral world that it implies. Paradoxical though it may be, the soul (as the unifying form of dutiful willing) turns out to be just as much a hanger-on to the unified manifold of moral consciousness for its own meaning as the soul (the unifying form 'I think') is on the objects of experience it constitutes.

Unraveling the conceptual knots of this paradox to spell out what we might mean by the (moral) soul is more of a conundrum than was doing so for its theoretical counterpart. Our moral awareness is always awareness in relation to empirical awareness. This means that we are appending a 'subject of consciousness' (soul)—which we conceive through the formal strictures of empirical consciousness—to the mental state of experiencing the effect of freedom. To use Kant's language, this will require us to make "a necessary assumption with reference to the subject as conforming to the objective practical laws of reason."[39] This assumption is that there is a possibility of a connection between the conditioned and its condition, which "belongs wholly to the supersensuous relation of things."[40] It makes sense to speak of the morally good soul and its world only when we presume a relation between the intelligible and the sensible, between the unconditioned and the conditioned. By virtue of a conceptual analysis, Kant continues, we are able to designate this supersensible relation with the idea of the "Intelligible Author of Nature."[41] As this mode of relation is neither spatial nor temporal, but instead a way of ordering that mediates between the unconditioned and the conditioned, we can, he thinks, meaningfully invoke the concept of God. But we can speak of the reality of God only insofar as it derives its meaning implicitly from its conjunction with the moral image of the world.

This is just another way of saying what happens in an explicit way when we subordinate everything to duty in the moral image of the world—or as Kant frequently calls it—the 'Highest Good.' Or what is the same, we subordinate happiness (spatiotemporally conditioned desire) to virtue (autonomy, or the unconditioned). The moral soul that has so willed thus discovers in the object that it constitutes how it has already constituted itself. Because the object (the Highest Good) it constitutes is an awareness of the effect of a spontaneous ordering that constrains desire in a way that prompts just conduct and happiness in the world, the soul "sees before its eyes" the effect of its a-temporal and a-spatial mode of ordering (God) and its "marks of permanence" or timelessness, otherwise known as "immortality."[42] Only in light of this insight can the soul be fully conscious of duty or, what is the same, of itself as exhibiting true respect for this ordering. So the soul can only 'see' itself in the image that it constitutes and then constitute itself with respect to the diligence its image exhibits. This is the fullest sense of what Kant means when he speaks of the moral soul as *conscience*.

And it is the reasoning that stands behind his claims that "the righteous man may say: I *will* that there be a God, that my existence in this world be also an existence in a pure world of the understanding," and "finally that my duration be endless."[43] Far from the overweening and Apollonian endeavor that Nietzsche construed it to be, this confession of Kant's righteous person is reflective insight into the life of the mind that is already experiencing moral awareness. That is, the mind already has constituted a moral image of the world, and insight into how that is possible brings into view the irresistible rational attraction of metaphysics. For from this perspective, metaphysical discourses provide a way of making intelligible what is otherwise incomprehensible. So it is that when the righteous person wills, the reality of her freedom has already impressed itself on her in a way that defines who she is and prompts her to articulate this definition. Because she is not deluded, she is not caught in the throes of desperation, which would thereby define her. Rather, because she enjoys freedom, she also enjoys a fuller sense of the life of the mind, whose definition of her she describes to herself as including both the reality of God and the immortality of her soul.

Our Blindness to Our Own Souls

We need no further probing of Kant's arguments to see how for him the concept of an object governs figuration. His point is twofold: 1) any concept of an object defines figuration; and 2) to avoid the impasses of both the empirical and the intuitional approaches to the religion of conscience, reconceiving the concept of an object is required. This is why he persists in the argument that because it is we who unite our representations into language, the language that we use to represent our souls to ourselves is the medium through which we discover what we take our uniting activity as souls to be. Thus where Hobbes and Rousseau think we encounter the soul in the ordinary engagement of living life, Kant demurs. He is convinced that a goodly measure of the life of the soul transpires within an ahistorical, fixed framework that in some way both undergirds and is set over against the contingencies of human experience.

Intransigent as he was about this fixity of framework—that the same ordering is both of the object and among objects—Kant did intimate that the soul assumes disparate forms. Yet however disparate the forms of the soul might be, we can only represent them to ourselves via the context of a single united consciousness. More than in anything else, it was Kant's commitment to how we conceive of objectivity that destabilized and upended the analogical and metonymic figures of the soul that we find in the Hobbesian and Rousseauian accounts. If there was some question in Hobbes and Rousseau about how much we could say of the soul, Kant drove home the point by saying that we are blind to our own souls, that we must thus make them out to be whatever our creations reflect back to us. But more, the soul, as Kant claims we must think it, endures a necessity that circumvents any other than proscribed imaging. Or as Ashbery has it:

> So as to create something new
> For itself, that there is no other way,
> That the history of creation proceeds according to
> Stringent laws, and that things
> Do get done in this way, but never the things
> We set out to accomplish and wanted so desperately
> To see come into being.[44]

A central problem for the makers of the modern religion of conscience was how, 'in between' the natural and intelligible worlds, and in the wake of the seeming loss of 'spirit,' the modern subject, suspecting both itself and God to be de-divinized, might conceive of the soul. The general solution to the problem was to play the use of figurative language off conceptions of objectivity. This strategy seemed to afford these thinkers a way of speaking about that for which there are no words, but it also proved to be one of disfiguration. Positively viewed, disfiguration led to the displacement of less than salutary ways of configuring the soul. It also contributed to the effacement of the soul. In configuring the soul analogically as a rational lifeform—or rationally articulated way of being in the world—of self-preservation whose own self-articulation issues in conscience, Hobbes also effaced the figure of the soul as naturally eternal. Rousseau's metonymic figure of the soul as the impulse to liberty (the constraint of conscience to remain in connection with objective reality) effaced the figure of the soul as imaginative life. When Kant effectively destabilized Hobbes' and Rousseau's tropological systems, he substituted something novel in their place by configuring the soul as the form of mind. He achieved this by what we have come to designate routinely as *transcendental theory*—the mutual implication of concepts of the mind with images of the world. But Kant's theory commits us to the view that the soul depends on the objects of thought that it constitutes to mirror its own form. Effectively sidelining the figure of the soul as 'inner sight,' Kant supplies instead a fixed figure that is 'empty' and 'blind' to itself. Kant's soul without a face affords us little option other than to characterize its conscience as a 'precipitate' of the soul's spontaneity.

Silvering the Soul

Had Kant heard John Keats describing the self as making the soul its "airy citadel" in which to dwell, he would have thought that Keats had it the wrong way round.[45] To say that the soul makes the self would be more apt. But what is the significance of putting the point in this way? I would like to conclude by touching on some of the ramifications of this question for the modern religion of conscience. In Kant's philosophy the tension between the soul as knower (I think) and the soul as moral agent (I dutifully will) manifests itself in the following dilemma: What is the soul? If, on the one hand, the soul is merely the unity of thought, then Kant's observations about religion could be little more than speculative possibilities, sliding in the direction of Hobbes' empirical analogies. If, on the other hand, the soul is merely the form of dutiful willing, then Kant's conception of religion becomes ethics without a face. This would amount to a meditation on the unconditioned, tipping in the direction of Rousseau's 'intuitional' states that show, but about which we can say nothing, apart from after-the-fact metonymic hints. Viewed from this perspective, it is possible to see how this dilemma in Kant's philosophy also serves to summarize the tension that riddles the entire modern religion of conscience: talk of the soul runs either too easily in the direction of the empirically familiar or evanesces into the vacuities of some sort of nonempirical awareness or intuitionalism. The oftheard complaint that what Kant virulently disallows in his epistemology he blatantly asserts in his ethics is a variant of this dilemma.[46]

This complaint, and the dilemma that stands just behind it, proceeds from a particular reading of Kant's conception of objectivity. Because, for him, objectivity is that in the concept of which a given manifold is unified, but the concept that unifies the manifold (the 'I think') is empty and thus unthinkable apart from the manifold it unifies, we must draw two inferences. The first is that the constitutive role the soul plays in empirical knowledge confines our thinking to certain truths about it. We can only speak of the soul in relation to what we know empirically, but we cannot speak meaningfully of it apart from such knowledge. For this reason, second, thinking (conceptual conditioning) about the unconditioned is self-contradictory. Put differently, thinking the unconditioned apparently requires some mode of nonconceptually saturated intuition, which is a contradiction, because thinking always entails the conceptual conditioning of any given manifold. Both inferences are therefore septic.

To see why these inferences are invalid, we need only review the course of Kant's figuration. The course begins with a linguistic procedure called *catachresis* and then shifts to the performative use of the trope of *anastomosis*. Catachresis is the tropological name for the use of a word with a known meaning to stand for that for which there are no words. The 'I think,' which we invoke to denote the 'I think' that we cannot think because it is empty, has a known significance from its relation to and association with other thoughts. To spell out this relationship between the 'I think' that is coherent and the 'I think' that is without significance, Kant traces the transfer of meaning from the one to the other. The performance of this transfer, which is analogous to the cognitive act of catachresis, is a form of anastomosis.

Broadly speaking, anastomosis is a linguistic procedure that designates the channeling between two independent entities, allowing one to support and vivify the other. It is an image that we derive from the cross-connections between separate lines of any branching system, such as in the veins of leaves. The channel connecting two entities may also be an entering of one vessel into another, so that one contains the other. As a figure of speech, for example, anastomosis is an insertion (of qualifying words) that renders one figure at once inside another and outside it. Such an insertion may occur within a space as contained as a single word or phrase. James Joyce's Spartan example of anastomosis in *Ulysses* is "underdarkneath"; Wallace Stevens's more expansive one in "The Red Fern" is the insertion of 'father' in the phrase, "the furiously burning father-fire." Both senses of anastomosis—either as the external connecting of channels or as the internal insertion of one figure at once inside and outside another—may also operate as performative tropes, as sequences of mental and linguistic procedures that link together distinct entities. Such is the form of anastomosis in Kant's theory of thinking and objectivity.

As a playing out of the performative trope of anastomosis, his theory turns on a kind of flowing together, in such a way that one entity, so to speak, contains the other. To say that the thinking soul accompanies all its thoughts is to represent the soul to ourselves in the same way in which we represent anything. Hence, we are using a known way of representing something to lend significance to that which we cannot represent (the thinking soul that is actually doing the thinking). This is the linguistic procedure of catachresis, a figure whose referent we cannot bring forth from the unknown. By way of analogue to catachresis, Kant spells out the kind of mental activity that this cognitive act presupposes. Specifically, to represent what is unknowable about itself, the soul has to unify the manifold of intuition by containing it. This 'containing' or form of the manifold—its unity—shines through our representation of the manifold. In turn, this representation contains the way in which we shape for ourselves the thinking self. So we may say that it is the effect of the soul's activity that contains our thoughts in a unity, and our thought, in turn, that contains the way in which we represent that activity to ourselves.

What emerges from these considerations is not the skeptical inference that we cannot think what the soul is apart from empirical knowledge. Instead, what becomes evident is that whenever we think about the soul, we go about it in the same way as we do *all our thinking*: in terms of a unity among diverse modes of thought that is at once applicable to every particular mode of thought. To see that this synthetic unity among our representations extends to all modes of thought is to see that hallowing one mode of knowledge misses the point. For only insofar as representations themselves possess sufficient order to be united in a single consciousness can they also express diverse modes of consciousness. The peculiar combinatory unity of which we are here speaking is nothing other than anastomosis. Hence, when we speak of the soul, we are not stepping outside all our representations and making a claim about it from a detached perspective. We are simply making another representation. And in doing so, we repeat, according to Kant's dynamic theory, the performative trope of anastomosis.

Just as the first inference that thinking about the soul is contained to certain truths proved mistaken in its skeptical sense, so also does the second inference that we cannot think the unconditioned come to ruin. For just as the first inference tacitly makes empirical knowledge the touchstone of objectivity, so also does the second. What the second complaint overlooks is that Kant builds analogously on this epistemological deployment of anastomosis to explicate moral awareness. So in moral awareness, the soul (dutiful willing) unifies the manifold of desire by containing it. The way in which we represent moral desire to ourselves stands under the effect of the same unity as does our image of the moral world. For illustrative purposes, we could say equally well that the unity of the moral world contains the unity of the moral self, or, perhaps better, the image that issues from inserting ourselves into the image of the moral world is the moral self. To illustrate the point in this way is akin to thinking of a glove into which we insert a hand: the glove contains the hand, but the hand, at the same time, 'contains' the glove. Each, so to speak, 'forms' and 'vivifies' the other.

There is, however, a certain disanalogy here, for as Kant never tired of reminding us, moral awareness announces itself in the context of empirical awareness. That is, only as we are proposing a course of conduct to ourselves do we become aware of a contrast between what we propose and what ought to be. This, of course, is the experience of conscience in which freedom, or the unconditioned, presents itself for consideration as the sole determinant of the will. And this is the point at which the analogy breaks down and Kant claims that a sort of intersection between two kinds of combinatory activity occurs. Here, as well, we find the occasion for the philosophical controversy over how we could ever think the unconditioned. But if we see this in terms of the performative trope of anastomosis, it becomes clear that this is no more than idle speculation, as this is not what Kant is claiming that we do. His claim is more circumspect. He says that the effect of spontaneous activity is a unity of which we are aware only by virtue of its contrast with empirically conditioned unity. There are credentials that Kant thinks we can marshal in support of designating this activity as the activity of freedom—it is, after all, not theoretically impossible—even though we cannot legitimate it. So an effect that can contain the manifold of desire, thereby giving rise to an image we name the moral world, is a figurative transfer of human terms that we have identified in epistemological anastomosis. And these, in turn, are already figurative transfers of natural terms, that is, the flowing together of distinct entities, as in the veins of a leaf. In this way we represent the soul to ourselves variously as the 'thinking self,' the 'moral self,' the 'sublime self,' or the 'radically evil self.'

Cleaning the slate of these mistaken inferences, by way of drawing out the performative dynamics of anastomosis, allows me to explain why I quipped that Kant would chide Keats for claiming that the self constitutes the soul. The anastomotic substitution of figure for figure in ceaseless interchange is characteristic of how Kant sees our soul, that is, as that within which the manifold of our representations is united, but of which we can but make another representation that we call the 'self.' The peculiarity of this definition lies in the absence of a substantial, preexisting soul. Instead, the soul, as empty, is an absence, an invisible possibility taking on one or another image. Hence we have no images of the soul, but see the soul everywhere reflected in the images of the world. Precisely because it is without face or figure, the soul spreads itself behind things, like the silvering of a mirror, figuratively transferring to itself all the objects it contains. So understood, the soul is thus a lusterless surface without which no reflection would be possible. By virtue of Kant's disfiguring trope of the soul, he is able to make the incoherence of the modern religion of conscience—that a self-legitimating self is both indispensable and impossible—appear to us as coherent. But the price of this coherence is a narcissistic imaging, an anastomosis flowing from the same to the same, the soul-emptying relation of the soul to itself, trapped in the melancholy of its own empty form, unable to conceive of or relate to the other. The solitude of its condition it marks in the objective sign of its own making: the self.

> This otherness, this
> "Not-being-us" is all there is to look at
> In the mirror, though no one can say
> How it came to be this way. A ship
> Flying unknown colors has entered the harbor.[47]

FOUR

Life Without Enigmatic Remainder

Our heart wanders lost in the dark woods.
Our dream wrestles in the castle of doubt.
But there's music in us. Hope is pushed down
but the angel flies up again taking us with her.

       —JACK GILBERT

Everything in the modern religion of conscience turns on the belief that the ends to which conscience directs us are not illusory, but can and will be realized. This belief, set within the conflict between the rationalities of a 'Christian worldview' and an 'Enlightenment worldview,' resonates with both ambitious and plaintive tones. However much the emerging Enlightenment perspective, by mastering the mysterious and inscrutable through calculation, sought to upend the claims of traditional religion, it could neither address nor quell longings for justice and peace in the world. Simultaneously, the prospect of capitulating to the dogma and cant of the Church, thereby abandoning the insights of the new sciences of the Enlightenment that were commensurate with the ethos of the time, seemed to many to be intellectually dishonest, if not untenable. Effectively barred from traditional ways of speaking of human aspirations, yet driven beyond the skepticism implicit in Enlightenment rationalism that construed the human presentiment toward metaphysics as illusory, if not fanatical, many modern thinkers found themselves steeped in loss.

What is novel about the response that the modern religion of conscience poses to this loss is its portrait of subjectivity. It suggests that the
subject is capable of a kind of moral self-assertion that purportedly dissolves the dilemma of mastery and loss. Because moral deeds were said to
issue in a new harmony, the conscience-governed conduct of the modern
subject could honor the legitimate perspectives of Enlightenment rationality, while still pursuing the aspirations for a just world. Thus the modern
subject's convictions about the authority of conscience appear to metamorphose its loss—that it no longer participated in the ordering that
tradition ascribed to divine revelation—into an asset: life without the vicissitudes of divine judgments, but under the stewardship of conscience,
would be life that culminated in harmonious repose. To live life under the
directives of conscience would balance the desire for happiness with the
imperatives of moral conduct. Such a claim entailed the requirement to
imagine the trajectory of eternal life, or, what is the same, to conceive of
life with enigmatic remainder.

The arguments that are supposed to support this conviction do not, as
we have seen, so much bolster the conviction as attempt to cover over a
gaping whole in the foundations of the theory. This lacuna gradually comes
to light when we follow the strategy of the modern religion of conscience
to exploit the figure of self-preservation. At first glance, the figure of self-
preservation expresses in a novel way the particular contingency that confronted early moderns. Self-preservation signals both the retreat of the
divine ordering of being from its hegemonic role in the interpretation
of public life and the advance of thoughts about the possibilities of self-
assertion. So the figure of self-preservation signifies the way in which some
modern thinkers, once they were no longer assured that they enjoyed preservation by virtue of being a part of a divinely ordained ordering, conceived
of themselves, instead, as being in some measure self-maintaining and as
creating their own ordering and aims. Consistent with this, the modern
religion of conscience holds that the world—not the divine ordering—is
first 'given' to the subject through the awareness of self-preservation. But
this begins to prompt the suspicion that something has gone awry. It leaves
open the question of what the relation of self-preservation to the world is.
To be sure, the interpretive strategy by which the makers of the modern
religion of conscience sought to fill in this lacuna is a limited speculative
metaphysics that exploits the structural features of self-preservation in
which the subject already finds itself, but only to the extent required to

make coherent sense of the experience. But this really doesn't do the job, either.

At one level, just as we begin to marvel over the limited metaphysical reflections of the makers of the modern religion of conscience, we sense, as well, a growing uneasiness that they have gotten off course. The ingenuity that we admire derives from the fact that these speculative interpretations boil down to interpolations of the basic structure of self-preservation: 1) force or power, 2) law or governing principle, and 3) the unity of the two.[1] Hobbes focuses on power; Rousseau, on the guiding principle; and Kant, on the unity as a whole. However compelling, these interpretations prove unsettling. They do so because they attempt to explicate the relation of self-preservation to the world through a speculative metaphysic that is itself merely an elaboration of the medium of self-preservation through which the world is first given to the subject. Doubtless, once the structure of self-preservation is operational, its basic features lend themselves to an arresting description of mental life. But such attempts falter, because the theories— emphasizing one or another of these structural features of self-preservation—omit from their purview the implicit dependence of self-preservation on something other than itself. Such features do not arise sui generis, but depend on certain conditions for their emergence. Hence, in themselves, they no more account for how the conditions of the functioning of self-preservation come into being than they assess the original relation of the structure of self-preservation to the world. So far from explicating these conditions, these speculative metaphysics at best intimate a domain of dependence, thereby effectively covering over a lacuna in the foundations of the modern religion of conscience.

To pinpoint where this covering over begins, we need to look at these speculative metaphysical reflections from the level that I explored in the previous essay. This is the level from which we may view them functioning strategically to disfigure traditional theological tropes. From this perspective, it becomes evident that the rule governing the figuration of the modern religion of conscience by which it upended traditional theological tropes is a particular conception of objectivity. And we know that Kant went to great lengths to make this conception explicit. But by now looking more closely at the rule of figuration—the conception of objectivity—that informed the way in which the modern religion of conscience routed traditional theological tropes, I think we can spot not only where the covering over begins, but also in what it consists: this is the view that the self-preserving subject constitutes its relation to the world, and that religion, objectively under-stood, mirrors this relationship by enshrining its ideal forms. If, however, the world is never anything more than a mirror of the strivings of the self-preserving subject, then is religion a collocation of the subject's fantasies about escaping the world of its own devising and so of escaping itself, as well, through exits of its own fashioning? Such a view of religion would appear to undermine the conviction that the ends to which conscience directs us can and will be realized, that a life lived under the stewardship of conscience will get us there, and that, accordingly, we can justify conceiving of eternal life—a life with enigmatic remainder—in order to render coherent our moral vision.

The collective force of these arguments prompts us to wonder if the bell has begun to toll for the modern religion of conscience. To draw such a conclusion might well be precipitous. Before we attend to its downfalls, I invite us to consider whether something could be profoundly *right* about the pivotal conviction of the modern religion of conscience: that there is a distinctive domain of mental life, about which it is difficult to speak apart from figurative, religious language, that directs us to just and harmonious ends of life. If we bear this conviction in mind, it will become evident that critics of this 'religion' succeeded not in deposing it, but rather in showing that its makers failed to say in what sense their conviction was correct. To show this, I am going to attempt an interpretation of this conviction, first by saying why the rule of figuration its makers used (the conception of 'objectivity') runs aground, and second, by lifting up what they covered over—the capacity for creating mental functioning in the face of loss—as an 'inverse' interpretive principle that can preserve what is right about the core conviction of the modern religion of conscience. I shall proceed with appeals to the insights of Wittgenstein, Freud, and Barth, each of whom reflected on the implications of this conception of objectivity from the perspective of post–World War I (traumatic) consciousness.

Reconsidering 'Objectivity'

If we want to know what it is about the conception of objectivity that makes it come to ruin, we might first look at what makes it attractive. This conception, which is a powerful aid to sifting through the problems of subjectivity, continues to command the respect of many philosophers. Kant made explicit what Hobbes and Rousseau had both assumed implicitly: we think of ourselves in the same way in which we think of the world. Kant radicalized this by holding that the unity within objects and among objects is the same, just as is the unity within a subject and among subjects. To put Kant's point in this pared-down form helps us to grasp his conviction that the task he was undertaking in the critical philosophy was to safeguard knowledge inside the bounds of experience. He did not, in other words, think it possible to elucidate what actually underlies and gives rise to our knowledge. Nevertheless, our knowledge within the bounds of experience always 'reflects' a certain threshold of pre-experiential conditions that we must acknowledge. Principal among these is the 'I think' that both justifies the possibility of knowledge and is "the highest point" to which the whole of transcendental philosophy must conform.[2] But to move from acknowledging this threshold to overstepping it in the pursuit of an exhaustive theory of the possible conditions of knowledge would be to "run riot in the transcendent."[3] Such speculative investigations inevitably would depart from the bounds of experience and so would compromise a theory whose sole purpose was to eliminate justified doubts from that domain of objects.

Just where this proviso leaves us when matters take a concrete turn is at first hard to tell. Consider, for example, our understanding about the 'I think' that Kant called the 'transcendental unity of apperception.' To say, as Kant does, that this transcendental consciousness differs from psychological self-awareness or that it corresponds to Cartesian self-certitude or that it is a spontaneous act is certainly to take us part of the way toward understanding what he has in mind. But it does not go far enough either to account for the conditions giving rise to the 'I think' or to specify how this particular principle becomes sufficiently determinate to qualify as falling within the boundaries of experience. This is tantamount to saying that under Kant's own provisos, we are left with an 'I think' that both distinguishes between itself and the content of the thought and knowingly relates itself to the thought in thinking it. While sorting out the import of this inference is far from a self-evident task, the significance of its difficulty brings home, paradoxically, Kant's point: once our aim becomes solely making sense of our experience, what matters is not that certain questions are unanswerable, but that we have no need whatsoever to answer them.

It would be difficult to imagine a more compelling argument than that we have no need of something. Such an argument commends to us the belief that pursuing what we do not need not only serves no purpose, but also, in some important sense, compromises us. And it does so with such force that we are apt to pass over its sticking point without noticing it. The sticking point I have in mind is determining in what sense something is said to count as a need. Or, better, I am referring to our tendency, in the absence of such reckoning, to generalize from a very specific and limited sense of the term to a more wide-ranging and encompassing sense. Thus we move from Kant's own claim that to be compelling, his argument about the nature of experience, or the domain of objectivity, requires no more than minimal accounts of the unity of subjectivity to a claim that Kant does not explicitly make—namely that nothing about experience requires us to think metaphysically. I do not dispute that many of the heirs to Kant's thinking did subscribe to this view (especially among the Neo-Kantians, who, in support of 'science,' embraced such a reading of their mentor). But I do think that this seemingly innocent faux pas opens the door to a more looming issue implicit within it: that the unity of which we necessarily speak in one domain of our awareness is the same in all domains of our awareness.

I take this to be the crux of the problem inherent within Kantian 'objectivity.' To imagine that from the outset we must necessarily conceive of unity in one way is to foreclose on transformations in life. Or worse, it commits us to clinging desperately to one way of seeing things that precludes both loss and new possibilities. An implicit extension of just this kind is, I suspect, what goes awry with the modern religion of conscience, especially in its attempt to bolster its conviction that the directives of conscience have positive outcomes. Far from standing open to the ramifications of the vicissitudes of life—to the disappearance of one unity and the appearance of another—the modern religion of conscience attempts to subdue the interruptions within life by containing them unenigmatically within its own principles of unity.

Wittgenstein: On the Limits of Kantian 'Objectivity'

To spell out what I mean by this, I want first to turn to Ludwig Wittgenstein's own assessment of this issue in his *Tractatus Logico-Philosophicus*.

Of the various ways of formulating the meaning of the Tractarian dictum "What can be said at all can be said clearly, and what we cannot talk about we must pass over in silence," I propose to pursue a quasi-Kantian reading. Here I follow, in part, Wittgenstein's own early immersion in the work of Heinrich Hertz, the Neo-Kantian philosopher of science. From Hertz, Wittgenstein became acquainted with the peculiarly Kantian kind of problem setting "How is an a priori science of nature possible?" I also adopt this way of reading, however, because there is a striking affinity between the two principal steps of Kant's transcendental deduction and the two parts of the Tractarian dictum: in the transcendental deduction of the first *Critique*, Kant claimed first that the condition of empirical knowledge is a fundamental unity combining sensations and concepts that becomes evident only in their combination; and second, that the application of this unity to any domain (the transcendent) apart from the combination of sensations and concepts yields no knowledge whatsoever. In other words, the unity of empirical knowledge is useless when directed to nonempirical matters. Correspondingly, Wittgenstein claims, first, that what we can say we can say clearly; and second, that what we cannot say clearly, we must pass over in silence. Viewed alongside the Kantian claim, the two steps of Wittgenstein's Tractarian dictum can be said to pursue a course with language that parallels Kant's course with knowledge. That is, Kant and Wittgenstein appear to share a commitment to solve philosophical problems by dissolving them through the careful delineation of limits. Or, what is the same, Wittgenstein seems to be echoing Kant's declaration that he had to limit knowledge in order to make room for faith. But Wittgenstein does this in a more radical and baffling way than did Kant. Whereas Kant circumscribed the limits of theoretical knowledge but left open the prospect that because freedom announces itself in the context of willed conduct, we can speak of rational belief and conviction, Wittgenstein declared that the limits of what we can express oblige us to remain silent about what lies beyond them, thereby foreclosing the options of descriptive ethics, faith, and aesthetics. Consistent with this, Wittgenstein maintained that the logic of descriptive language—strictly observed—mortgages those options to the domain of the ineffable.

I think that I can make clear what Wittgenstein is driving at, although of course the widely disparate reception of his arguments continues to be punctuated with open-ended debate. We might begin with the observation that if the relation of self-preservation to the world functions in some way to 'give the world to us' in a manner that is not merely an elaboration of the structure of self-preservation, then there must be some logical correlation between self-preservation and the world. On Wittgenstein's reading, such an observation is equivalent to the claim that the logic of the way in which we represent linguistically to ourselves real states of affairs and the logic of the world are identical. One task of the *Tractatus*, accordingly, is to elucidate the meaning of this claim.

Wittgenstein sought to demonstrate that all philosophy is a "critique of language."[4] The principal steps of his argument can be summarized along the following lines. First, he argued that we construct for ourselves linguistic propositions whose form models the form of the states of affairs that they depict.[5] Indeed, because the form is the possibility of the states of affairs in which objects occur, to know an object is simultaneously to know all its possible occurrences: new possibilities cannot be discovered later.[6] Accordingly, the form or relation between the elements of a model is determinate.[7] In Wittgenstein's view, it is the logic inherent in ordinary language that comprises this determinate relation among the elements and constitutes the nexus in terms of which names have significance.[8] Hence, the possibility of all models of expression is contained in the logic of modeling itself.[9] The 'world' as we know it is possible precisely because the logic of our language constitutes it:

> Logic is not a body of doctrine, but a mirror image of the world.[10]
>
> It is obvious that an imagined world, however different it may be from the real one, must have something—a form—in common with it.[11]

But of this form, Wittgenstein offered the caveat that we can say nothing about it: "A model cannot model the form of modeling; it displays it."[12] Just as Kant had claimed that we cannot know the unity of self-consciousness directly, but only as its form is manifest in our representations, so Wittgenstein now maintained that the form of the logic of our language is manifest only in language but cannot be stated through some independent means. So he concluded that philosophy, as a critique of language, arrives at the limits of language, demarcating, by showing, what language cannot say from what it can.

With respect to the question of the relation of self-preservation to the world, this account of the relation between language and the world provides a helpful insight: for Wittgenstein, the form of the world would show through the model of self-preservation. Inasmuch as the model of self-preservation exhibits the form of modeling, as does our model of the world, there is a sense in which the form of modeling of the world 'shows' through the model of self-preservation. To be sure, we can only speak of this figuratively. But in effect, Wittgenstein's account actually resolves the question of the relation of self-preservation to the world by dissolving it. On his reading, no literal, theoretical account of the language/world relation is possible. A 'language' independent of the form of modeling that language is remains unimaginable.[13] For Wittgenstein, this amounts to the claim that because we often misunderstand the constraints of the logic of our language on what we can meaningfully say, we misconstrue the nature of our questions. In this case, we pursue the question of the relation of self-preservation to the world on the mistaken assumption that the form of self-preservation and the form of the world differ.

A corollary of such dissolution brings another aspect of Wittgensteinian 'showing' into view. Just as we are unable to speak of the relation between language and the word, so also are we unable to speak of the "sense of the world."[14] We are unable, in other words, to speak of 'value' in the world, because everything 'in the world' is determinate. The form of modeling consists of all possible occurrences of states of affairs, to which new possibilities may not be subsequently added. Questions of value are indeterminate and therefore fall outside the purview of the logic of modeling, precisely owing to the determinate nature of its form. It is apparently for this reason that Wittgenstein claimed that "it is impossible for there to be propositions of ethics."[15] Or again, "It is clear that ethics cannot be put into words . . . (Ethics and aesthetics are one and the same)."[16] 'Showing' in the theoretical case refers to the form of the model that is manifest in language, but cannot itself be said (without an infinite regress of 'showing through the language'); 'showing' in the ethical and aesthetic domain refers to the illumination of the limits and inapplicability of the determinate language of theorizing to the indeterminate aesthetic and ethical domain.

These brief and admittedly too-formal summary remarks serve as a backdrop for interpreting the last passages of the *Tractatus*, especially those having to do with the enigma of eternal life.[17] Here Wittgenstein articulates what he takes to be the metaphysical temptations to which we are drawn and the reasons why the ways in which we think about them are wrong-headed. The specific way that Wittgenstein has in mind is what he calls 'the modern conception of the world':

> The whole modern conception of the world is founded upon the illusion that the so-called laws of nature are the explanations of natural phenomena.[18]
>
> Thus people today stop at the laws of nature, treating them as something inviolable, just as God and fate were treated in past ages.
>
> And in fact both are right and both are wrong: though the view of the ancients is clearer in so far as they have a clear and acknowledged terminus, while the modern system tries to make it look as if everything were explained.[19]

Wittgenstein's complaint is that we routinely confound the form of model-ing with the model: "Laws are about the net and not about what the net describes."[20] Just as Kant had delineated the limits of theoretical reason in order to prevent us from running riot into the transcendent—that our ways of thinking about empirical experience did not thereby extend legitimately to the nonempirical—so also Wittgenstein observes the distinction between logical necessity and explanations of natural phenomena, thereby disallow-ing our warrant both to speak even analogously of metaphysical ordering, and, in turn, to pander to nonsensical claims. By means of this distinction, Wittgenstein exposes the failing of modern ways of speaking about the laws of nature (meaning by this Newtonian laws of causality). In such speech, moderns purport to be establishing something that is true about the world and the laws of conservation. But the import of this claim rests on a sleight of hand that actually subverts the alleged 'inviolability' of natural laws. Here is what Wittgenstein thinks we really learn: inasmuch as our thinking is conducted through a series of connections that are already subject to laws, what we discern is actually something about the way that these laws supply "the bricks for building the edifice of science."[21] Put simply, we learn the laws of the logic of language, not the laws of nature. This insight is analo-gous to Kant's teaching that the relations among objects derive not from empirical observation, but from conditions of the operations of thought in the human mind. To grasp this insight is to be in a position to appreciate what Wittgenstein thinks is 'right' about the 'modern conception.' Properly speaking, the laws of nature cannot themselves be said, but instead make themselves manifest in our language. And this, in turn, amounts to the claim, reminiscent of Kant, that there are no grounds for believing that "the simplest eventuality will be in fact realized"[22] or that there is "some compulsion making one thing happen because another has happened."[23]

Observing the strictures of the logic of our ordinary descriptive language sharply delimits what we can say meaningfully. But this 'modern' demarcation might cause us to pass over Wittgenstein's salient observation, put forward elsewhere, that there was something right about the ancients' formulation of God and fate. To speak of God and fate as *Unastastbarem* (Wittgenstein's emphasis in his 5 June 1916 entry into his *Notebooks*, which were prefatory explorations of the thesis that he spelled out in the *Tractatus*) as "Inviolable" was to conceive of them as the "terminus," as that in terms of which all explanation proceeds. The terminus itself, however, is beyond explanation. In this sense, Wittgenstein thinks that the ancients are 'clearer.' In his view, the ancients grasp the radical nature of the limit in a way that moderns do not. For moderns (rightly understood) think that what is said or is manifest in language exhausts what matters in life. Where ancients differ is in their contention that what matters most cannot be said. To be sure, Wittgenstein thought that the ancients had faltered as well, insofar as they tried to say what cannot be said when they spoke of God in a manner that placed God 'in' the world of facts.

On my reading, Wittgenstein here suggests that the locus of inviolability differs for moderns and ancients, with moderns placing it within the world, ancients outside the world. He is contemptuous of the modern presumption that our delineation of the inviolable displaces that of the ancients, thereby abetting our attempt "to make it look as if *everything* is explained."[24] But rather than seeing this as one configuration among others, Wittgenstein wants to tilt this difference in another direction. By its means, he intends to mark the distinction between the two senses of 'showing' toward which he is inexorably moving:

> The sense of the world must lie outside the world. In the world everything is as it is, and everything happens as it does happen: in it no value exists—and if it did exist, it would have no value.
>
> If there is any value that does have value, it must lie outside the whole sphere of what happens and is the case. For all that happens and is the case is accidental.
>
> What makes it non-accidental cannot lie within the world, since if it did it would itself be accidental.
>
> It must lie outside the world.[25]

To say that "in the world everything is as it is and everything happens as it does happen" is to say that the logic of our language, though itself unsayable without an infinite regress, is manifest in the determinate models that we make for ourselves about states of affairs: "Propositions show the logical form of reality."[26] On Wittgenstein's own grounds, we are obliged to conclude that because logic cannot be stated propositionally, it is transcendental.

Now over against this stands the question of value, which for Wittgenstein "lies outside the world." The project of ethics is at loggerheads with the world because all propositions address only what is in the world, and it is impossible for there to be propositions about what is outside the world (values, ethics). In much the same vein, Wittgenstein wryly notes that "the world is given to me, i.e., my will enters into the world completely from the outside."[27] Accordingly, because the will confronts the world as a given totality, and the activity of the will is, on this view, not in the world, "it is clear that ethics cannot be put into words."[28] Or, as Wittgenstein puts it, "Ethics is transcendental."[29] His idea is simple enough: just as the form of logic is transcendental and only shows itself, so also the form of values is transcendental and only shows itself. Neither can be reduced to or supplanted by the other. Less simple is how the form of values shows.

Wittgenstein's celebrated answer is this:

> If the good or bad exercise of the will does alter the world, it can alter only the limits of the world, not the facts—not what can be expressed by means of language.
>
> In short the effect must be that it becomes an altogether different world. It must, so to speak, wax and wane as a whole.[30]

This passage is baffling. On first glance, the central point seems to be that the will affects the limits but not the facts of the world—a point turning on the earlier claim that "the world is independent of my will."[31] Given this purported independence of will from world, the effects of the will could not possibly alter the facts of the world. In this sense, the effects of the will could not be said to be in the world. But this construal amounts to conceding that the will is powerless: "I cannot bend the happenings of the world to my will: I am completely powerless."[32] On further reflection, however, the central point of the passage appears to metamorphose into the will making the world "altogether different." This emphasis appears to turn on the claim that "when an ethical law of the form, 'Thou shalt . . .' is laid down, one's first thought is, 'And what if I do not do it?' . . . There must be something right about the question we posed."[33] To be sure, what is 'right' could not refer to the outcomes of willing—the will is, after all, impotent—in the usual sense. So there must be some other sense in which the will is not powerless, in which its effects alter the limits of the world. And the will must do so in a way that permits a "waxing and waning of the whole," despite the linguistic inexpressibility of this movement.

This seems to be the point of ethical reflection in which the form of the ethical would show. Wittgenstein gives a cryptic clue about what this 'showing' might entail: "The world of the happy man is a different one from that of the unhappy man."[34] The injection of happiness flags our attention. It would be seductive to imagine that what Wittgenstein has in mind here is some sort of satisfaction of our desires in the world. But clearly that will not do. For although "the willing subject would have to be happy or unhappy . . . happiness and unhappiness could not be part of the world."[35] In other words, just as the ethical subject is transcendental, so also is happiness or unhappiness. It is important, just now, to see that Wittgenstein is not delving into some philosophical sleight of hand, but instead attempting to drive home a penetrating and unsettling point. What counts as happiness or unhappiness is not some quixotic fulfillment of our desires, but is instead a matter of our will's being in "agreement with the world."[36] But such a harmony has no objective mark that can be described. Instead, it is transcendental,[37] and insofar as it is, the will's agreement can be nothing other than the attitude that it adopts toward the world: "The will is an attitude of the subject to the world."[38] Indeed, it is by virtue of such attitude that "things acquire 'significance.'"[39] To construe the will in this fashion is to prepare the way for the view that what 'shows' is the agreement or disagreement with the world—the happiness or unhappiness with the world—which, in turn, alters the significance of the facts of the world. In this sense, happiness is not *in* the world, but an agreement of the transcendental subject's will with the world, which, strictly speaking, lies *outside* the world.

Wittgenstein's remarks thus far seem to suggest that it is perfectly coherent to interpret fundamental changes in our lives with reference to a manifest but unspeakable form that itself is said to be constant. Only in this way could the will as attitude alter the significance of the facts. But the power of purchase of these remarks turns entirely on their transcendental status: the 'subject' transcends the world, 'value' transcends the world, and 'alteration' transcends the world. It is thus tempting to draw the conclusion, as many of the positivists did, that nothing is being said here, or that on Wittgenstein's own grounds, strictly speaking, ethics cannot be talked about. This interpretation, however 'true,' falls short. If Wittgenstein is attempting to make philosophically accessible what cannot be said, and this, in turn, renders possible a way to think about ethics, what is gestured toward in the notion of transcendence is a structuring condition of the world of our ethical possibilities. The agreement of the will with the world is the condition of ethical possibilities, but this structural alignment is itself transcendental.

To see this, we need only turn to Wittgenstein's remarks on conscience.

> When my conscience upsets my equilibrium, then I am not in agreement with Something. But what is this? Is it *the world*?
> Certainly it is correct to say: Conscience is the voice of God.[40]

In the lexicon of the *Notebooks*, Wittgenstein associates 'God' with the question of the meaning of life. To understand the question about the meaning of life, to see that the facts of the world are not all that there is, and to see that life has a meaning is to believe in God.[41] Inasmuch as the world is given to us, it is altogether natural that we should "have the feeling of being dependent upon an alien will."[42] Wittgenstein goes on to say that "*however this may be*, at any rate we *are* in a certain sense dependent, and what we are dependent on we can call God."[43] We have already said that happiness is transcendental agreement or disagreement with the world. We are now in a position to see that to be in agreement with the world entails being in agreement with the 'alien will' on which we appear to be dependent. So a will agreeably disposed toward the world could appropriately say, "I am doing the will of God."[44]

This is no aside, no philosophical throwaway, but a way of articulating a structuring condition of the universe of ethical possibilities. The voice of God is conscience—the correlation of the ethical subject and the givenness of the world (or what Wittgenstein calls the "two godheads") that constitutes the structural condition of my being able to assesses the totality of facts of the 'given' world, including my own particular willing.[45] This is why, according to Wittgenstein, we are able to speak of a will divided against itself: "It makes me unhappy to think that I have offended such and such a man."[46] I appeal to "the voice of God" to assess a view of the world as a whole, but for the ethical relevance of this assessment, my eye must turn entirely toward the integrity of the will's alignment with the world.

Again, we need to bear in mind Wittgenstein's contempt toward the idea that there is a logical connection between the will and the world that undergirds the belief that what we wish for can happen. The ethical aim of the Tractarian project, accordingly, is never about the supposed physical connection between the will and the world or about the idea that we could will it.[47] Instead, the ethical aim is about viewing the world as a whole—*sub specie aeterni*—and about altering its limits.[48] In keeping with this commitment, Wittgenstein maintains that we can be happy only through the life of knowledge,[49] meaning by this, naturally enough, the knowledge of our limits as shown in the *Tractatus* that pave the way for understanding what good conscience is:

> The good conscience is the happiness that the life of knowledge preserves.
> The life of knowledge is the life that is happy in spite of the misery of the world.
> The only life that is happy is the life that can renounce the amenities of the world.
> To it the amenities of the world are so many graces of fate.[50]

To summarize, Wittgenstein proposes a way of structuring our world of ethical possibilities by assigning ethics and the will to the domain of the transcendental. The ethical will can be conceived as being happy or unhappy depending on the conformity of the will with conscience, or the voice of God. The effect of the will is the alteration of the limits of the world, but not the facts of the world that can be expressed in language. At one level, this set of claims begs the question of coherence: if ethics cannot be talked about, then all of what Wittgenstein claims is meaningless; if it *can* be talked about, and the ethical subject is in some sense in the world, then ethics in the transcendental sense ceases to exist. But if we set aside the question of coherence and incoherence, and move instead to the point where the disruption in intelligibility becomes manifest, then the point that I have been trying to make comes into view: the task of the *Tractatus* is not to change life in the world, but to alter what can be meant by 'the structure of the possibilities in which ethical life can be lived.'

If we recall what Wittgenstein deemed to be the illusion on which the whole modern conception of the world is founded—confounding the form of modeling with the model, or what is the same, confounding the world and the laws of conservation with the ways in which we speak of them—we find ourselves in a position to see how deeply he rejects the modern religion of conscience. We see this, in part, by moving beyond the affinities between Wittgenstein and Kant and comparing more closely the Wittgensteinian notion of 'showing' with the Kantian notion of 'unity.' Kant argued that there is a single principle—the transcendental unity of apperception—to which all other knowledge must conform. He conceived of this unity as a principle of combination (joining concepts with sensible intuitions) both consonant with the laws of nature and manifest in all of our representations. Moreover, this unity, which is the condition for all possible experience, both can be said and invoked as a critical principle for limiting knowledge, as, for example, in establishing the organizing role for human knowledge of such ideas as God, self, and world. Wittgenstein, however, thought that unity of experience derives not from some mental activity, but from the logic of our language. This logic is manifest in all that we say, but cannot itself be said. Hence, in his view, the Kantian presumption of coincidence between the transcendental unity of apperception and Newtonian physics is mistaken; rightly understood, the logic of language provides the laws in terms of which we build the framework of scientific theory. Wittgenstein's corrective amounts to the claim that Kant has overstepped his own limits in thinking that he can say what transcendental knowledge is.

Turning to the ethical affords us a view of how sharp this contrast becomes. Still bounded by the principle of the unity of experience, Kant is obliged to argue that an empirically conditioned consciousness can become aware of an unconditioned principle. In other words, a human subject in the world can become aware of an unconditioned principle (freedom or the moral law) that, by itself, can determine a human action in the world. For Kant, this principle, freedom, is the lens through which moral action in this world may be rightly seen. Hence, we see as free an action whose origin is in the intelligible world but whose effect appears in the sensible world, alongside other sensible effects. And we construe the conditions for completing the moral task beyond this world by virtue of belief in God and in the immortality of the soul. On Wittgenstein's reading, this second move begins to look a bit desperate. Strictly speaking, the unconditioned or the absolute is unsayable, so any attempt to render it intelligible is to convert the unconditioned into the conditioned, whereby it loses its ethical value.

In effect, the 'ethical' in the Kantian scheme becomes relativized, because Kant does not conceive the absoluteness of freedom radically enough. To imagine that the principle of freedom can enter into the world, as Kant does, is to make it both a condition of the world and an item in the world, thereby subordinating it to the logic of language. Wittgenstein is pointing up the Kantian inability to conceive movement from the unity of experience to an entirely different unity—freedom; or what is the same, Wittgenstein is arguing that the Kantian strictures of knowledge require a more radical kind of 'showing' than Kant allows if absolute freedom is to become manifest. It is precisely this failing that permits Kant to extend the principle of unity (and its concomitant principle of causality) analogously to the 'beyond,' postulating belief in the immorality of the soul—a rational exposition of the conditions under which moral good would prevail over evil.

Wittgenstein counters starkly: "Not only is there no guarantee of the temporal immorality of the human soul, that is to say of its eternal survival after death; but, in any case, this assumption completely fails to accomplish the purpose for which it has always been intended. Or is some riddle solved by my surviving for ever? Is not this eternal life itself as enigmatic as our present one? The solution of the riddle of life in space and time lies *outside* space and time."[51] The purpose for which at least Rousseau and Kant had intended the assumption of immortality was to render coherent the moral authority of the self-legislating self, thereby countering nihilism. By assuring humans that the just ordering of God's goodness will prevail and not the evil that, as Rousseau put it, 'everywhere seems to prosper,' the assumption encouraged humans to believe that their striving to be just was not in vain. In the time to come, not only would the ethical order be manifest but one's own place in it also would become clear. So in order to see the significance in what we do now, we are compelled by the sense of our inchoate convictions to speak of a 'remainder'—a life beyond life—in which God will embrace the good and punish the evil. Life with enigmatic remainder is a life that compensates for the injustice and loss of the temporal life.

However appealing such claims might be, they are, in Wittgenstein's view, based on a series of missteps. The first misstep is the notion that God, as that which lies beyond understanding, can be contained within rational structure of interpretation. To attempt to do so, of course, would be to overstep the ancient insight about God as 'terminus,' as inexplicable. The second misstep, which follows from the first, is the thought that one can speak of eternal life at all. To speak of eternal life is to make it subject to the logic of language. It also vitiates the very difference from temporal life that 'eternal life' purports to signify. This gives rise, in turn, to the third misstep. Here we imagine that formulating a way to understand the significance of our striving to be just solves the enigma of eternal life. But by virtue of the previous errors, we now see that all the notion of 'eternal life' could possibly mean would entail repeating the riddles of our present life, or so Wittgenstein is insinuating. Once we correct these missteps, it becomes quickly evident that rightly understood, the question of an 'enigmatic remainder' to life cannot even be framed:

> When the answer cannot be put into words, neither can the question be put into words.
> The *enigma* does not exist.
> If a question can be framed at all, it is also *possible* to answer it.[52]
>
> The solution to the problem of life is seen in the vanishing of the problem.[53]

By walking us through what amounts to the basic framework of the modern religion of conscience, Wittgenstein leads us to the view that this religion cannot possibly be rightly conceived. And paradoxical as it may be in the end, this attempt to cast light on the illusory claims of the modern religion of conscience itself proves (by Wittgenstein's own accounting) "nonsensical": "My propositions serve as elucidations in the following way: anyone who understands me eventually recognizes them as nonsensical, when he has used them—as steps—to climb up beyond them. (He must, so to speak, throw away the ladder after he has climbed up it.)"[54] Wittgenstein radicalizes the Kantian lines of the modern human predicament—that we are neither suspended from heaven nor anchored on earth—with his notion that this dilemma is *unsayable*. He also gestures toward the absence of a way (on the Kantian telling) to account for the disruption in thinking—the 'loss of the ladder,' which we may readily overlook—wherein conscience *shows* changing structures of possibilities in which life can be lived. Neither the nature of this disruption to understanding nor the changing structures of life possibilities can be subsumed under our ordinary notions of ourselves. Therein Wittgenstein lifts up the unspeakable dilemma of the interiority of the modern religion of conscience: the well of interiority, from which it is drawn, and through which it shows, cannot be said. The showing of conscience halts ordinary thought and speech.

Freud: 'The Diseased Conscience'

One way to approach this dilemma is to ask if there might be a conceptualization of conscience that incorporates the Kantian omission to which Wittgenstein thought that we could only gesture: the disruption to thought. To pose the issue in this way brings to my mind Freud's own attempts to unravel the conceptual knots that are bound up with the notion of an original unity, and that become indissolubly linked with conscience. Freud's principal efforts in this regard appear in two of his meta-psychological essays, "On Narcissism: An Introduction" (1914) and "Mourning and Melancholia" (1917); further elaborations appear in lectures VIII and XI of *Group Psychology and the Analysis of the Ego* (1921) and Lecture XXVI of *Introductory Lectures on Psychoanalysis* (1916–17).[55] Freud's reflections supply a new criticism of the modern religion of conscience: he argues that conscience without disruption issues in a destructive attachment to a self-ideal that is deadly.

Translating "Zur Einfuhrung des Narzissmus" literally as "On the Introduction of the Concept of Narcissism" brings to the fore Freud's concern with the conceptual issues of a fundamental unity. He aims to introduce a concept of self-referential unity (ego) as the achievement of an ingenious introspective process (the interplay of sexual and ego instincts that attach to the world, while simultaneously withdrawing and redirecting them to the ego), whose interruptive character issues in self-respect (conscience). The conceptual difficulty Freud faces is how to introduce the disposition of withdrawing from the world and attaching to the ego (narcissism) in a way that avoids both presupposing an original fixed self-referential unity and asserting something that cannot be said.

Explanations of self-reference frequently come to ruin because they presuppose themselves. Self-reference in some sense always assumes 'knowledge' that the reference is to itself and not something else. Much philosophical ink has been spilled trying to account for this assumption, with the results either dubious (e.g., Bertrand Russell)[56] or tortuously speculative (e.g., J. G. Fichte).[57] Such efforts notwithstanding, the threat of infinite regress continues to haunt anyone who chooses to invoke a notion of a self-referring unity.[58] Freud notoriously berated philosophers and philosophy, often for this flaw, but he was not without philosophical sensibilities of his own. Doubtless he had good clinical reasons to insist that his concept of narcissism not be thought of as foundational, but he had philosophical reasons as well. By inviting us to think of narcissism as a "coping stone"— literally, the top or headstone of a building that is clear for all to see—Freud positions himself not only on what he takes to be the sound ground of clinical observation, but also on more promising philosophical ground. Now he could say that in some sense, narcissism functions (figuratively) as the crowning or finishing touch of the achievement of the ego, and not as its starting point or foundation. Insofar as self-reference is conceived of as an achievement, it is not immediately susceptible to the charge of circularity that accrues to more foundational metaphysical theories that begin with a self-referring unity. And the transparency of the achievement opens the prospect that self-reference can enjoy a kind of justification that speculative metaphysics cannot proffer.

To get clear about what this claim is about we need to know something about Freud's method in the *Papers on Metapsychology*, to trace the steps of his argument, and then to draw out the significance of Freud's insight. Let us begin with method. Freud's mode of argumentation, viewed philosophically, is 'transcendental.' That is to say, Freud starts with a range of behavioral observations and then asks what the underlying conditions would have to be in order for those behaviors to occur. He looks as much at the pathological instances of schizophrenia, hysteria, or obsession as he does at the mental life of "primitive peoples" and children. And he notes that in each instance, there occurs a withdrawal of sexual interests from the external world and a redirecting of these energies inward. He sees that obsessional neurotics or hysterics abandon their relation to reality, as do schizophrenics—thereby not only precipitating megalomania, but also limiting their susceptibility to psychoanalytic influence—just as he discerns that "primitive peoples" and children overestimate the power of their wishes and the omnipotence of their thoughts—believing in the totemic virtue of words, they often subscribe to magical thinking as a way of dealing with the outer world.[59] Persons suffering from organic disease who tend to withdraw and to attend to themselves; hypochondriacs who withdraw and concentrate on some bodily ailment; and persons who fall in love, who vacillate between overestimation of the object of their love (thereby depleting themselves) and the withdrawal from the love object (thereby falling into a state of self-sufficiency and inaccessibility) do not escape Freud's purview. Indeed, such broadly based, exaggerated phenomena suggest to Freud a *hidden, prior condition of mental functioning* (primary narcissism) in terms of which the diverse movements of attachment and withdrawal that he has observed become possible. Or, put another way, Freud begins with the pathological and its distortions because he thinks that these amplifications bring the ordinary course of mental life—which otherwise escapes our notice—into view.

The import of these methodological observations is twofold. First, Freud's exposition follows the contours of certain pathologies, permitting him the opportunity to strike distinctions among them as he proceeds. Hence, for example, the difference between the withdrawal of interest from the external world in organic disease and hypochondria lies in the source of distress in the body: organic or libidinal (erotogenetic) changes. Second, Freud's order of exposition is therefore not identical with his order of argumentation. From his analyses of the contours of various psychopathologies, Freud derives a series of points about their *underlying structure*, which conjointly form the basis of his claims about narcissism. By working from the outside in, so to speak, Freud hopes to get to an important truth. But the logical ordering of those points, from the inside out—a fundamental thinking without which we might fail to grasp Freud's argument and fundamental claim about narcissism—remains a task for the reader.

Let us, accordingly, take up what, on my reading, are the five basic steps of Freud's argument in his essay "On Narcissism."

First, sexual instincts and ego instincts, although distinct, exist side by side in the individual in their primordial form. Primary narcissism denotes the "existence of an epoch and a mental state in which the two groups of instincts are acting in harmony with each other, inseparably blent."[60] So construed, narcissism is "the libidinal complement to the ego instinct of self-preservation."[61] In the service of self-preservation, the ego initially attaches its interest on itself (self-regard) rather than on others. However much protection a strong egoism may be, the ego must begin to love in order to live. Therein, the basic antithesis between ego instincts and sexual interests surfaces, as the ego surrenders part of its self-attachment as it attaches to others (caregivers, providers, and feeders) to further the interests of self-preservation. This activity of attaching, withdrawing, and reattaching to ego and others is ongoing, issuing in a continuum of reciprocity. Freud invokes the figure of the body of the protoplasmic animalcule and its relation to the pseudopodia that it puts out to illustrate the relation between fundamentally persisting primary narcissism and subsequent attachments to the external world.

Second, narcissism, in its secondary form, is the withdrawal of interests from the external world and the redirection of that interest toward the ego. Freud suspects that the secondary form is superimposed on the primary one, although he concedes that this is hypothetical.[62] In any event, by virtue of this withdrawal of interest, the ego ceases to be susceptible to outside influence. Freud's hypothesis of the superimposition of the secondary form on the primary one and the insusceptibility of the ego to outside influence gives us a clue to what secondary narcissism is fundamentally about: it is part of an effort to live well by attempting to recover the lost original harmonious blend between sexual and ego instincts.

Third, in the attempt to restore balances, the return of sexual interests to the ego precipitates a "working over" of stimuli in the mind, with the ensuing attempt to master the "damming up" of 'ego libido.' When the turning of sexual interest away from reality toward the life of fantasy—in which the ego creates new structures of wishes (introversion)—exceeds a certain degree, these energies become dammed up.[63] If sexual interests are redirected away from objects of fantasy to the ego, liberation from this frustration of damming up sexual interests issues in the forms of megalomania or hypochondria (what Freud terms 'paraphrenic disorders'); if sexual interests are not so redirected, the process of introversion persists, issuing in transference neuroses. When, however, sexual interests are emancipated from the ego, their redirection toward external objects represents an attempt at recovery, even if in a hysterical or obsessional manner.

Fourth, the non-pathological release of ego-libido occurs through the formation of an ego ideal—self-respect—which is the condition for repression.[64] Idealization, simply put, is the mind's exaltation and aggrandizing of an object. The form of the ideal functions not only to delineate the ideal, but also to delimit the sphere of possible conduct. As Freud says elsewhere, the ego ideal is "the sum of all limitations in which the ego has to acquiesce."[65] Parental criticism, the training of teachers and friends, and public opinion inform the content of the ego ideal. Self-love is now directed toward the ego ideal, deemed the "possessor of all perfections," which displaces the lost narcissism of childhood. This increases the demands on the ego, precipitating repression of sexual interests that conflict with the ego ideal, or what is the same, self-respect. The gratification in maintaining and fulfilling the ideal is (heightened) self-regard.

Fifth, and finally, to secure this gratification, intense critical self-observation must keep in view both the ego ideal and the actual ego, deflecting interests away from sexual aims incompatible with the ideal (sublimation). The distinctive activity of self-respect that joins self-love and self-regard with the aim of restoring happy love (corresponding to the primal harmony of sexual and ego instincts) is conscience.⁶⁶ By means of self-observation and self-criticism, conscience strives to regulate and balance the residual, primary self-regard, the self-esteem that accompanies the experienced fulfillment of the ego ideal, and the self-enrichment or exaltation that follows gratification (being loved) of appropriate sexual interests. However much akin to the primal harmony of sexual and ego interests, the happiness herein sought diverges significantly, insofar as it is the achievement of a greater unity in which the ego is able to relate to itself as an ego.

Here is Freud's succinct summary of these steps:

> The development of the ego consists in a departure from the primary Narcissism and results in a vigorous attempt to recover it. This departure is brought about by means of the displacement of libido to an ego ideal imposed from without, while gratification is derived from attainment of this ideal.
>
> At the same time, the ego has put forth its libidinal object-cathexes. It becomes impoverished in consequence both of these cathexes and of the formation of the ego-ideal, and it enriches itself again both by its gratification of its object and love and by fulfilling its ideal.⁶⁷

It is tempting to think of Freud's argument as sketching the underpinnings of a severe personality disordering, the illness of a person who is so internally fragile that their efforts to sustain attachments to the external world prove so injurious that they precipitate a manner of navigating life that holds the world at bay; the defenses of this person are akin to an impregnable fortress. There is certainly a sense in which this is so, but Freud is also attempting to say something more and different. Narcissism, in essence, is a disposition of the mind that aims at *health*, especially healthy self-respect. It is not merely that sexual instincts and ego instincts operate in oppositional tension, but also that the addition of a measure of self-regard makes possible the task of balancing of these opposing instincts in a way that is conducive to flourishing in life.

To see how this is so, we must be willing to strike a distinction between narcissism in its narrow sense, and narcissism in its broader reach. Narrowly construed, narcissism is the (hypothetical) passionate attachment of interest to the task of self-preservation (primary narcissism). In an amplified view, narcissism is a recapitulation of this passionate attachment, evident in withdrawing sexual interests from external attachments and redirecting them back on the ego (secondary narcissism). But in its broadest reach, narcissism not only embodies the structural features of primary and secondary narcissism, but also clearly extends to incorporate self-regard, self-love, and self-respect manifest in the activity of conscience. With the broader notion of narcissism in mind, it becomes possible for us to notice that the withdrawal of interests from the external world characteristic of secondary narcissism constitutes an interruption of psychical energy from one aim and a redirection toward another. Against the backdrop of this larger picture, the essential character of interruption for navigating the course of attachments comes into full relief. A disproportionate vesting of psychical energies toward the external world depletes the ego; a disproportionate vesting of psychical energies toward the ego over-exalts it. Only with the interruption of the flow of psychical energies—either toward object or toward ego—does the attempt to recover the original harmony between ego instincts and sexual instincts become possible.

We might better call this attempt an imaginative recovery, entailing as it does the "working over of stimulae" in the mind. From this 'working over,' new attempts at psychical attachment emerge "from another level and under different conditions."[68] New construals or word presentations of the object occur, as part of the initial attempt at recovery.[69] In such construals, we are not only rethinking the objects, but also rethinking ourselves, in the sense of re-imagining what we are like. Naturally enough, the epitome of such re-imagining is the formation of an ego ideal. By means of the ideal, we can effect a critical assessment of who we are, and govern our sexual interests that are incompatible with whom we think we ought to be. Through the censure of repression or the redirection of sublimation, we are able to align our sexual interests with our ideal of ourselves, thereby enjoying the satisfaction of fulfilling the ego ideal.

As may now be evident, our critical self-assessment is telling only insofar as it encompasses an historical reconstruction of the patterns of conduct that we have pursued. Loving what one once was but no longer is, or loving what one would like to be, or again, loving another who possesses the excellences that one does not have, presupposes a self-critical awareness not only of who one has been, or hopes to be, but also of how far one has fallen short of one's ideals.[70] Such self-critical awareness would scarcely be salutary, however, if it did not incorporate recognition of the patterns of conduct in which our efforts to love ourselves and others were bodied forth. However significant it might be to say, for example, that one has longed to be loved and acknowledged, but has fallen wide of the mark, this claim lacks full power of purchase. To say, however, that in the need for recognition one has exhibited a pattern of over-attaching to others and then, in hurt and disappointment, of retreating repeatedly into oneself—erecting one fortress-like barrier after another, which, while purportedly protecting oneself, proves off-putting because it renders one unavailable to others—is telling. This is why Freud thinks that we can fill in the often-hidden significance of our words about ourselves and others by attending to our patterns of conduct. By this means we can we develop a more penetrating picture of who we actually are.

Drawing the various threads of our discussion together will permit me to recast the significance of Freud's claim that the ego is an achievement. To see why Freud's claim that the ego is an achievement might better read, "Narcissism is the coping stone by which we are able to see aright the achievement of the ego," we would now note the parallel between Freud's metaphors of the 'protoplasmic animalcule' with extended pseudopodia and the 'coping stone.' Each serves to underscore that the original or foundational structure of the mind is hidden from us; borrowing a page from Wittgenstein, we might say that each alludes to something of which we cannot speak. Nonetheless, and again following Wittgenstein, what cannot be said does show itself. The premise of original self-referring sexual instincts (autoeroticism) or ego instincts (self-preservation) would itself prove circular if they were regarded as foundational. We could no more explain how it is that the sexual or ego instincts are self-referring than we could say that the ego knows itself from the outset. So to this premise, Freud asserts, "There must be something added—a new psychical action."[71] In its initial conception, this new psychical action consists in an interrupting of attachments either by their withdrawal from the world or from their sanctuary of retreat within the ego. But the elaboration of this conception issues in the notion that the ego, in attempting to reach beyond itself, constantly attempts to maintain or restore a balance between its inner harmony and the rhythms of the world. The evidence Freud adduces in support of his hypothesis is the myriad patterns of attachments in which the ego either surfeits or depletes itself—the most dramatic of which are the paraphrenic disorders or the transference neuroses. But however much these patterns exhibit distortion, what shows through them is the constant activity of attaching and withdrawing of interests in the pursuit of *health*. Still more, these interruptions give occasion not only to delineate the patterns of attaching and withdrawing, but also to construct an ego ideal. Based, in part, on our patterns of attaching and withdrawing, and, in part, on our social historical location, the ego ideal of our 'own' constructing actually says as much of who we are as of who we would strive to be. It is our attempt to achieve healthy self-respect. When we resist the temptation to construe the narcissistic component of our psyche pathologically, we see instead that, by the lights of its contours, the real achievement of the ego's self-knowledge comes into view: the ego strives for flourishing.

Parsing out this insight in Freud's argument is hardly the pursuit of some philosophical adiaphora. On the contrary, if we failed to do so, we would miss the peculiar nature of the claim that Freud is advancing. He is implying that the apparently self-referring features of the ego instincts and the sexual instincts are an insufficient and misleading basis for understanding self-knowledge. They are insufficient because they lead either to infinite regress or to speculative aerial gymnastics devoid of empirical verification; they are misleading because they conceal more than they reveal about self-knowledge. By way of contrast, Freud is urging us to see that we first begin to understand the nature of self-knowledge by becoming aware of the narcissistic patterns of attachment and withdrawal that show through our interactions with the world. By noticing these patterns, we may then, second, discern within their interruptive deficits the ongoing attempt of psychic life to establish a balance between inner repose and the rhythms of social existence. Only as we can articulate these patterns and balances in a conception of an ideal ego are we able, finally, to introduce the prospect of self-reference to the oversight of our conduct. And this gives us a clue about how to think more perceptively about the ego: it is an activity that emerges within psychic life whose achievement is to frame a concept that refers to the process of which it is a part, and by so 'governing' it, to bring the process into relation with itself.

Now if, as I have been suggesting, narcissism is the 'coping stone' that has helped us begin to apprehend what kind of achievement Freud thought that the ego represented, are there are other features of narcissism that can help us to fill out the picture? Here we may recall, first, that Freud distinguishes narcissism from ego and sexual instincts. He did not consider either instinct a sufficient basis for interpreting the complex unity of the ego: some "new psychical apparatus" had to be added to his analysis.[72] What is distinctive about narcissism is that Freud construed it both as the conception of forging toward an ideal balance (self-regard) and as the passionate attachment to (rather than the mere acknowledgement of) that ideal as a standard for self-interpretation (self-love).[73] Accordingly, we may now say with Freud that narcissism is both a motivated activity and a limit: in striving to maintain a primordial, but to us unknown, "happy love"—a harmony in which subject and object are indistinguishable—the psyche creates an ideal to displace the "lost" harmony that serves to limit its striving. But the 'limit' reflects certain curtailments of this ideal, as well. The ideal may well be a form of rationality, but it is a form that, by purporting to represent rationally the 'primordial harmony,' disguises or hides the inaccessible character of that harmony from reason. To see that the ideal distorts the primordial harmony by rationalizing it is not to require the abolition of the ideal because it is deceptive. Instead, it is to see that the ideal functions as a critique of reason, limiting reason as it makes room for imagination. From this perspective, the character of the ego's achievement—self-knowledge—appears in full relief: self-knowledge is the imaginative act that joins self-regard (the ego instinct) with self-love (the libidinal instinct) in an ideal that governs one's conduct as self-respect (conscience).

Above, I indicated that Freud's notion of narcissism might afford us a way to incorporate 'disruption' into the conception of unity in a way that neither Kant nor Wittgenstein could do. We are now in a position to see how this might be so. By casting the 'unity of the ego' as an imaginative achievement, Freud was not far afield from one kind of claim that Kant was making about the constructive role of the imagination to the unity of thought. By construing the ego ideal as an imaginative construct that attempts to 'say' what only can be 'shown'—and thereby keeping in view language's distortion of the primordial harmony of the psyche—Freud also observed something of the harrowing restrictions that Wittgenstein found inherent in 'modeling' discourse. But Freud no more thought of the unity of the ego as an original principle of reason (Kant) than he thought of it as something over which we must pass entirely in silence (Wittgenstein). Instead, he transformed the imaginative achievement into a critical principle. The ego ideal honors what only can be 'shown' by exposing the limitations that (Kant's) reason encounters in attempting to explain the form of an original unity. At the same time, the imaginative achievement modifies Wittgenstein's radical court of silence with the recognition that what 'shows' inevitably disturbs the 'rationality' of the ego ideal, precipitating more imaginative changes. In a word, Freud attempted to show that it is characteristic of the ego ideal to undergo change. And because change entails loss, this is tantamount to claiming, contrary to Kant, that the achievement of the ego ideal entails a measure of conflict between the original harmony and the ego ideal, which is expressed in the life of the mind, both through imaginative creations and through the discontent of loss and uncertainty.

It is within the broader context of what ordinarily we think of as loss—that of a loved person—that Freud takes on the loss of "some abstraction . . . such as an ideal."[74] A significant form of loss, which Freud calls 'mourning,' precipitates feelings of "dejection, cessation of interest in the outside world, loss of the capacity to love, [and] inhibition of all activity."[75] Freud thinks that these feelings express opposition (which may grow to considerable intensity) to the requirement to withdraw attachment from the lost 'object.' Ordinarily, such opposition wanes over time, permitting the individual to form new attachments. But this is not always the case. There is another form of reaction to loss, one that consists not only in the seeming refusal to surrender the lost 'object,' but also in "an extraordinary diminution of self-regard."[76] Freud is pointing to a form of grieving that diminishes the ego instinct—a form that he calls 'melancholia.' Incorporated in this notice is something of a paradoxical claim. Freud argues that the mind actually attacks its own functioning. It does so "by an overcoming of the instinct which compels every living thing to cling to life."[77]

This claim needs explanation and qualification. On first look, we should find little difficulty in determining that this is an expression of conscience, or what is the same, an occasion in which the ego ideal stands in judgment of the ego, pronouncing moral disdain. But upon closer viewing, this pronouncement gives us pause. The basis on which this moral judgment rests does not come clear: how does the loss of an object to which the ego has attached suddenly metamorphose into a devastatingly harsh moral criticism of the ego? We begin to suspect that this is an instance of conscience gone wrong, if not run aground. Freud confirms this by observing that this is "conscience . . . become diseased on its own account."[78]

In its healthy instantiation, the ego attaches passionately to an ideal that it has constructed from what it loves, has loved, or should love. This ideal, in turn, represents what Freud describes as that lost primordial harmony in which subject and object were indistinguishable. By representing in rational guise what cannot be represented rationally, this ideal functions in some measure as a cover. Insofar as it is a cover, the ideal therein limits the pretensions of reason to absolutize itself, and so makes room for the imaginative, adaptive governing of conduct. The healthy conscience is a conscience that acknowledges loss and leaves room for the unknown.

By way of contrast, Freud argues, in the unhealthy conscience, the ego that has lost its ideal object resolutely refuses to acknowledge the loss of what it has loved. Instead, it absolutizes its ideal. The ego fails to see that its ideal—and the concomitant moral judgments that rain down on the ego, purporting to be self-criticism—do not a represent a lost primordial harmony, but instead cover a derogatory reproach toward the ideal. In the unhealthy conscience, ambivalence marks the passionate attachment to the ideal. The subject ardently desires to possess the object, but simultaneously expresses resentment over a perceived slight that the ego has suffered in the loss of the relationship to the forsaken object. Inasmuch as this forsaken object bodies forth as much of who we are as who we should like to be, its loss is shattering. And in the instance of the unhealthy conscience, although the attachment of the subject is withdrawn from the object, the subject does not reattach elsewhere. Instead, the subject works to establish an identification between itself and the lost object: "Thus the shadow of the object fell upon the ego, and the latter could henceforth be judged by a special agency, as though it were an object, the forsaken object."[79] Accordingly, as the subject transforms the loss of its ideal object into the loss of itself, the former conflictual ambivalence between the subject and its ideal is also metamorphosed—thereby preserving the passionate attachment from extinction.[80] It now becomes a conflict between the conscience and the ego (altered by its identification with the lost ideal). Failing to attach to new (ideal) objects, but instead withdrawing its passionate attachment inside of itself, the altered ego succumbs to the cannibalizing conscience. The concealed aggressiveness toward the lost object (hatred that the loved object is gone) is now revealed as the judge that holds within itself the intolerable other in order to continue to possess it by destroying it.

The psychological significance of this diseased conscience is not so much the loss of the object or the subsequent manifestations of ambivalence— both of which are as characteristic of mourning as they are of melancholia—as it is the retreat of the passionate attachment of the ego into itself.[81] This withdrawal, carried out in the name of preserving passionate attachment, distorts self-love and imperils self-regard, even as it vitiates self-respect: the conscience entombs the ego in omnipotent devouring. "We must begin to love," Freud reminds us, "lest we fall ill, and are bound to fall ill when we are no longer able to love."[82] In the absence of love, the mind attacks its own functioning, destroying its own achievement.

It seems to me difficult to overestimate the philosophical importance of Freud's portrait of the unhealthy conscience, even though Freud seems to have been understated about, if not dismissive of, its significance. If the unity of the mind is an achievement of conscience-governed conduct that can only be understood in terms of 1) the interruption of the ego's attachments, 2) the withdrawal of those attachments into itself, 3) the establishment of new attachments, and 4) the ego's imaginative capacity to represent those oscillating patterns in an ideal that 5) can function critically, we don't really know how tenuous the business of self-knowledge is until we understand the power of our terror over the loss of love: such terror can bring it and ourselves to ruin. As paradoxical as it might seem, when the modern forgers of the religion of conscience covered over that terror by conceiving of a fixed original unity as the veritable bedrock of passionate attachment, and so of conscience, they unwittingly enshrined as emancipatory what Freud would later deem as diseased. A fixed principle of freedom is the mirage within which the narcissist admires himself; the hidden face of the narcissist of which he is unaware is his melancholia, which carries him away to death.

Recasting the Question of Conscience

At the beginning of this essay, I suggested an insight that the makers of the modern religion of conscience opened up but did not fully grasp: in the face of loss, it is possible to conceive of an emancipatory vision of life in which its conflicting tendencies eventually would resolve in peaceful repose. What they failed to see was that this need not be the equivalent of life in which all the loose ends are gathered up, or what is the same, of eternal life—that is, life with enigmatic remainder. They failed, in part, because they conceived of self-preservation as a particular kind of unity that not only is original and manifest in our conception of objectivity, but also serves as a guide to the forging of our own ends. And they also failed because however much this structure could interpret powerfully the multidimensional experiences of self-preservation—not only making sense of a panoply of forces and principles in which the modern subject found itself imbricated, but also commending itself as a sure compass to conscience-governed life—it could not account for the relation of self-preservation to the world on which the subject depends. Despite the attempts of the authors of the modern religion of conscience to fill in this gap by elaborating a limited speculative metaphysic derived solely from the structural features of self-preservation, they nonetheless hit wide of the mark. If one does not emphasize the loss, there is no basis for conceptualizing striving as an attempt to restore an earlier harmony, even if in 'subjective' teleological guise. And if there is no basis for seeing the striving as inherently tending toward the preservation of an original state, then there is no basis for conceiving the striving as essentially preservative. So a conception of self-preservation that glosses over loss also eclipses the question of its relation to the world. And even the limited metaphysics that purports to fill in this lacuna does no more than repeat the covering over, because in according primacy to the striving to sustain the unity eternally, it neglects to incorporate loss. Thereby, limited metaphysics of this speculative stripe set into motion the vision of life that necessitates the assumption of an enigmatic remainder: of a life *after* this life that restores a lost justice.

To travel in the company of Wittgenstein and Freud is to become clear about just why so much of this strategy is illusory. It is to learn from Wittgenstein that the issue of the relation of self-preservation to the world is resolved by dissolving it. It is to see, by his lights, how much a fallacy it is to think that we can somehow adopt a standpoint independent of this relation from which to state it. And it is to recognize that because our conception of the relationship is always embedded in—and shows through—the logical structure of language, the relationship cannot itself be stated. In much the same way, it is to learn from Freud that is wrongheaded to con-found the apparently original self-referential character of self-preservation or of self-love with the unity of the ego. And it is to discern, instead, that the unity of the mind is the achievement of the ego's imaginative capacity to create a field of mental functioning, which links self-love with self-regard and self-respect.

Still more, it is to discover that a vision of life with enigmatic remainder is chimerical. Wittgenstein taught us that we cannot even frame linguisti-cally the problem of either an unenigmatic or enigmatic remainder to life, without converting it into an issue *within* life; what purports to be a puzzle isn't a puzzle at all. On somewhat different grounds, Freud maintained that our clinging to the image of a life in eternal harmonious repose absolutizes an ideal that is actually an imaginative, critical notion that symbolizes what can't be said. Hence, for him, the absolutizing of the ideal is a case of con-science gone bad; it is not so much the ideal to which we cling, as it is to what the ideal covers: our (self-) resentment over the loss of the ideal.

One should read these complaints, I think, less as an attack on the possi-bility of developing a theory of the conscience-governed life, and more as the possibility of forming one. Neither Wittgenstein nor Freud doubted that the theoretical efforts of the makers of the modern religion of con-science had run aground. But neither wanted to abandon the centrality of conscience. To do this, each sought ways to avoid the Kantian confusion of linking our conception of objectivity to an original (transcendental) princi-ple of (subjective) unity, which eventually obliges us to think of conscience in the same way that we think all other objects of our experience. This meant redrawing the lines of the Kantian conception of the modern subject: if the Kantian conception cast the subject as neither suspended from heaven nor anchored on earth, the Wittgensteinian conception portrayed the sub-ject as suspended between what can be said and what can only be shown, or better, between the limits of language and silence; the Freudian conception depicted the subject as situated between self-love (desire) and self-regard (self-preservation), striving to effect self-respect (the construction of an imaginative, critical ego ideal to govern its conduct).

Such shifts in the portrayal of the dilemma of the modern subject make it clear that both Wittgenstein and Freud thought that something lies 'out-side' the reach of rationality that is indissolubly linked with conscience. At the same time, both were at pains to find ways to express this without misconstruing it. Wittgenstein's 'silence' and Freud's 'unknown' (the unconscious) are domains outside the bounds of rationality, which though theoretically resisting any discursive exposition whatsoever, nonetheless find themselves (paradoxically) the subject of extensive comment. So their attempts to counter the established patterns of the modern religion of conscience, especially in its Kantian form, only take us part of the way to recasting the structure and reach of the question of conscience.

To take us the rest of the way, it is now time to make good on the promise I made at the outset of this essay to introduce 'an inverse principle of interpretation.' I hope to set out what remains of note in the modern religion of conscience, despite the justified indictments of it that I have posed throughout the essays in this volume. To do this, I propose to turn to Karl Barth's *Römerbrief* in which he uncovers an important structural truth about the unknowable.

Barth: On the "Void Become Visible"

Like Wittgenstein and Freud, Barth accepted and then revised the Kantian claim that we are neither suspended from heaven nor anchored on earth. What he recognized was that Kant's formulation had become for many moderns the paradigmatic way of self-interpretation; indeed, he reckoned that because there was no way around Kant, one had no choice but to find a way through Kant.[83] What he revised was the widely touted emancipatory significance of that Kantian conception of the homelessness of the mind: Barth deemed it 'criminal arrogance.' He accomplished this by exposing the ambiguity of Kant's formulation in light of the radical Otherness (and its implications) on which the paradigm tacitly rested; paradoxically, he exploited the very limits of the intelligibility of Christian religious discourse that Kant adumbrated to drive home his point.

In the "Third Introduction" to the *Römerbrief*, Barth wrote:

> It seems to me impossible to set the Spirit of Christ—the veritable subject matter of the Epistle—over against other spirits . . . Rather it is for us to perceive and to make clear that the whole is placed under the KRISIS of the Spirit of Christ. . . . The Spirit of Christ is not a vantage-point from which a ceaseless correction of Paul—or of anyone else—may be exercised schoolmaster-wise. No human word, no word of Paul, is absolute truth . . . But what does the relativity of all human

speech mean? Does relativity mean ambiguity? Assuredly it does. But how can I demonstrate it better than by employing the whole of my energy to disclose the nature of this ambiguity? . . . It is precisely the hidden things, inaccessible to sense perception, that are displayed by the Spirit of God.[84]

Barth was claiming that he had woven together certain thematic issues with a specific methodological approach. Less clear, perhaps, is the extent to which it is the specific methodological approach that lends an edge to—if not decisively constituting the significance of—these themes. To see this, we need only remember Barth's widely cited claim: "If I have a system, it is limited to a recognition of what Kierkegaard called the 'infinite qualitative distinction' between time and eternity, and to my regarding this as possessing negative as well as positive significance: 'God is in heaven and thou art on earth.' The relation between such a God and such a man, and the relation between such a man and such a God, is for me the theme of the Bible and the essence of philosophy."[85] On the surface, this claim is straightforward enough, standing as it does in the long line of theological claims stemming from the Protestant 'Reformation.' To speak of the "infinite qualitative distinction" is to speak with Calvin of a human relation with God so sundered that it is inconceivable for humans to imagine in what its restoration might consist. To invoke the phrase "God is in heaven and thou art on earth" is to recognize with Luther that no human artifice can bridge the gulf between the world and God. To focus on the relation between "such a man and such a God" is to reflect with Bucer on our guilt over our desertion from God that is sin and our consequent destiny that is death. And to lift up with Zwingli the prospect of a relation between "such a God and such a man" is to venture believing that the Gospel of the Resurrection comes to humans from God, proclaiming the forgiveness of our sin, and the transformation of our captivity to the world—our death—into the freedom both to discern our boundedness and to await the new righteousness—our true life.

But this reading is not complete. By managing to insinuate clarity into what is unclear, comprehensibility into what is incomprehensible, and strength of conviction into what is the negation of all conviction, it minimizes Barth's ambition to "employ the whole of (his) energy to demonstrate the nature of the ambiguity of the whole of human speech."[86] I propose instead that we attend to the Barthian delineation of the boundaries of what can and cannot be said. Such an attending would lend a much-needed corrective to the reading that merely places Barth in the line of 'Reformation' themes; it would also bring into view Barth's perspective on the modern religion of conscience. In order to accomplish this corrective, we would begin with the recognition that Barth observes the Kantian strictures on the spatially and temporally conditioned character of all experience and on the conformity of all knowledge to the conditions of self-consciousness. Indeed, we would note that he pursues the implications of these strictures with Wittgensteinian zeal and scruple. So for him, humans stand in organic relation with society as it exists in history. And for him, all that is known exists within the plane of "the world of men, of time, and of things—our world."[87] By way of contrast, all that does not conform to the conditions of our experience of the world is unknown: "the world of the Father, of the Primal Creation, and of the final Redemption."[88] All theological words—for example, Primal Origin, Creation, Grace, Faith, Resurrection, Redemption, and the like—signify that which is incapable of direct apprehension. For inasmuch as they are beyond historical definition, they are beyond human comprehension.

Thus far, there is little in Barth's distinction between the known and the unknown to distinguish it from the tradition of Kantian epistemological strictures. But where Barth differs, and, indeed, is novel, is in his claim that the unknown is not merely empty but also shows itself as unknown: "a void becomes visible."[89] Barth speaks of this showing as KRISIS, or the "disquieting" that occurs when the boundedness of our knowledge by the incomprehensible becomes evident. In KRISIS, the unknown places everything we know into question, thereby dissolving the confidence with which we formerly embraced our knowledge.

To expound on the difference of this claim from its Kantian forbearer is to begin to bring into view Barth's structural insight about the unknown. In Kantian epistemology, it is axiomatic that the synthetic or combinatory activity of the mind brings sensible intuitions under concepts of the mind in the form of a judgment. What fails to conform to the concepts of the mind—or more specifically, to the highest principle of their unity (the transcendental unity of apperception)—is for Kant the unknowable. In effect this means that the human mind establishes the boundary between the known and the unknown, which, of course, is the basis of the Kantian 'Copernican Revolution.' But Barth inverts this claim, arguing instead for the primacy of the *unknown*.

The Unknown, he says, has to establish the boundary between the known and the unknown in order to escape the illusion that human designation is sufficient to delineate what remains wholly distinct from ourselves.[90] Barth here departs from two indispensable assumptions of the Kantian project—the givenness of that which we intuit and the givenness of our own lives—but radicalizes their implications, thereby turning them in a very different direction. Whereas Kant thought it speculatively injudicious to comment on these assumptions, Barth discerned in them not only intimations of a dependence on something other than ourselves (as Schleiermacher had taught), but also a showing of the presuppositionless presupposition (the *Abpunkt*: the primal form of judgment. To follow Barth's thinking, we need to see that the function of the terms 'Primal Origin' and 'Primal History' (to which he refers repeatedly) is to signify the primacy of this unknowable domain over the human domain. Once we recognize this, it becomes possible for us to espy a critical dimension in his claim that it is the unknowable domain "that bestows life and breath and all things" and on which we depend.[91] So alerted, we might be prepared to discern that the unknowable, which is not of our own devising, could only make itself known *as Unknown*. But this move, in turn, is possible only on the 'presuppositionless presupposition' that what shows itself is an wholly *other* form of judgment. For Barth the unknowable as other than ourselves becomes the criterion under which all claims to knowledge stand, or the negation before which all certitude dissolves. Only then could it become evident why the unknown as negation—as precipitating a "shattering halt" to the advance of our claims to know, and constituting a "boundedness of the world by a truth that contradicts it"—*shows* an wholly other primal form of judgment: the unknown *as* unknown.[92]

We can now begin to appreciate why Barth thinks that "God is in heaven and thou art on earth" is a phrase rife with ambiguity. If we were honest with ourselves, most of us would have to admit that we no more know what it means to say "God is in heaven" than we do "thou art on earth." Given our organic relationship with human society as it exists in history, we must acknowledge that the significance of 'God' and of 'heaven' lies beyond our ken. So, too, because we have no way to adopt a standpoint independent of our historical situatedness, we must admit that the significance of "thou art on earth" escapes us. Whatever meanings we ascribe to these phrases fall wide of the mark. We here begin to suspect, following Barth, that we are caught in a hall of mirrors, seeing no more than what we ourselves project (a dilemma that might with equal aptness be cast as the Feuerbachian diagnosis of the Kantian project).[93] But neither such scruples nor such suspicion could awaken within us if our boundedness did not become visible to us. Whether we apprehend our barrier or come to see ourselves as prisoners depends entirely on that unknown act wherein the unknown discloses itself as unknown to us, calling into question every truth that we have embraced. Seeing ourselves as prisoners depends on seeing ourselves as bounded, or as held captive by something other than ourselves.

Naturally enough, as we have moved toward Barth's insight about the structural truth of the unknown, we have also moved toward the limits of language's ability to express coherent thought and have encumbered ourselves with the risk of introducing terms that only appear to mean something. This is precisely the tension that Barth wants to exploit in his exposition of Paul's epistle to the Romans. Because for Barth, Paul's theological language, rightly conceived, embodies the paradox of comprehensibility and incomprehensibility, he thinks that it is the key to the interpretation of Paul's letter. More narrowly, this paradoxical *theological* language is peculiarly apt for Barth's critical assault on the modern religion of conscience, precisely because such language maintains a tension that this distinctively modern expression of religion attempted to suppress.

The Theme of Paul's Letter to the Romans

Here is what Barth claims to be the theme of Paul's epistle to the Romans: the Gospel is the truth of God, "the Word of the Primal Origin of all things . . . the clear and objective perception of what eye hath not seen nor ear heard."[94] It declares a God utterly distinct from humans, manifest in the name Jesus Christ:

> In this name two worlds meet and go apart, two planes intersect, the one known and the other unknown. The known plane is God's creation, fallen out of its union with Him and . . . is intersected by another plane that is unknown—the world of the Father, of the Primal Creation, and of the Final Redemption . . . The name Jesus defines an historical occurrence and marks the point where the unknown world cuts the known world . . . Jesus as the Christ, as the Messiah, is the End of History . . . In this declaration and appointment—which are beyond historical definition—lies the true significance of Jesus.[95]

Inasmuch as we who stand in the world are incapable of knowing any-thing of the Other World, the Resurrection is the point of transformation at which is established from above the declaration of the revelation of Jesus as the Christ. The Gospel of the Resurrection is "the supreme miracle, by which God, the unknown God dwelling in light unapproachable, the Holy One, Creator, and Redeemer, makes Himself known."[96] In the strictest sense, the assumption that Jesus is the Christ is an assumption void of any content that we can comprehend. And any attempt on our part to fill this void vitiates all our relation to the power of God, leaving instead a "reli-gious survival" in which humans surround themselves with comfortable il-lusions about their knowledge of God to satisfy their religious needs.[97]

Not only is the power of God "the disclosing of his effective pre-eminence over all gods,"[98] but it is also the opening up of the final perception, proceeding outward from God, that the Resurrection is both barrier and exit.[99] It is barrier, Barth says, insofar as it marks the frontier of a new world; it is exit inasmuch as it is redemption from our captivity, our transformation from prisoner to sentinel, the turning point from our creatureliness to our freedom. Because the power of God is so distinct from—and utterly un-known by—us, it can only appear, be received, and be comprehended as contradiction.[100] How else to speak of the God who affirms himself by deny-ing us as we are, whose mercy is his judgment of us, whose redemption of us as prisoners is to maintain the distance by which we are separated from him? Those who stand in awe in the presence of this Contradiction, hon-estly allowing themselves to be set to wait under the judgment of God en-counter the faithfulness of God even as it establishes their fidelity.

Yet, for Barth, we remain fugitives in the Night of our own devising. He describes this as the Night that befalls us as we become caught up in self-exaltation, ascribing to ourselves what only can be ascribed to God, thereby secretly identifying ourselves with God. What then do we worship other than ourselves, "the little god . . . [that] must, quite appropriately, dispossess the great God?"[101] And in doing so, Barth asks rhetorically, do we not trim the truth of God to our own measure, making it "ordinary, harmless and useless . . . transforming it into untruth?"[102] So to honor this idol, we see it as the light by which we would kindle our own lights, rebelling against the unapproachable Light.[103] By reckoning the no-god as the pretender to the throne of God, we extinguish the light in us, beckoning darkness and sur-rendering ourselves to the mercy of the powers of this world.

Seduced by the 'wisdom' of the Night—the simple and straightforward confidence that our view of life corresponds with its practical requirements and the vicissitudes of its standards—we imagine ourselves to be emancipated from our distinctness, our separation, from God. The world takes the place of God, and, indeed, becomes God, and the God who dwells beyond this is given up.[104] But this forgetting of God breaks loose the wrath of God against those who turn away:

> Once the eye . . . has been blinded, there arises in the midst . . . a mist or concoction of religion, in which, by a whole series of skilful assimilations . . . the behavior of men . . . is exalted to be an experience of God. In this mist, the prime factor is provided by the illusion that it is possible for men to hold communication with God . . . But . . . if the experience of religion is more than a void . . . it is a shameless and abortive anticipation of that which can proceed from the unknown God alone. In this busy concern with concrete things, there is always a revolt against God. For in it, we assist at the birth of the "No-God," at the making of idols . . . The confusion avenges itself and becomes its own punishment . . . The enterprise of setting up the "No-God" is avenged by its success.[105]

The religious worldview that begins as "mist," wherein we assist at the birth of the "No-God," soon mushrooms into "a veritable sea of clouds" that shrouds humans in a "nimbus of security."[106] This is the more pronounced form of the rebellion of humans against God, what Barth decries as the "criminal arrogance of religion."[107] Unable to reckon with anything beyond the limits of experience, humans engage in spiritual sophistry, deifying unbroken naturalness as "the necessity of nature" or what is highest in human society—duty and fellowship—as the Kingdom of God (or ethical commonwealth) on earth.

Even so, the awe that the "starry heavens above" or the "moral law within" (Kant) steadfastly elicits from the human mind is never wholly independent of the basic relic of the secret of God—the Unknown asserting itself in that amazement. To turn a blind eye to the last warning of our recollection of the Unknown—to the awe that we profess to acknowledge—is, Barth says, to embrace the wisdom of the Night. Thereby, to affirm the edifice that humans have built upon earth, to align our desires with its continued existence, and to establish ourselves as its guardians is to commit ourselves to the end to which the forgetfulness of Night delivers us—Death.[108]

Barth concludes that the relation with God can only be reestablished by a "breaking in" of the eternal, the awe in the presence of the Unknown, and the faith in the "clearly seen memory of eternity breaking in upon our minds and hearts"[109] that we have been set to await the faithfulness of God.[110] In a penetrating play on Kant's dictum on the 'solution to the problem of metaphysics,' Barth sets the stage for the good news of the Gospel of the Resurrection. Apart from this good news: "Heartless, perceiving without observing, and therefore empty, is our thought: Thoughtless, observing without perceiving, and therefore blind, is our heart. Fugitive is the soul in this world and soulless is the world, when men do not find themselves in the sphere of the knowledge of the unknown God, when they avoid the true God in whom they and the world must lose themselves in order that both may find themselves again."[111]

Dispossessing the 'Unknown God'

Barth's argument is as simple as it is elegant: by confounding the known with the unknown, time with eternity, religion with faith, humans have made themselves gods, dispossessing the Unknown God. Ungodliness is thus an inescapable disposition for every living creature, thrusting them into very new forms of unrighteousness. Against such ungodliness, the Unknown God can only be revealed as the Wholly Other Unknown that condemns the apostasy of the world: the kingdom of humans can never be the Kingdom of God. Yet such condemnation, which Barth construes as God's judgment, may awaken a new disposition, namely, awe in the face of the incomprehensible void, the impossible possibility—faith—quickened by the presence of the Unknown God. In this way, the collapse of our values that are vehicles of aggression against ourselves may portend our emancipation from our captivity to self-destructiveness.

Even so, the dissolution of our values in the face of divine judgment can lead to an even more horrific outcome. The more compelling the presence of God that stills us, the more we attempt to still ourselves through the exercise of those spiritual disciplines that cultivate the gifts of discernment. By internalizing the judgment, we hope in our distress to divine the meaning of life. However correct this spiritual exercise appears to us, and however much it conforms to the facilitations of Judeo-Christian culture, it comes to naught, because the encounter of grace depends upon no human possession.

By stating the simplicity of Barth's argument in this way, it becomes possible for us to grasp the magnitude of its sweep. Not only the traditions of nineteenth-century culture Protestantism (which seeks the eternal in the midst of time) and Christian conservatism (which purports to grasp the eternal, despite the constraints of time), but also nineteenth-century survivals of earlier 'mystical,' 'spiritual intuitional,' and 'ecstatic' traditions (which claim to possess a special preserve of spiritual perception) fall under Barth's critical gaze. Each of these traditions claims more for the powers of human perception—and so, in some sense divinizes them—than Barth (closely following Kant) is prepared to allow.

While I hope this is an apt summation of the effects of Barth's argument, a proper understanding of the argument itself—or at least of its trenchant significance—tilts one in a somewhat different and deeper direction. I have already pointed up the alignment of Barth's epistemological strictures with Kant's, and it is not difficult to see that his criticism of culture Protestantism, Christian conservatism, and Christian 'mystical' traditions turns on his adoption of Kant's admonition against running riot in the transcendent. On this sort of Kantian reading, both culture Protestantism and Christian mysticism would be portrayed as purporting to grasp intuitions beyond the bounds of experience, while Christian conservatism would be depicted as claiming to grasp concepts without experiential content. Yet even this is not the full story. For however much Barth aligns his epistemological caveats with Kant, he also turns those limits against him. For example, consider again his riff on Kant's celebrated dictum that 'intuitions without concepts are blind, and concepts without intuitions are empty':[112] "Heartless, perceiving without observing and therefore empty is our thought: thoughtless, observing without perceiving, and therefore blind, is our heart."[113] The very formula that Kant thought secured knowledge from skepticism Barth construed as the figure of the Titan, whose thought, however critical, remains only formal and empty, and therefore unproductive. The epistemological triumph of Kant's empty self—freedom from metaphysical illusion—is for Barth the epistemological folly of emptiness—the delusion of dispossessing the Unknown Other. To read Barth in this light helps us understand that his argument turns on both its structural affinities with—and condemnation of!—the Kantian estimate that what marks the modern age is the (Titanic) capacity of humankind to engage in critical thinking. Nowhere does this come more clearly into view than in Barth's interpretation of ethics: "Pure ethics require—and here we are in complete agreement with Kant—that there should be no mixing of heaven and earth in the sphere of morals."[114] What comes to mind here is Kant's claim in the *Groundwork of the Metaphysics of Morals* that we are neither suspended from heaven nor anchored on earth, underscoring the indispensable role of conscience for moral-religious guidance.[115] Conscience, in other words, is self-legitimating, pure reason of itself made practical, the law that we give to ourselves in the moment that our freedom announces itself to us. When Kant's view is stated in just this way, Barth cannot travel the entire distance with him. True, Barth can agree with Kant that humans are neither suspended from heaven nor anchored on earth. But while humans may be "stretched into some conceivable possible middle world betwixt here and there," they cannot escape the form of this world and its pressure toward possession, power, and perfection.[116]

So where Barth parts company with him is at the point where Kant claims that conscience is what interrupts or disturbs us. Barth construes Kant's conception of the categorical imperative to act according to duty alone as yet another pressure toward works. In contrast to Kant, Barth contends that Grace stands over against this pressure. On his reading, Grace alone is competent to provide a truly ethical disturbance, because it alone is the presupposition, the unobservable origin of the truth of God that interrupts all human being and having. For this reason, it is Grace that is "the axe laid at the root of the good conscience,"[117] "the axe laid at the root of our haphazard conceits."[118] What else could Kantian conscience be, queries Barth, but the thinking that proffers itself as justified?[119] "The root from which our conceits spring, the secret which lies behind all human exaltation, is disclosed in the persistent regularity with which men crown themselves with the security of some absolute answer. By putting an end to all absolute ethics, Christianity puts an end to all the triumph and sorrow that accompanies the occupation of any human eminence."[120]

In the absence of the absolute triumphalism that funds our conceits, Grace emerges, in Barth's reading, not as meaning the possibility of good conscience, but as the recognition that a bad conscience must be *assumed* in the daily routine of the world.[121] So understood, Barth claims, such recognition allows the possibility of a *consoled* conscience.[122] What consoles the human conscience is "being confronted by that which is common to all . . .

namely, by the eternal distinction of God.''[123] Our comfort emerges from the recognition that all humans stand before the God whose 'infinite qualitative distinction' negates our pretentions. In this negation of all human conduct lies the sole protection against its great error, its subtle and ever-present penchant toward 'Titanism.' As such, the negation is that love (Agape) which is the question addressed to the questions of good and evil:

> Love is therefore both sweet and bitter. It can yield; but it can also be harsh. It can preserve peace; but it can also engage in conflict. "All the good works that I might perform on behalf of my neighbor and all the love that I might display towards him ought to be governed by the will of God. Should I be able to make the whole world happy for one day, nevertheless I must not do so—if it be not God's will" (Luther). Only the love that is strong enough to abhor that which is evil can cleave to that which is good. Love forgets—and knows; forgives—and punishes; freely receives—and utterly rejects.[124]

If, then, Barth maintains that Grace is that act by which the hidden, Unknown God disturbs fundamentally the vitality of the known humans of this world, what happens to the motive power of human action that we call 'conscience?' The picture that Barth paints is one of utter deprivation: "We are deprived by The Truth of the energy with which we immerse ourselves in a truth . . . We are deprived by The Victory of the vast excitement with which we await a victory here or there . . . Death is the inevitable lot of everything which lies on this side of the discouragement of our courage . . . There is no such thing as a 'good conscience' either in war or in peace."[125] Conscience as the directive issuing from the Kantian question "What ought I do?" is on Barth's telling supplanted by the ground and purpose of all human action, transforming it into a question to which only the action of God is the answer: an action is ethical only when approved by the unobservable One. To the extent that an action must conform to the principle of truth, the principle by which human society is constituted, rather than being directed to some secret principle of happiness, Barth retains formal affinities with Kant.[126] But whereas Kant thought that an ethical action construed others as ends-in-themselves, for Barth ethical action reminds us that in our whole conduct toward others, it is God who must be honored. And this, in turn, means honoring God's perpetual renewing and reconstituting of others' minds, which action, while remaining unobservable to us, prompts us to regard in others the Other who is One in all. Then (reconstituted) Conscience not only reminds us that we are evil, but also "does not allow us to

rise up from the severity of our lives—but pronounces the end of the grim
cycle of evil . . . leading us out of the turmoil of human suffering, back to
our Primal Origin . . . God.''[127] Reconstituted conscience does not afford us
a vantage point above the fray of human existence from which to glimpse
the prospect of a harmonious life that we somehow might fashion. Instead,
reconstituted conscience glimpses the invisible harmony of just life in the
Origin of our life—God.

The effect of Barth's ethics of deprivation is nothing less than an aggres-
sive assault on the Kantian metaphysics of freedom. By embracing Kant's
epistemological strictures and then turning them against him, Barth paves
the way for unseating Kant's claim that what disturbs and interrupts our
lives of desire is freedom's announcement of itself through conscience. Giving ourselves the law is, in Kant's mind, what interrupts our captivity to the
unbroken laws of Nature. Barth, noting Kant's own boundaries of thought,
observes that no act of thought or of will, no matter how pure, ever escapes
the form of the world that is stamped on it. Only that which is Other than
the world, and incomprehensible to the world, can "disturb" the form of the
world. The 'Titanism' of Kant's moral religion is its 'criminal arrogance'; its
freedom, our captivity. Believing that our free striving can issue in a just
society is the delusion of our bondage to ourselves.

We arrive again at Barth's metaphor of 'the prisoner become sentinel'
with which we began, but now its deeper significance can come into view:

> The prisoner becomes sentinel. Bound to his post as firmly as a prisoner to his
> cell, he watches for the dawning of the day: *I will stand upon my watch, and set me
> upon the tower, and will look forth to see what he will speak with me, and what he will
> answer concerning my complaint. And the Lord answered me and said, Write the vision,
> and make it plain upon tables, that he may run that readeth it. For the vision is yet for
> the appointed time, and it hasteth toward the end, and shall not lie: though it tarry, wait
> for it; because it will surely come, it will not delay.* (Hab. ii. 1–3)[128]

The manifest content of this metaphor is that there is a difference between
lives lived as prisoners and lives lived as sentinels. And there are in this
metaphor many resonances with Plato's claim that behind the visible lies
the invisible, which is the origin of all concrete things. Who, then, is the
prisoner? The prisoner is the Kantian human, neither suspended from
heaven nor anchored on earth. Bound by experience to the visible, the
Kantian human confesses ignorance of the invisible. But when embracing
conscience as its self-given moral compass, the Kantian human thinks that

it has been disturbed by the invisible, and strives to subordinate everything to that which the law commends. The God of the Kantian moral agent is the guarantor of the ethical enterprise, the assurance that the wicked shall not prevail. But by assigning God the highest place in the world, the Kantian moral agent ostensibly positions God in line with the aspirations of human freedom; in point of fact, the Kantian moral agent subordinates God to human freedom, aligning God with that freedom's requirements. Indeed, by setting God on the throne of the kingdom on earth, edging the invisible toward the tolerable measure of the visible, the Kantian moral agent means by 'God' nothing other than its exalted self. The Kantian moral agent is thus prisoner to its own reflection, captive to its conscience's hall of mirrors. Unable to surrender its own ideals, the Kantian moral agent succumbs to the melancholic death of the diseased conscience of narcissism.

And who is the sentinel? The sentinel, for Barth, is the Kantian human for whom the Unknown interrupts the unbroken chain of thought—much as for Weber's watchman—and in this Void reveals itself as unknown. From the perspective of the Pauline tradition, Barth claims, the sentinel is the one who, hearing the Gospel of the Resurrection and standing in awe of the Unknown, sees in the Void the Judgment of God on the no-gods. The sentinel is the one for whom the Void calls into question all previously held truths that Kantianism has enthroned. Thereby, the sentinel knows itself to be limited and its pretence to be dissolved, its own brilliant lights extinguished by the Light. Gone is its previously cherished conscience, its moral compass in a world of evil, displaced by the Graceful recognition that God alone is the truth. The conduct of the sentinel proceeding alone from the great divine disturbance bespeaks the reconstituted Conscience that appears in the wake of the conscience that has been shattered by the freedom of God. So detached from the unity and freedom of Kantianism, the Conscience of the sentinel sees in the freedom brought by the Unknown Other the unjustifiability of everything that Kantianism deemed life, and the appearance of a new Unity. In this perception, Conscience is set not against faith, but is our faith. Indeed, by virtue of this perception, the sentinel espies in others the Other, the One whose dissolving and reconstituting of them leads them as well to the end of conscience and the Primal Origin of Conscience. But to see this is for the sentinel to renounce as well the exalted depiction of itself as neither suspended from heaven nor anchored on earth. For the Pauline Christian, Barth contends, Jesus as the Christ becomes the emblematic figure that expresses the incomprehensible fact that the known plane of our world and Unknown plane of Creation and Redemption intersect. Hence the Pauline Christian by faith discerns in the Void that Jesus as the Christ is the one in whom the two worlds come together and go apart, which shatters the perception that we occupy the center suspended between two spheres. (See Dalí, *Corpus Hypercubus*, Figure 7.) So it is that in the barrier of the Void, the exit becomes visible to the sentinel, marking the sentinel as the guard at the threshold of divine reality. Mourning the loss of its ideals, the sentinel is freed by Grace to detach from them and to await new life in the Unknown Unity that has begun to appear.

Dissolving Life's 'Enigmatic Remainder'

As I have set them forth, the arguments of Wittgenstein, Freud, and Barth are just so many knots on a string. Thus far, they are bearings, marking places along the trail where these inquirers paused to puzzle in their own distinct ways over aspects of the modern religion of conscience. Yet our walking back with them has brought us to a point of arriving: looking over the course that we have traveled, we may now draw together their insights, and, seeing them as a constellation of problems, say for ourselves a little more.

If it was the singular achievement of the modern religion of conscience to exploit the contours of a fundamental unity (self-preservation) in ways that yielded a comprehensive interpretation of life in the ethos of freedom, its apparent methodological monism (Kant's multidimensional approach notwithstanding) was also its most costly commitment. However novel its epistemological claim that the measure of all intelligibility consisted in the conformity of the world to the basic structure of the human mind, the problems of how self-preservation was related to the world and of how, given the strictures of this basic unity, one could speak of anything (e.g., eternal life) beyond the bounds of experience, even if by way of a 'limited' metaphysic that lent coherence to the picture of a self-legislated moral life, remained.

Wittgenstein helps us to resolve these problems by dissolving them. The problem of the relation of self-preservation to the world proves chimerical, once we understand that we have confounded our linguistic modeling of

Figure 7: Dalí, *Corpus Hypercubus* (1955). (Image copyright © The Metropolitan Museum of Art / Art Resource, NY; © 2008 Salvador Dalí, Gala-Salvador Dalí Foundation / Artists Rights Society [ARS], New York.)

each of them with the idea of an independent model: the logic that underlies the linguistic structure of self-preservation is the same as the logic that underlies the linguistic structure of the world. Figuratively speaking, then, the 'model' of the world already shows through the 'model' of self-preservation, because each is a particular instance of linguistic modeling in general. In this wise, Wittgenstein dissolves as well the problem of eternal life. We cannot speak of conscience in terms of the logic of our language. Conscience disrupts our ordinary way of speaking by showing a way of living life, a disposition toward the world, that differs from what life in the world is like. So even attempting to speak of what is beyond life in the effort to lend coherence to a moral perspective is misguided. It amounts to nothing more than subjecting and subordinating the 'eternal' beyond life to the original unity that logic lends to the language of this life, thereby positioning the eternal in this world.

Wittgenstein not only exposed the illusory features of the modern religion of conscience, but also, by the radical character of his position, pointed the way toward the necessity of reconceptualizing it. It was altogether evident that both the notion of 'unity,' which undergirded the modern religion of conscience, and that of 'disruption,' which is indissolubly linked to the intervention of conscience on the ordinary exercise of language, needed to be recast if they were not to be felled by the Wittgensteinian axe.

To put the matter in this way is to open the prospect for understanding Freud's conceptual contributions to the constellation of problems surrounding the modern religion of conscience. His way of conceptualizing unity as the achievement of the ego, and not as a foundation from which one could only speculatively proceed, is pivotal. By conceiving of self-love (sexual instincts), self-regard (ego instincts), and self-respect (conscience) as distinct components that nonetheless may join together in a complex unity, Freud minimized—if not dissolved—the interpretive value of the apparent (albeit inexplicable) simple self-reference pertaining to each of them. Noting that such simple self-reference, to borrow a Wittgensteinian way of talking, 'shows,' Freud privileged instead the oscillating 'narcissistic' feature of external attachment and internal withdrawal evident in patterns of relating. By virtue of this conception, he was able to introduce 'disruption' into his construal of the process of ego formation. What was novel about this conception was Freud's paradoxical exploitation of it: disrupted attachments actually advanced the search for *healthy* balance between inner repose and the rhythms of social existence. For him, the unification of self-love, self-regard, and self-respect thus signified the successful outcome of this sequence of disrupted attachments and the acceptance of their loss (mourning): the 'achievement of the ego' is the self-knowing, conscience-governed activity that unifies this process. By means of the same conceptual components, Freud was able to account for the numerous (pathological) ways in which the process of disrupted attachments could run aground. Again, paradoxically, any attachment that becomes absolutized signals the vitiation of the search for health. Freud's preeminent example is the conscience that, turning against itself because it cannot accept the loss of its ideal (melancholia), becomes the rogue, diseased conscience that cannibalizes the process of healthy ego formation. On this reading, the idea of an enigmatic remainder to life, despite its august pretensions to render coherent a moral image of the world, is the work of a diseased conscience that holds tenaciously to its commitment to an original unity. Eternal life is an idea that we form to harbor our rage against the loss of our ideals and to refuse resolutely the end of life.

Once we recognize that Wittgenstein discredited the utility of the notion of an original unity to render intelligible the sensibilities of conscience-governed life, and as soon as we acknowledge that Freud construed the adamant embrace of such a notion as the work of a diseased conscience that savaged self-respect, then we are in a position to see—conceptually speaking—that Barth was a kindred spirit. For, just as did Wittgenstein and Freud, Barth both subscribed to the sharp divide between the knowable and the unknowable and accorded a privileged position to the role of the unknowable in shaping what we can claim to know.

But Barth differed in his commitment to demonstrating the ambiguity of the *whole* of human speech, owing to the absolute primacy of the Unknown over the known that shows itself as an wholly other form of judgment. As soon as we recognize Barth's perspicuous assessment that Kant reckons heteronomy inconceivable—both epistemologically and morally—then we can conclude with him that the affirmations of the modern religion of conscience to discern God in ancillary support of its ambitions for freedom can be no more than forms of self-worship. The incoherence of self-legislating moral religion becomes wholly evident only in the face of real heteronomy, of an Other than is not constituted and legitimated by a subject's self-relating. Such an Other, as inconceivable, precipitates the collapse of the faith that we can all become perfectly transparent to one another. The inconceivable wisdom of the Other, the unknowability of God, is a placeholder 'outside' the Kantian conception of religion within the boundaries of reason alone. As such, it signifies the negative judgment of the Unknown God that calls into question the determination of the religion of conscience to translate the relation between self and other into a relation between self and ideal self. Making ourselves gods is, after all, the equivalent of exhibiting our ungodliness, as is our penchant to lend coherence to the afterlife to cover over the incoherence of self-legislating moral religion.

To such ungodliness, God could only be revealed as utterly distinct. God's revelation condemns our self-worship as expressing the apostasy of the world. To pursue this line of thinking is to conceive of God's grace as the ultimate disturbance of human conscience, if not the upending of it, and as the consequent prompting that we regard in others the Other that alone can renew and reconstitute conscience. Herein lies the reappropriation of what the modern religion of conscience had denied: transformations of conscience are not self-directed, but depend entirely on the inexplicable otherness of the Unknown, from which all life emerges and to which it returns. And herein lies, as well, a path of escape from the unhealthy narcissistic overtones of the modern religion of conscience: making the Void instead of the self the center between two worlds (emblematically expressed in Pauline Christian discourse as 'Jesus Christ') succeeded in making 'visible' a ground that is distinct from, and thereby in principle critical of, the self-mirroring of the modern religion of conscience.

Embracing this conclusion is not a comfortable affair. It demands the recognition that the gods to whom modern thinkers have given homage—even if merely in support of their ideals—are lost, and that they can not escape the disenchanted state of mourning their departure. Despite the sad power of the soul's departure from the gods, it remains for us who are heirs of this legacy to be tempted by our pace of being to hold fast to the mystery that we know. So our loss can again become the refraction of our own souls, of the inflection of our own minds. We could totter between melancholia and mourning, between the unredeemed conscience's hall of mirrors (the criminal arrogance of religion) and the painful, but tolerable, loss of the visible (Grace). But if disrupted, our conscience could recognize that the Unknown Other can govern our notice, and that our conscience-governed freedom would therefore become moving where we are moved to go. Freed from the need to frame God in our own image, we could entertain a conception of life without enigmatic remainder. Therein, the harmony and just repose of life would be the eternal ruling activity of the Unknown Other. The ends of life would be those of our Primal Origin who alone can renew and reconstitute conscience. In the Oneness that emerges, as our own disappears, lies the end of our nervous clinging to and mourning for the autonomy of modern culture. And in that place, the beginning of life as God's prisoner—and freedman.

Epilogue: The Shattered Mirror

We find out the heart only by dismantling what
the heart knows. By redefining the morning,
we find a morning that comes just after darkness.
We can break through marriage into marriage.
By insisting on love we spoil it, get beyond
affection and wade mouth-deep into love.
We must unlearn the constellations to see the stars.

—JACK GILBERT

It has become a commonplace in many philosophical, theological, and literary circles to depict the 'modern subject' as the self-conscious activity of self-assertion that issues in strategies of domination. The picture looks something like this: anchored in the (Cartesian) certitude that the only reliable thing is that which the subject presents to itself, the modern subject valorized its own self-objectification. Through this subjection of the object, in turn, the modern subject exercised mastery over everything that is other than itself: only that which is presented to consciousness by the subject's *own activity* of representing objects can be present to self-consciousness. By means of such representation, the modern subject in effect transformed the world into its own image. Thereby, the modern subject pursued a path of (Baconian) self-enhancement, domesticating all forms of otherness through its (interrogating/negating) practices of representation. Wary of religious dogma and cant, as well as various forms of religious institutional exploitation, the modern subject exploited the contours of its own self-conscious representation to chart a path of emancipatory enlightenment. Guided by its self-legislated course, the modern subject sought to stave off the threat of encroachments of others to its own desires and inclinations. Although emerging from a reconsidered Christian heritage (in the shape of 'Reformation'), the modern subject drifted from its origins to become either non-Christian or anti-Christian. In its (Nietzschean) apogee, the modern subject swallowed up objectivity, not only by removing the barriers that Christianity erected to protect itself from Enlightenment, but also by eliminating that which *is* itself, independent of the parameters of self-consciousness— the killing of God. In this act, the modern subject transformed itself, turning against itself. Its enlightened respect for dignity metamorphosed into moral nihilism; its tempered skepticism, epistemological nihilism; its august valuing of the person, rampant totalitarianism. What was once humanism consonant with at least some of Christianity now became secular humanism incompatible with any recognized form of Christianity.

The essays in this book have attempted to complicate this picture, which turns, tacitly, on the view that liberty consists in safeguarding individual expression against external threat. I have explored instead a movement within modernity whose thinking is reminiscent of St. Paul's dictum that we fight against principalities. It construes the issue of liberty from the threat of various fanaticisms, both political and religious, as a conflict rooted primarily *within* the individual. Overcoming the threat of coercion was thus a matter of conforming one's desires and inclinations to the voice of conscience, through which, it was thought, God spoke. The progenitors of this view— the modern religion of conscience—Hobbes, Rousseau, and Kant, each appealed to 'ordinary consciousness,' and claimed, albeit in differing ways, that reflection on its contents shows that self-legislating authority and liberty are coterminous. The commonplace picture lifts up this self-conscious self-assertion and valorizes it. But it omits from mention the awareness that the subject of the modern religion of conscience harbors: that the threat to conscience is the seduction of inscrutable otherness. Heteronomy lays bare the incoherence of the self-legislating self that is indispensable to the modern religion of conscience: the self thrusts its autonomy into its loss of relation to the *other*, but at the cost of a world that can ever evoke words from it. Dialogue devolves into soliloquy. So the commonplace picture does not portray the frantic determination of the subject of the modern religion of conscience to cover over its incoherence by routing the various fanaticisms of religious practices. Balancing, by affirming, the limits of natural reason and the place of free will, the subject of the modern religion of conscience attempts to effect salutary moral and spiritual transformation.

Not alien to, but resonant with the main body of Christian teaching that opposes certitude about human perfection, such efforts at balance hold at bay the prospect of an ultimate solution that lies within our ken. By over-looking the determination of the subject of the modern religion of con-science to establish balance, the commonplace picture fails to notice the extent to which this subject—no longer conceiving itself to be linked onto-logically to the divine order of being—found itself situated between the languages of Christendom and the languages of Enlightenment scientific rationality in a way that destabilized each discourse. Accordingly, the com-monplace picture says little about—or misconstrues—the significance of Weber's observation that the subject of the modern religion of conscience discovers that it is positioned in a stance of disenchantment: this subject does not so much displace a religious worldview with a scientific worldview as it lives precariously between the two. Hence, the difficulties that the subject of the modern religion of conscience encountered in articulating its uncertain position—issuing in a sustained effort to disfigure and refigure inherited Christian tropes, in order to cover over its incoherence—receive scant mention in the commonplace picture.

By emphasizing the advance of the tyranny of the will and its strategies of domination, the commonplace picture veils the struggles of the subject of the modern religion of conscience to cope with its loss of a sense of Spirit or of the significance of its soul. In sum, this picture covers over the spiritual movement of modern subjectivity that, in the grips of helplessness and con-fusion, overstepped the bounds of what it could say, only to discover that by questioning its way of telling its own history, it could begin to reassess its significance.

The commonplace picture intimates that the modern subject is narcissis-tic, ensnared in its own grandiosity. But this picture shows only part of the narcissist's dilemma; the flair of its portrayal is won at the cost of pathologi-zing narcissism. Doubtless, the peril of narcissism is the diseased conscience and the imminence of melancholia, wherein self-righteousness and the righ-teousness of the just community are confounded. But there is, as I have attempted to recount, not only the subject's delicate and painful detachment from its own incoherent translation of the relation between self and other into self-relating, but also its journey to the acknowledgment that autonomy is never fully secured in the *other*. So there is hope. The oft-overlooked promise of narcissism is its role in the ego's achievement of balancing self-respect, self-love, and self-regard. Apart from acknowledging an *otherness* that is constitutive of itself, however, and apart from resisting appropriating such *otherness* into the terms of self-consciousness, this achievement of the modern subject would remain chimerical.

To portray the subject of the modern religion of conscience as caught in the throes of understanding human religiousness—battling dogmatisms and fanaticisms of every stripe, even as its seeks a new mooring in conscience—is to perceive the pathos of much of modern self-criticism. It is to eschew facile, discerptible characterizations of the seductions of self-presence that accrue to the commonplace picture. And in their stead, it is to attend to a different tenor of modern self-critical subjectivity: as the certitude and coherence of self-reflective self-presence shattered (as Picasso's *Girl Before a Mirror* dramatically expresses; see Figure 8), the subject of the modern religion of conscience now dramatically turned its original criticisms of traditional religion against its *own* foundling formulations of religion. Accordingly, the early modern identification of the self-relatedness of conscience with the self-consciousness of the individual proved illusory. Conscience did not, as was first thought, refer to the individual or *its* ordering. Instead, conscience *dissolves* this formulation, as it *shows* itself to be referring to an (*other*) ordering to which the individual is related and by which the individual is reconstituted. Only by thinking in this wise could the subject of the modern religion of conscience remain true to its critical search for identity *and* discern the problematic character of its own grounding.

It is a fault of the narcissist to be life without substance. And it is a fault of the narcissist's God to be substance without life. By attending intensely to his own reflection, the narcissist fixates entirely on a surface of who he is. He neglects the requirements of the body. The rustling of the leaves underfoot or the soaring of the eagle above are of no account to him. He desires only to possess himself, but in this desire he is frustrated. To ameliorate his frustration, the narcissist conceives of a God who links appearance and reality. By naming *his* lack 'God,' the narcissist confers a restrictive identity upon God. He limits the being of God to the fulfillment of *his* desire, and brooks no insubordination from God. Believing that *his* longing outranks the desires of everybody else, the narcissist projects his own dilemma on eternity. Here is what narcissistic eternity consists of: perpetual

Figure 8: Picasso, *Girl Before a Mirror* (1932). (Digital Image © The Museum of Modern Art/Licensed by SCALA / Art Resource, NY; © 2008 Estate of Pablo Picasso / Artists Rights Society [ARS], New York.)

longing to be possessed. In this eternity, the narcissist is not separated from the ideals that he has fashioned to recover the primordial happy love in which subject and object are inseparably blended. He invents a domain in which the privations of his childhood shall be returned and perpetually honored. This idea of eternity is born of a mind deranged by solitude, by want of food and sleep. For just as the narcissist cannot possess himself, so also the God born of the narcissist's self-fashioning cannot possess him. So the narcissist's religion positions him 'in between'—between mourning and melancholia, between the loss of God and the loss of himself. Only as an Wholly Other manifests itself to the narcissist as Unknown, shattering the narcissist's mirror; and only as the narcissist acknowledges the loss of his reflected ideal, thereby surrendering himself to the Unknown; only then do self-respect, self-regard, and self-love reappear in a conscience whose true ground is *otherness*, and opens a new perspective.

Only then, indeed, can the forgotten outcome of the narcissist's struggle show itself as a new light in the darkness of religious and political fanaticism. The narcissist who criticizes the ways of God is not left altogether without an answer. The dilemma of liberty may not lie so much in the capacity to choose whatsoever one desires without censure and the right to defend those choices. The dilemma may reside instead in our penchant to frame and to disguise incoherent moral images. And this, in turn, may be the inevitable outcome of the magnetic fascination and repulsion of that inalienable desire within conscience not to be perfectly conscientious. But the narcissist can learn from the threat of the inconceivable that the answer may emerge in the dissolution of—and emancipation from—what he first took the question of liberty to be.

PROLOGUE: THE LOOKING GLASS RELIGION

1. Hans-Georg Gadamer, *Truth and Method*, trans. from 2d ed. Garrett Barden and John Cumming (New York: Seabury, 1975); H. G. Gadamer, *Philosophical Hermeneutics*, trans. and ed. David E. Linge (Berkeley and Los Angeles: University of California Press, 1976).

2. By the "Hobbesian-Rousseauian-Kantian" outlooks, I have in mind the shared structural features of their accounts that proceed from 'ordinary consciousness' and discern a depth structure in terms of which such consciousness is possible. I do not, of course, want to suggest that their outlooks are identical.

3. Immanuel Kant, *AA* 10:177; *Cor*, 153.

4. Paul de Man, *Blindness and Insight: Essays in the Rhetoric of Contemporary Criticism*, 2d ed., rev., vol. 7 of *Theory and History of Literature* (Minneapolis: University of Minnesota Press, 1983).

5. Gordon D. Kaufman, *In Face of Mystery: A Constructive Theology* (Cambridge, Mass.: Harvard University Press, 1993); Richard Rorty, *Contingency, Irony, and Solidarity* (Cambridge: Cambridge University Press, 1989).

6. Michel de Certeau, *The Writing of History*, trans. Tom Conley (New York: Columbia University Press, 1988).

1. UNSCAFFOLDING RELIGIOUS "MADNESS"

1. I. Kant, *AA* 10:177; *Cor*, 152.

2. I. Kant, *AA* 10:179; *Cor*, 154.

3. I. Kant, *AA* 10:176–77; *Cor*, 152–53.

4. I. Kant, *AA* 10:176; *Cor*, 152.

5. I. Kant, *AA* 10:177; *Cor*, 152–53.

6. I. Kant, *AA* 8:41; *QeE*, 21.

7. Leszek Kolakowski, "Modernity on Endless Trial," in *Modernity on Endless Trial* (Chicago: University of Chicago Press, 1990), 3.

8. I. Kant, *AA* 4:Axi; *AA* 4:Axi, n; *CPR*, 100.

9. R. Rorty, *Contingency*, 3.

10. My wording echoes Lewis White Beck's adroit reprisal, "The *Critique* seems to be suspended from nothing in heaven and supported by nothing on earth," and Robert Pippin's cleverly inverted rephrasing—"supported by nothing on earth and suspended from nothing in heaven"—of Kant's own claim in the *Groundwork of the Metaphysics of Morals*. See Lewis White Beck, *Essays on Kant and Hume* (New Haven, Conn.: Yale University Press, 1978), 30; and Robert B. Pippin, *Modernism as a Philosophical Problem: On the Dissatisfactions of European High Culture*, 2d ed. (Oxford: Blackwell, 1999), 54.

11. I. Kant, *AA* 4:425; *G*, 77.

12. I. Kant, *AA* 3:B760–80; *CPR*, 640–50.

13. Salomon Maimon, *Versuch über die Transcendental Philosophie*, in *Gesammelte Werke*, ed. V. Verra (Hildesheim: Georg Olms Verlagsbuchhandlung, 1965–1971); Friedrich Heinrich Jacobi, *David Hume über den Glauben, oder Idealismus und Realismus, Ein Gespräch* (Breslau: Gottl. Löwe, 1787); L. W. Beck, *Essays*; R. B. Pippin, *Modernism*.

14. I. Kant, *AA* 4:Ax; *CPR*, 100.

15. I. Kant, *AA* 29:940; *LM*, 286.

16. I. Kant, *AA* 4:Axii; *CPR*, 101.

17. Dieter Henrich, *Between Kant and Hegel: Lectures on German Idealism*, ed. David S. Pacini (Cambridge, Mass.: Harvard University Press, 2004), 33.

18. I. Kant, *AA* 4:Avii–viii; *CPR*, 99.

19. I. Kant, *AA* 3:B154; *CPR*, 258.

20. I. Kant, *AA* 7:134n; *A*, 23n19.

21. I. Kant, *AA* 3:B134n, B135; *CPR*, 247n, 248.

22. I. Kant, *AA* 8:35; *QeE*, 17.

23. I. Kant, *AA* 8:35; *QeE*, 17.

24. I. Kant, *AA* 4:446–63; *G*, 94–108.

25. I. Kant, *AA* 3:Bxiii; *CPR*, 109.

26. I. Kant, *AA* 5:31; *CPrR*, 164.

27. I. Kant, *AA* 5:74ff; *CPrR*, 200–211.

28. I. Kant, *AA* 5:119; *CPrR*, 236.

29. I. Kant, *AA* 20:144.

30. Manfred Kuehn, *Kant: A Biography* (Cambridge: Cambridge University Press, 2001), 71.

31. Ibid; see also Frederick C. Beiser, *The Fate of Reason: German Philosophy from Kant to Fichte* (Cambridge, Mass.: Harvard University Press, 1987).

32. Howard Caygill, "No Man's Land: Reading Kant Historically," *Radical Philosophy* 110 (November–December 2001): 31.

33. I. Kant, *AA* 8:144; *O*, 16.

34. I. Kant, *AA* 8:145; *O*, 16.

35. I. Kant, *AA* 8:145; *O*, 16.

36. I. Kant, *AA* 6:26–28; *Rel*, 74–76.

37. I. Kant, *AA* 6:21n; *Rel*, 71n.

38. I. Kant, *AA* 6:48; *Rel*, 92.

39. I. Kant, *AA* 6:21; *Rel*, 71.

40. I. Kant, *AA* 4:408; *G*, 62.

41. I. Kant, *AA* 4:425; *G*, 77.

42. I. Kant, *AA* 20:45.

43. I. Kant, *AA* 3:B779; *CPR*, 649.

44. I. Kant, *AA* 3:B780; *CPR*, 650.

45. For further discussion see Howard Caygill, "No Man's Land"; Frederick Beiser, *The Fate of Reason*; Manfred Kuehn, *Kant: A Biography*; Allen W. Wood, introduction to Immanuel Kant, *Religion and Rational Theology* (Cambridge: Cambridge University Press, 1996).

46. M. Kuehn, *Kant*, 363.

47. I. Kant, *AA* 8:145, *Rel*, 17.

48. I. Kant, *AA* 8:145, *Rel*, 17.

49. Friedrich Heinrich Jacobi, *Über die Lehre des Spinoza in Briefen an den Herrn Moes Mendelssohn* (Breslaü: Gottlieb Löwe, 1785).

50. I. Kant, *AA* 10:414; *Cor*, 231.

51. I. Kant, *AA* 10:432; *Cor*, 243.

52. I. Kant, *AA* 10:428; *Cor*, 237.

53. I. Kant, *AA* 10:442; *Cor*, 251.

54. Thomas Wizenmann, *Die Resultate der Jacobischen und Mendelssohnischen Philosophie, kritisch untersucht von einem Freywilligen* (Leipzig: Göschen, 1786).

55. I. Kant, *AA* 8:133–46; *Rel*, 7–18.

56. I. Kant, *AA* 10:428; *Cor*, 237–38.

57. I. Kant, *AA* 10:428; *Cor*, 237–38.

58. I. Kant, *AA* 5:3–4; *CPrR*, 139.

59. I. Kant, *AA* 8:441; *Rel*, 333.

60. I. Kant, *AA* 20:311.

61. I. Kant, *AA* 10:340; *Cor*, 198.

62. I. Kant, *AA* 11:311; *Cor*, 396. Kant's own infelicities of language in the first *Critique* (e.g., A19/B33; A50/B74) lend warrant to the criticism that he merely postponed the problem of skepticism from the subject/object relation to the relation between representations and things in themselves. But in correspondence with Jacob Sigismund Beck, who was working on an abstract of Kant's critical writings, Kant elucidates his meaning in response to Beck's concerns that the definition of intuition as a representation relating to objects is problematic. Kant concurred with Beck's view that intuition is "nothing more than a manifold accompanied by consciousness" (*AA* 11:311; *Cor*, 396) and that "the activity of the mind whereby this union of representation is represented is what we mean by relating them to the object" (*AA* 11:314; *Cor*, 399). In other words, *givenness* of the manifold of sensation can only be cognized as 'objects' in relation to their principle of composition that the mind produces.

63. I. Kant, *AA* 3:B419; *CPR*, 451.
64. I. Kant, *AA* 3:A108; *CPR*, 233.
65. I. Kant, *AA* 10:346; *Cor*, 203.
66. I. Kant, *AA* 8:140; O, 13.
67. I. Kant, *AA* 8:140–41; O, 13–14.
68. I. Kant, *AA* 8:142; O, 14.

2. DISENCHANTMENT AND THE RELIGION OF CONSCIENCE

1. Maurice Merleau-Ponty, *Phenomenology of Perception*, trans. Colin Smith (New York: Humanities Press, 1962).

2. Richard Rorty, in *Contingency, Irony, and Solidarity*, suggests provocatively that we substitute one vocabulary for another; I am merely adding to this the proviso that what is left unsaid is as telling as what is articulated, and fills out the significance or import of the new vocabulary.

3. René Descartes, *Discourse on the Method of Rightly Conducting One's Reason and Seeking Truth in the Sciences*, in *The Philosophical Writings of Descartes*, trans. John Cottingham, Robert Stoothoff, and Dugald Murdoch (Cambridge: Cambridge University Press, 1984), 1:142–43.

4. Benedict de Spinoza, *The Ethics*, in *The Chief Works of Benedict de Spinoza*, trans. R. H. M. Elwes (New York: Dover, 1955), IV, 2:187.

5. Thomas Hobbes, *Lev*, I.10, 62.

6. For an analysis of the centrality of the concept of self-preservation for the interpretation of modernity, see Wilhelm Dilthey, "Weltanschauung und Analyse des Menschen seit Renaissance und Reformation," and "Der entwicklungsgeschichtliche Pantheismus nach seinem geschichtlichen Zusammenhang mit den älteren pantheistischen Systemen" in *Wilhelm Diltheys Gesammelte Schriften*, vol. 2, ed. Georg Misch (Leipzig: Teusbner, 1921–36); Dieter Henrich, "Die Grundstruktur der modernen Philosophie," in *Subjectivität und Selbsterhatung: Beiträge zur Diagnose der Moderne*, ed. H. Ebeling (Frankfurt am Main: Suhrkamp Verlag, 1976); David S. Pacini, *The Cunning of Modern Religious Thought* (Philadelphia: Fortress, 1987). I have developed new features of my analysis that appear in the body of this essay.

7. See R. Descartes, "Les Meteores," in *Œuvres de Descartes*, ed. Charles Adam and Paul Tannery (Paris: Léopold Cref, 1902), 6:230–66.

8. Voltaire, *Candide or Optimism*, trans. Burton Raffel (New Haven, Conn.: Yale University Press, 2005). See also Voltaire's "Poem on the Lisbon Disaster," in Candide *and Related Texts*, trans. David Wootten (Indianapolis: Hackett, 2000), 99–108.

9. I. Kant, *AA* 6:26; *Rel*, 74.

10. Max Weber, WB, 578ff; Sci, 139ff.

11. R. Descartes, *Discourse*, 113–14. See also Stephen Greenblatt, *Marvelous Possessions: The Wonder of the New World* (Chicago: University of Chicago Press, 1991).

12. Georg Lukács, *Theory of the Novel: A Historico-philosophical Essay on the Forms of Great Epic Literature*, trans. Ana Bostock (Cambridge, Mass.: MIT Press, 1977), 84.

13. T. Hobbes, *Lev*, I.2, 16.

14. On the issue of 'origins' or the attempt to mark an absolute beginning in time, see Hans Blumenberg, *The Legitimacy of the Modern Age*, trans. Robert M. Wallace (Cambridge, Mass.: The MIT Press, 1983), especially pp. 63–179; Martin Heidegger, "The Age of the World Picture," *The Question Concerning Technology and Other Essays*, trans. William Lovitt (New York: Harper and Row, 1977), 115–54; Jürgen Habermas, *Reason and the Rationalization of Society*, vol. 1 of *The Theory of Communicative Action*, trans. Thomas McCarthy (Boston: Beacon, 1984), 143–271.

15. William Shakespeare, *King Lear*, III.i.5; III.ii.5.

16. Samuel Purchas, *Purchas His Pilgrimes in Five Books* (London: William Stansby for Henrie Fetherstone, 1625), 10.

17. Godfrey Goodman, *The Fall of Man, or the Corruption of Nature, Proved by the Light of Our Naturall Reason* (London: Felix Kyngston, 1616).

18. For an extended treatment of alchemy, albeit from an eclectic perspective, see Titus Burckhardt, *Alchemy: Science of the Cosmos, Science of the Soul*, trans. William Stoddart (Baltimore: Penguin, 1971).

19. Francis Bacon, *The New Organon*, ed. Lisa Jardine and Michael Silverthorne (Cambridge: Cambridge University Press, 2000), Book I, Aphorism lxxxiv, 68.

20. John Donne, "An Anatomie of the World," in *John Donne: Complete Poetry and Selected Prose*, rev., ed. John Hayward (London: Nonesuch, 1972), 202.

21. John Wilkins, *The First Book: The Discovery of a New World. Or a Discourse Tending to Prove That 'Tis Probable There May Be Another Habitable World in the Moon. With a Discourse Concerning the Possibility of a Passage Thither. The Third Impression* (London: John Norton for John Maynard, 1640).

22. For an extended art historical analysis of Fuseli's *The Artist Moved to Despair by the Grandeur of Antique Fragments*, and its relation to cases of the body in pieces, see Linda Nochlin, *The Body in Pieces: The Fragment as a Metaphor of Modernity* (London: Thames and Hudson, 1994).

23. Friedrich Schlegel, "Athenaeum Fragments," in *Friedrich Schlegel's Lucinde and the Fragments*, trans. Peter Firchow (Minneapolis: University of Minnesota Press, 1971), 189.

24. M. Weber, *From Max Weber: Essays in Sociology*, trans. and ed. H. H. Gerth and C. Wright Mills (New York: Oxford University Press, 1958), 129–56.

25. M. Weber, WB, 578ff; Sci, 139ff.

26. M. Weber, WB, 578ff; Sci, 139ff.

27. I take this reading to conform to Peter Homans's interpretation in *The Ability to Mourn: Disillusionment and the Social Origins of Psychoanalysis* (Chicago: University of Chicago Press, 1989); and Anthony J. Cascardi's in *The Subject of Modernity* (Cambridge: Cambridge University Press, 1992).

28. M. Weber, WB, 595; Sci, 154.

29. M. Weber, WB, 588; Sci, 148.

30. M. Weber, WB, 569; Sci, 132.

31. M. Weber, WB, 569; Sci, 132.

32. M. Weber, WB, 589; Sci, 149.

33. Is 53:1b–2 (RSV).

34. M. Weber, WB, 588; Sci, 148.

35. M. Weber, WB, 593; Sci, 152.

36. Isaiah Berlin, *The Crooked Timber of Humanity*, ed. Henry Hardy (New York: Knopf, 1991), 6.

37. I. Berlin, *Four Essays on Liberty* (Oxford: Oxford University Press, 1969), 134.

38. F. Bacon, *The New Organon*, Book I, Aphorism lxxxiv, 68.

39. David Hume, *A Treatise of Human Nature*, ed. L. A. Selby-Bigge (Oxford: Oxford University Press, 1967), II.3.3, 415.

40. For an analysis of the formation of the "American canon," see Bruce Kuklick, "Seven Thinkers and How They Grew: Descartes, Spinoza, Leibniz; Locke, Berkeley, Hume; Kant," in *Philosophy in History: Essays on the Historiography of Philosophy*, ed. Richard Rorty, J. B. Schneewind, and Quentin Skinner (Cambridge: Cambridge University Press, 1984), 125–39.

41. T. Hobbes, *Lev*, I.12, 76.

42. T. Hobbes, *Lev*, I.12, 79.

43. T. Hobbes, *Lev*, I.12, 79.

44. T. Hobbes, *Lev*, I.13, 89.

45. T. Hobbes, *Lev*, III.32, 255–56.

46. T. Hobbes, *Lev*, III.33, 260.

47. Here Hobbes expresses his accord with the Westminster Confession of 1646, which delimited revelation solely to the Bible. But although Hobbes was willing to maintain with the Confession that there are many things in God's word above reason, he takes exception to it, insofar as he maintains that nothing in God's word is contrary to human reason.

48. T. Hobbes, *Lev*, III.33, 260.

49. T. Hobbes, *De corpore: elementorum philosophiæ sectio prima*, ed. Karl Schuhmann (Paris: J. Vrin, 1999), II.8.10, 87.

50. Jean-Jacques Rousseau, *Ém*, 3:16; CSV, 231.

51. J. J. Rousseau, *Ém*, 3:58; CSV, 254.

52. J. J. Rousseau, *Ém*, 2:92–93; *E*, 174. See also *Discourse on the Origin of Inequality*, trans. G. D. H. Cole (London: J. M. Dent and Sons, 1973), 41.

53. J. J. Rousseau, *Ém*, 2:92–93; *E*, 174.

54. J. J. Rousseau, *Ém*, 3:57; CSV, 253.

55. J. J. Rousseau, *Ém*, 3:31; CSV, 239.

56. J. J. Rousseau, *Ém*, 3:32; CSV, 239.

57. J. J. Rousseau, *Ém*, 3:38–39; CSV, 243.

58. J. J. Rousseau, *Ém*, 3:55; CSV, 252.

59. J. J. Rousseau, *Ém*, 3:42; CSV, 245.

60. J. J. Rousseau, *Ém*, 3:43–44; CSV, 246.

61. J. J. Rousseau, *Ém*, 3:61; CSV, 255.

62. I. Kant, *AA* 5:452; *CJ*, 318.

63. The paths Kant pursued to arrive at this insight were numerous (and often tortuous), as his thinking remained in constant motion, and he continued to revise his views both during and after the period in which he was actively publishing. But a suitable interpretation of Kant's corrective to Rousseau's religion of conscience requires that we adopt one of his later viewpoints. For it is only here in his first preface to *Religion Within the Boundaries of Mere Reason* that we find Kant incorporating the idea of a synthetic connection between conscience and purpose that precipitates the image of moral order.

64. I. Kant, *AA* 6:49–50; *Rel*, 93–94; *AA* 22:130; *OP*, 209.

65. I. Kant, *AA* 6:26–28; *Rel*, 75–76.

66. I. Kant, *AA* 6:26–28; *Rel*, 75–76.

67. I. Kant, *AA* 6:26–28; *Rel*, 75–76.

68. I. Kant, *AA* 6:26–28; *Rel*, 75–76.

69. I. Kant, *AA* 6:31; *Rel*, 79.

70. I. Kant, *AA* 6:29–31; *Rel*, 77–78.

71. I. Kant, *AA* 6:43; *Rel*, 88.

72. I. Kant, *AA* 6:43; *Rel*, 88.

73. I. Kant, *AA* 6:49–50; *Rel*, 93–94.

74. I. Kant, *AA* 6:48; *Rel*, 93.

75. I. Kant, *AA* 6:3; *Rel*, 57.

76. I. Kant, *AA* 6:6–8n; *Rel*, 59–60n.

77. I. Kant, *AA* 6:6n; *Rel*, 59n.

78. I. Kant, *AA* 6:6n; *Rel*, 59n.

79. I. Kant, *AA* 6:7n; *Rel*, 59n.

80. I. Kant, *AA* 6:6–8n; *Rel*, 59–60n.

81. I. Kant, *AA* 6:8n; *Rel*, 60n.

82. I. Kant, *AA* 5:124; *CPrR*, 239–40.

83. See above, chapter 1, "Unscaffolding Religious 'Madness, especially pp. 28 31.'"

84. W. Dilthey, "Weltanschauung und Analyse des Menschen seit Renaissance und Reformation," and "Der entwicklungsgeschichtliche Pantheismus nach seinem geschichtlichen Zusammenhang mit den älteren pantheistischen Systemen"; Ernst Troeltsch, "Historiography," in *Encyclopædia of Religion and Ethics*, ed. James Hastings (New York: Scribner's, 1914), 6:716–21; M. Weber, *Essays*; Dieter Henrich, "Die Grundstruktur der modernen Philosophie." The

reader may also wish to pursue my own analyses in *The Cunning of Modern Religious Thought*, especially pp. 45–62, where I offer a more detailed account of classical Stoicism.

3. DISFIGURING THE SOUL

1. I have in mind here, among others, the works of Descartes, Spinoza, Leibniz, Fénelon, and Mendelssohn.

2. G. E. Moore, "The Refutation of Idealism," *Mind* 12 (October 1903): 433–53.

3. T. Hobbes, *Lev*, III, 255–82.

4. J. J. Rousseau, *Ém*, 3:32; CSV, 239.

5. I. Kant, *AA* 6:40n, 6:79n; *Rel*, 86n, 118n.

6. John Ashbery, "Self-portrait in a Convex Mirror," in *Self-portrait in a Convex Mirror* (New York: Penguin, 1976), 69.

7. T. Hobbes, *Lev*, I.2, 19.

8. T. Hobbes, *Lev*, I.12, 80.

9. T. Hobbes, *Lev*, I.12, 80.

10. T. Hobbes, *Lev*, I.12, 80.

11. T. Hobbes, *Lev*, III.44, 424.

12. T. Hobbes, *Lev*, III.44, 425.

13. T. Hobbes, *Lev*, II.30, 244.

14. T. Hobbes, *Lev*, I.12, 76.

15. J. Ashbery, "Self-portrait," 72.

16. J. J. Rousseau, *Ém*, 3:27; CSV, 236.

17. J. J. Rousseau, *Ém*, 3:37; CSV, 242.

18. J. J. Rousseau, *Ém*, 3:57; CSV, 253.

19. J. J. Rousseau, *Ém*, 3:32; CSV, 239.

20. J. J. Rousseau, *Ém*, 3:58; CSV, 254.

21. J. J. Rousseau, *Ém*, 3:25; CSV, 236.

22. J. J. Rousseau, *Ém*, 3:31; CSV, 239.

23. J. J. Rousseau, *Ém*, 3:43–44; CSV, 245–46.

24. J. J. Rousseau, *Ém*, 3:45; CSV, 246.

25. J. Ashbery, "Self-portrait," 71.

26. These may be traced to Fichte's articulation of the circularity of the reflection model of consciousness that he detailed in the various editions of the *Wissenschaftslehre*. See especially "Vorläufige Anmerkung," in "Wissenschafts-lehre nach den Vorlesungen von Herr Professor Fichte," in "Wissenschaftslehre nova methodo," in *Gesamtausgabe der Bayerischen Akademie der Wissenschaften*, ed. Reinhard Lauth, Hans Jacob, and Hans Gliwitzky (Stuttgart-Bad Cannstatt: Frommann-Holzboog, 1978), vol. IV, 2, 30.

27. I. Kant, *AA* 3:A15/B29; *CPR*, 152.

28. I. Kant, *AA* 3:A51/B75; *CPR*, 193–94.

29. I. Kant, *AA* 3:B129–69; *CPR*, 245–66.
30. I. Kant, *AA* 3:B129–69; *CPR*, 245–66.
31. I. Kant, *AA* 3:B132; *CPR*, 246.
32. I. Kant, *AA* 3:A108; *CPR*, 233.
33. I. Kant, *AA* 3:B133–34; *CPR*, 247.
34. I. Kant, *AA* 3:A402; *CPR*, 442.
35. I. Kant, *AA* 3:A402; *CPR*, 442.
36. J. Ashbery, "Self-portrait," 77.
37. I. Kant, *AA* 4:403; *G*, 57.
38. I. Kant, *AA* 5:103; *CPrR*, 222–24.
39. I. Kant, *AA* 5:11n; *CPrR*, 145n.
40. I. Kant, *AA* 5:119; *CPrR*, 236.
41. I. Kant, *AA* 5:115; *CPrR*, 232.
42. I. Kant, *AA* 5:133; *CPrR*, 246.
43. I. Kant, *AA* 5:143; *CPrR*, 255.
44. J. Ashbery, "Self-portrait," 80.
45. Keats to J. H. Reynolds, February 19, 1818, *Selected Letters of John Keats*, rev., ed. Grant F. Scott (Cambridge, Mass.: Harvard University Press, 2002), 92.
46. This theme was first sounded by Friedrich Heinrich Jacobi in his revised *Über die Lehre des Spinoza in Briefen an den Herrn Moes Mendelssohn*, 2d ed. (Breslau: Gottlieb Löwe, 1789).
47. J. Ashbery, "Self-portrait," 81.

4. LIFE WITHOUT ENIGMATIC REMAINDER

1. See above, chapter 2, "Disenchantment and the Religion of Conscience," 88–90.
2. I. Kant, *AA* 3:B134; *CPR*, 247.
3. I. Kant, *AA* 5:57; *CPrR*, 186.
4. Ludwig Wittgenstein, *TLP*, 4.0031, 62–63.
5. L. Wittgenstein, *TLP*, 2.1, 38–39.
6. L. Wittgenstein, *TLP*, 2.0123, 32–33.
7. L. Wittgenstein, *TLP*, 2.14, 38–39.
8. L. Wittgenstein, *TLP*, 3.3, 50–51.
9. L. Wittgenstein, *TLP*, 4.015, 64–67.
10. L. Wittgenstein, *TLP*, 6.13, 168–69.
11. L. Wittgenstein, *TLP*, 2.022, 34–35.
12. L. Wittgenstein, *TLP*, 2.172, 40–41.
13. L. Wittgenstein, *TLP*, 3.001, 42–43.
14. L. Wittgenstein, *TLP*, 6.41, 182–83.
15. L. Wittgenstein, *TLP*, 6.42, 182–83.
16. L. Wittgenstein, *TLP*, 6.421, 182–83.
17. L. Wittgenstein, *TLP*, 6.362–67, 178–89.

18. L. Wittgenstein, *TLP*, 6.371, 180–181.

19. L. Wittgenstein, *TLP*, 6.372, 180–181.

20. L. Wittgenstein, *TLP*, 6.35, 176–77.

21. L. Wittgenstein, *TLP*, 6.341, 174–75.

22. L. Wittgenstein, *TLP*, 6.3631, 180–81.

23. L. Wittgenstein, *TLP*, 6.37, 180–81.

24. L. Wittgenstein, *TLP*, 6.372, 180–81.

25. L. Wittgenstein, *TLP*, 6.41, 182–83.

26. L. Wittgenstein, *TLP*, 4.121, 78–79.

27. L. Wittgenstein, *NB*, 8.7.16, 74.

28. L. Wittgenstein, *TLP*, 6.421, 182–83.

29. L. Wittgenstein, *TLP*, 6.421, 182–83.

30. L. Wittgenstein, *TLP*, 6.43, 184–85.

31. L. Wittgenstein, *TLP*, 6.373, 180–81.

32. L. Wittgenstein, *NB*, 11.6.16, 73.

33. L. Wittgenstein, *TLP*, 6.422, 182–83.

34. L. Wittgenstein, *TLP*, 6.43, 184–85.

35. L. Wittgenstein, *NB*, 2.8.16, 79.

36. L. Wittgenstein, *NB*, 8.7.16, 75.

37. L. Wittgenstein, *NB*, 30.7.16, 78.

38. L. Wittgenstein, *NB*, 4.11.16, 87.

39. L. Wittgenstein, *NB*, 15.10.16, 84.

40. L. Wittgenstein, *NB*, 8.7.16, 75.

41. L. Wittgenstein, *NB*, 8.7.16, 74.

42. L. Wittgenstein, *NB*, 8.7.16, 74.

43. L. Wittgenstein, *NB*, 8.7.16, 74.

44. L. Wittgenstein, *NB*, 8.7.16, 75.

45. L. Wittgenstein, *NB*, 8.7.16, 74.

46. L. Wittgenstein, *NB*, 8.7.16, 75.

47. L. Wittgenstein, *TLP*, 6.374, 180–81.

48. L. Wittgenstein, *TLP*, 6.45, 186–87.

49. L. Wittgenstein, *NB*, 13.8.16, 81.

50. L. Wittgenstein, *NB*, 13.8.16, 81.

51. L. Wittgenstein, *TLP*, 6.4312, 184–85.

52. L. Wittgenstein, *TLP*, 6.5, 186–87.

53. L. Wittgenstein, *TLP*, 6.521, 186–87.

54. L. Wittgenstein, *TLP*, 6.54, 188–89.

55. Sigmund Freud, *GW*, 10, 13, 11; N, M, GP (especially pp. 111–16, 129–33), LN.

56. Bertrand Russell, *The Problems of Philosophy* (New York: Oxford University Press, 1959).

57. Johann Gottlieb Fichte, *Grundlage der gesammten Wissenschaftslehre* (Leipzig: Christian Ernst Gabler, 1794–95).

58. Kant's own formulation of the 'I think' appears to many critics, including Fichte and more recently, Dieter Henrich, to suffer from the problems of circularity. For an alternative reading of this circularity in Kant, see Rudolf Makkreel, *Imagination and Interpretation in Kant: The Hermeneutical Import of the Critique of Judgment* (Chicago: University of Chicago Press, 1995), 147.

59. S. Freud, *GW*, 10:140; N, 75.

60. S. Freud, *GW*, 10:159; N, 92.

61. S. Freud, *GW*, 10:138–39; N, 73–74.

62. S. Freud, *GW*, 10:142; N, 77.

63. S. Freud, *GW*, 8:323–324; O, 232.

64. S. Freud, *GW*, 10:161; N, 94.

65. S. Freud, *GW*, 13:147; GP, 131.

66. S. Freud, *GW*, 10:167; N, 99–100.

67. S. Freud, *GW*, 10:167–68; N, 100.

68. S. Freud, *GW*, 10:153; N, 86–87.

69. S. Freud, *GW*, 10:302–3; U, 203–4.

70. S. Freud, *GW*, 10:168; N, 101.

71. S. Freud, *GW*, 10:142; N, 77.

72. S. Freud, *GW*, 10:142; N, 77.

73. S. Freud, *GW*, 10:160; N, 93.

74. S. Freud, *GW*, 10:429; M, 243.

75. S. Freud, *GW*, 10:429; M, 244.

76. S. Freud, *GW*, 10:431; M, 246.

77. S. Freud, *GW*, 10:432; M, 246.

78. S. Freud, *GW*, 10:433; M, 247.

79. S. Freud, *GW*, 10:435; M, 249.

80. S. Freud, *GW*, 10:444–45; M, 257.

81. S. Freud, *GW*, 10:445–46; M, 258.

82. S. Freud, *GW*, 10:151–52; N, 85.

83. Karl Barth, *Protestant Theology in the Nineteenth Century: Its Background and History*, trans. Brian Cozens (London: SCM Press, 1972), 266.

84. K. Barth, *Röm*, xx–xxiii; R, 17–20.

85. K. Barth, *Röm*, xiii; R, 10.

86. K. Barth, *Röm*, xxii; R, 20.

87. K. Barth, *Röm*, 5; R, 29.

88. K. Barth, *Röm*, 5; R, 29.

89. K. Barth, *Röm*, 9; R, 33.

90. K. Barth, *Röm*, 9; R, 33.

91. K. Barth, *Röm*, 11; R, 36.

92. K. Barth, *Röm*, 14; R, 39.

93. See Ludwig Feuerbach, *The Essence of Christianity*, trans. George Eliot (Amherst, N.Y.: Prometheus, 1989).

94. K. Barth, *Röm*, 4; *R*, 28.
95. K. Barth, *Röm*, 5; *R*, 29.
96. K. Barth, *Röm*, 11; *R*, 35.
97. K. Barth, *Röm*, 13; *R*, 37.
98. K. Barth, *Röm*, 11; *R*, 35.
99. K. Barth, *Röm*, 13; *R*, 38.
100. K. Barth, *Röm*, 14; *R*, 38.
101. K. Barth, *Röm*, 20; *R*, 45.
102. K. Barth, *Röm*, 20; *R*, 45.
103. K. Barth, *Röm*, p. 23; *R*, 47.
104. K. Barth, *Röm*, 26; *R*, 51.
105. K. Barth, *Röm*, 25–26; *R*, 49–51.
106. K. Barth, *Röm*, 25–28; *R*, 49–52.
107. K. Barth, *Röm*, 13, 28; *R*, 37, 53.
108. K. Barth, *Röm*, 29; *R*, 54.
109. K. Barth, *Röm*, 23; *R*, 48.
110. K. Barth, *Röm*, 16; *R*, 41.
111. K. Barth, *Röm*, 24; *R*, 48.
112. I. Kant, *AA* 3:A51/B75; *CPR*, 193–94.
113. K. Barth, *Röm*, 24; *R*, 48.
114. K. Barth, *Röm*, 418; *R*, 432.
115. I. Kant, *AA* 4:425; *G*, 77.
116. K. Barth, *Röm*, 419; *R*, 433.
117. K. Barth, *Röm*, 416; *R*, 430.
118. K. Barth, *Röm*, 450; *R*, 466.
119. K. Barth, *Röm*, 412; *R*, 426.
120. K. Barth, *Röm*, 450–51; *R*, 466.
121. K. Barth, *Röm*, 414; *R*, 428.
122. K. Barth, *Röm*, 414; *R*, 428.
123. K. Barth, *Röm*, 427; *R*, 442.
124. K. Barth, *Röm*, 439; *R*, 454.
125. K. Barth, *Röm*, 451–55; *R*, 466–71.
126. K. Barth, *Röm*, 453; *R*, 468.
127. K. Barth, *Röm*, 474; *R*, 490–91.
128. K. Barth, *Röm*, 13–14; *R*, 38.